Street by Street

C000195738

COVEN...
RUGBY
BEDWORTH, BIRMINGHAM NEC, KENILWORTH

Baginton, Balsall Common, Brownsover, Bulkington, Dunchurch, Hampton in Arden, Hillmorton, Long Lawford, Meriden, Tile Hill, Wolston

3rd edition October 2007
© Automobile Association Developments Limited 2007

Original edition printed May 2001

 This product includes map data licensed from Ordnance Survey® with the permission of the Controller of Her Majesty's Stationery Office. © Crown copyright 2007. All rights reserved. Licence number 100021153.

The copyright in all PAF is owned by Royal Mail Group plc.

Published by AA Publishing (a trading name of Automobile Association Developments Limited, whose registered office is Fanum House, Basing View, Basingstoke, Hampshire RG21 4EA. Registered number 1878835).

Produced by the Mapping Services Department of The Automobile Association. (A03506)

A CIP Catalogue record for this book is available from the British Library.

Printed by Oriental Press in Dubai

The contents of this atlas are believed to be correct at the time of the latest revision. However, the publishers cannot be held responsible or liable for any loss or damage occasioned to any person acting or refraining from action as a result of any use or reliance on any material in this atlas, nor for any errors, omissions or changes in such material. This does not affect your statutory rights. The publishers would welcome information to correct any errors or omissions and to keep this atlas up to date. Please write to Publishing, The Automobile Association, Fanum House (FH12), Basing View, Basingstoke, Hampshire, RG21 4EA. E-mail: *streetbystreet@theaa.com*

Ref: ML34y

Key to map pages	ii-iii
Key to map symbols	iv-1
Enlarged map pages	2-3
Main map pages	4-71
Index – towns & villages	72
Index – streets	73-86
Index – featured places	87-89
Acknowledgements	89

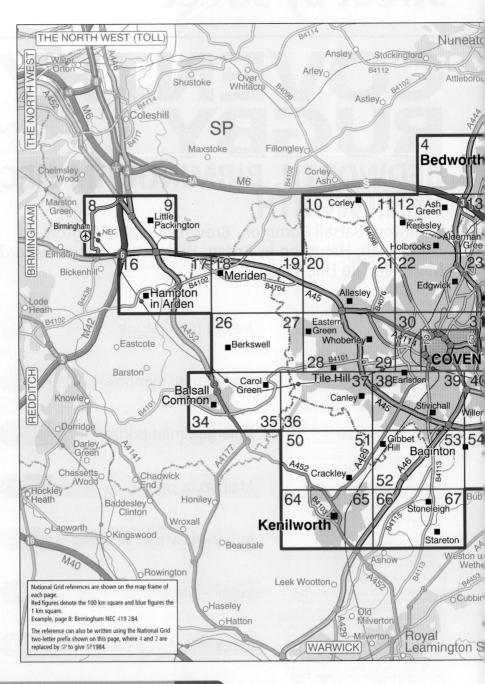

THE NORTH WEST (TOLL)

THE NORTH WEST

BIRMINGHAM

REDDITCH

Water Orton

Shustoke

Over Whitacre

Ansley

Stockingford

Arley

Astley

Attleboro

Nuneato

Coleshill

SP

Maxstoke

Fillongley

Corley Ash

Bedwort

4

Chelmsley Wood

Marston Green

Birmingham

NEC

Elmdon

Bickenhill

Lode Heath

8

9

Little Packington

10

Corley

11 12

Ash Green

Keresley

Holbrooks

Alderman Gree

13

Eastcote

Barston

Knowle

Dorridge

Darley Green

Chessetts Wood

Hockley Heath

Lapworth

Kingswood

16 17 18

Meriden

19 20

6

Hampton in Arden

26

Berkswell

27

Allesley

Eastern Green

Whoberley

21 22

23

Edgwick

30

COVEN

5

34

Balsall Common

Carol Green

28

Tile Hill

37 38

29

Canley

Earlsdon

39 40

35 36

Stivichall

Willer

Chadwick End

Honiley

50

51

Gibbet Hill

Baginton

53 54

Baddesley Clinton

Wroxall

Crackley

52

67

Beausale

64

65 66

Stoneleigh

Rowington

Kenilworth

Stareton

Bub

Ashow

Weston u Wethe

Leek Wootton

Old Milverton

Cubbi

Haseley

Milverton

Royal

Hatton

WARWICK

Leamington S

National Grid references are shown on the map frame of each page.
Red figures denote the 100 km square and blue figures the 1 km square.
Example, page 8: Birmingham NEC 419 284

The reference can also be written using the National Grid two-letter prefix shown on this page, where 4 and 2 are replaced by SP to give SP1984.

Scale of enlarged map pages 1:10,000   6.3 inches to 1 mile

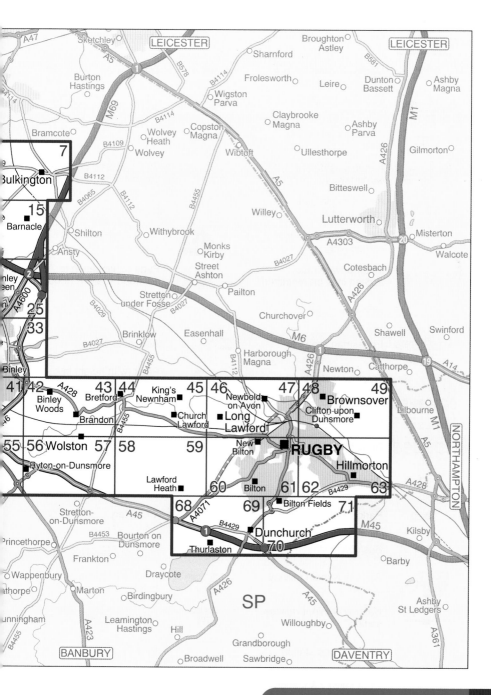

iv

Junction 9	Motorway & junction	*LC*	Level crossing
Services	Motorway service area	•——•——•——•	Tramway
	Primary road single/dual carriageway	- - - - - - -	Ferry route
Services	Primary road service area	....	Airport runway
	A road single/dual carriageway	— · — · — · —	County, administrative boundary
	B road single/dual carriageway	▼▼▼▼▼▼▼▼▼▼	Mounds
	Other road single/dual carriageway	**17**	Page continuation 1:15,000
	Minor/private road, access may be restricted	**3**	Page continuation to enlarged scale 1:10,000
← ←	One-way street		River/canal, lake, pier
	Pedestrian area		Aqueduct, lock, weir
- - - - - -	Track or footpath	465 ▲ Winter Hill	Peak (with height in metres)
	Road under construction		Beach
	Road tunnel		Woodland
P	Parking		Park
P+🚌	Park & Ride		Cemetery
🚌	Bus/coach station		Built-up area
	Railway & main railway station		Industrial/business building
	Railway & minor railway station		Leisure building
⊖	Underground station		Retail building
⊖	Light railway & station		Other building
+++++++++	Preserved private railway	**IKEA**	IKEA store

Symbol	Description	Symbol	Description
City wall		Castle	
A&E	Hospital with 24-hour A&E department	Historic house or building	
PO	Post Office	Wakehurst Place (NT)	National Trust property
Public library		M	Museum or art gallery
i	Tourist Information Centre	Roman antiquity	
i	Seasonal Tourist Information Centre	Ancient site, battlefield or monument	
Petrol station, 24 hour Major suppliers only		Industrial interest	
†	Church/chapel	Garden	
Public toilets		Garden Centre Garden Centre Association Member	
Toilet with disabled facilities		Garden Centre Wyevale Garden Centre	
PH	Public house AA recommended	Arboretum	
Restaurant AA inspected		Farm or animal centre	
Madeira Hotel	Hotel AA inspected	Zoological or wildlife collection	
Theatre or performing arts centre		Bird collection	
Cinema		Nature reserve	
Golf course		Aquarium	
Camping AA inspected		Visitor or heritage centre	
Caravan site AA inspected		Country park	
Camping & caravan site AA inspected		Cave	
Theme park		Windmill	
Abbey, cathedral or priory		Distillery, brewery or vineyard	

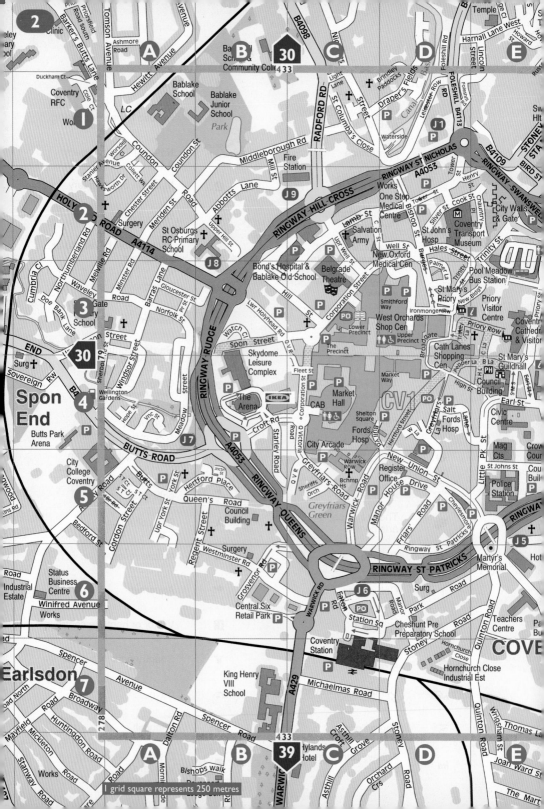

2

Coventry RFC

Ashmore Road

Duckham Ct

Coventry Clinic

Hewitt Avenue

Tomson Avenue

Cole Ct

Priorsfield Road South

Barker's Butts Lane

A

1

B

30

Bablake School & Community Colle

B4098

C

D

Temple

Harnall Lane West

Howard Street

Lincoln Street

E

Bablake School

Bablake Junior School

Park

Middleborough Rd

RADFORD RD

B4098

St Columba's Close

Light Lane

Brindley Paddocks

Draper's Fields

Canal Basin

LEICESTER ROW

FOLESHILL RD

B4113

Foleshill Rd

J1

B4109

RINGWAY SWANSWELL

STONEY STA

BIRD ST

Swi Hlt

Waterside

Coundon St

Coundon Rd

Mill St

Fire Station

RINGWAY ST NICHOLAS

A4053

Tower St

Works

One Stop Medical Centre

Bishop St

Silver St

Cook St

Chauntry Pl

M

City Walls & Gate

Coventry Transport Museum

Trinity St

2

HOLYHEAD ROAD

A4114

Stanley Avenue

Hawks Worth Dr

Worsdell St

Collett Wk

Chester Street

Meriden St

Upper Hill St

J9

RINGWAY HILL CROSS

Lamb St

Upr Well St

Salvation Army

New Oxford Medical Cen

Well St

Burges

St John's Hosp

Palmer La

Hales Street

St Mary's Priory

New Bldgs

Pool Meadow Bus Station

Priory Visitor Centre

Coventry Cathedral & Visitor

Surgery

St Osburgs RC Primary School

J8

Bond's Hospital & Bablake Old School

Belgrade Theatre

Corporation Street

Smithford Way

Ironmonger RW

Trinity La

Priory Row

St Mary's Guildhall

3

Minster Road

Barras Lane

Gloucester St

Norfolk St

Hill St

Lwr Holyhead Rd

Spon Street

PO

Lower Precinct

Upper Precinct

West Orchards Shop Cen

Gate

Pepper La

B La

PH

Cath Lanes Shopping Cen

High St

Council Building

St Mary's

GATE

Gulson Rd

END

Sovereign Rw

Surg

30

Windsor Street

Sherbon St

Watch Close

RINGWAY RUDGE

Skydome Leisure Complex

Fleet St

The Precinct

Market Way

CV1

Earl St

Civic Centre

Mag Cts

Crow Cour

Spon End

Wellington Gardens

4

Vnc St

Hope St

The Arena

IKEA

CAB

Market Hall

Shelton Square

Fords Hosp

Hertford Street

Greyfriars Lane

Salt La

PO

Fords Hosp

Little Pk St

St John's St

Cou Buil

Butts Park Arena

J7

Meadow Road

Croft Road

Starley Road

A4053

City Arcade

Warwick Row

Register Office

New Union St

Manor House Drive

Cheylesmore

Police Station

5

City College Coventry

Butts

York St

Hertford Place

Inchn St

Queen's Road

RINGWAY QUEENS

WARWICK RD

Greyfriars Green

Sheriffs Orch

Warwick Road

Bchmpl Hs

Friars' Road

Ringway

Quinton Road

J5

Bedford St

Gordon Street

Upr York St

Regent Street

Council Building

Westminster Rd

Surgery

Grosvenor Rd

Ringway St Patricks

Martyr's Memorial

Hot

6

Status Business Centre

Winifred Avenue Works

Central Six Retail Park

WARWICK RD

Eaton Rd

J6

PO

Station Sq

Surg

Park Road

Manor Road

Cheshunt Pre Preparatory School

Teachers Centre

Pa Bu

Road Industrial Estate

Spencer Avenue

King Henry VIII School

Spencer Road

A429

Coventry Station

Michaelmas Road

Stoney

Hornchurch Close

Hornchurch Close Industrial Est

COVE

Earlsdon

7

Broadway

Dalton Rd

Mornll St

Bishops walk

A433

A

B

39

Hylands Hotel

Asthill Grove

C

Asthill Croft

Orchard Crs

Stoney Road

D

Quinton Road

Wrighsm St

Thomas La

Joan ward st

E

The Mart

Mayfield

Mickleton Road

Huntingdon Road

Stanway Works

WARWICK

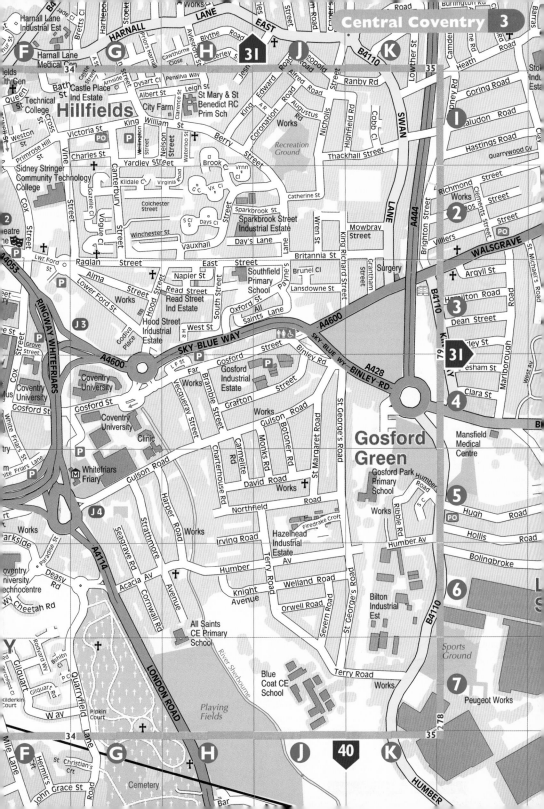

4

A B C D

Cowley Wood

433 34

1

Sole End Farm

Astley Lane

Cow Lees

Bedworth Lane

Woodlands Lane

88

Dove Cl

Way

2

Bedworth Woodlands

Taffs Farm

87

3

Astley Hall Farm

Smorrall Lane

The Lawns

Astley Lane

Bedworth Heath

Juniper Cl
The Pines
The Willows
The Laurels
The Alders
Laburnum Wy
The Limes
The Beeches

Buttercup Wy
Daisy
Bluebell Dr
Orchid Cl
Milw Cr
Onion
Fern Gv
Bluebell Dr

Wilder Rd
Marriott Rd
Lndl Sq
Daffodil Dr
Speedwell
Larkspur Gv
Primrose Cl
Columbine
Foxglove
The Wy
Bellairs Av
Bluebell Dr

Highfield House Farm

286

4

Ashington Road
Blyth Cl
Whitburn Rd
P C
R R C
Cardigan Road
Tenby Cl

Market End

Smercote Cl

Smorrall Lane

Newdigate Primary School

Anderton Road
Blair Dr

Newcomen

Keenan Dr

Keenan Dr

Dark Lane

Glebe Rd
Martins Rd
Kathleen Av
Cashmore Rd
Hammersley St
Hearne
Todps

5

Goodyers End

Hospital Lane

Mayor

Raynor Cfs
Dowty Cts
Howells
Newey Av
Drive

Road

Robinson Rd
Melros Av
McMahon Rd
Potters Rd
Henson Rd

End Lane

Goodyers End Prima School

Maynard Av
Jeffrey Close
Humphrey Cw
Moat Dr
Acorn Farm
Goodyers
End

M6

433 34

A B C D

Newland Hall Farm

Breach Brook

Royal Oak Lane

Newland

Police

12

1 grid square represents 500 metres

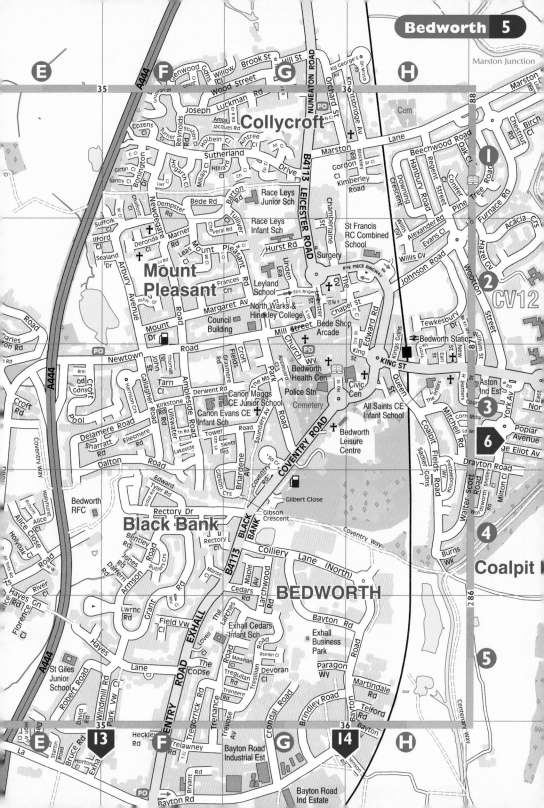

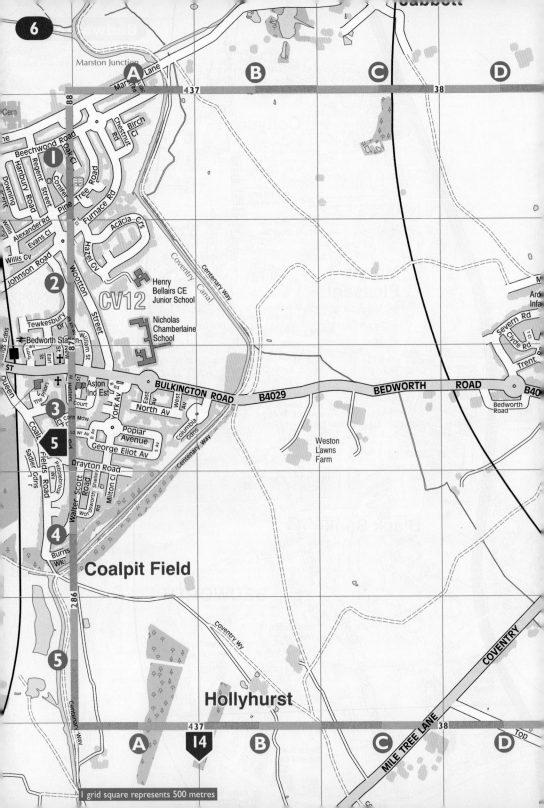

6

Marston Junction

A **B** **C** **D**

Marston Lilac Lane Road

437

88

38

Cem

Beechwood Road Oak Cl

1

Downing Crescent

Regent Street

Hanbury Road

Conifer Cl

Chestnut Rd

Birch Cl

Pine Tree Road

Furnace Road

Acacia Crs

Alexander Rd

Evans Cl

Willis Gv

Hazel Gv

Johnson Road

Coventry Canal

Centenary Way

2

Wootton Street

CV12

Henry Bellairs CE Junior School

Tewkesbury Dr

William St

Earl St

Thomas

Nicholas Chamberlaine School

Bedworth Sta.

88

ST

Queen St

The Priory's

Hatters

Court

Aston Ind Est

Bd

York Av

East Av

West Av

North Av

BULKINGTON ROAD

B4029

BEDWORTH ROAD

B40

Severn Rd

Clyde Rd

Trent

Ard Infa

M

3

5

Coalpit

Corn Mdw

La Wr Av

Poplar Avenue

Columbia Gdns

Bedworth Road

George Eliot Av

Sadler Gdns

Fields Road

Pebblebrook Wy

Drayton Road

Walter Scott Road

Cosworth

Shelley

Milton Cl

Centenary Way

Weston Lawns Farm

4

Burns Wk

Coalpit Field

286

Coventry Wy

5

Hollyhurst

COVENTRY

MILE TREE LANE

Top

Centenary Way

A **14** **B** **C** **D**

437

38

1 grid square represents 500 metres

E F G H

21 22

I

85

2

3

School La

Garden
Centre

A446

2

Little
Packington

Fishpool Lane

Packington Lane

River Blythe

†

84

Packington
Hall

Park Farm

Warwickshire County

Solihull

Hall Pool

4

Middle Bickenhill Lane

CHESTER ROAD

The Mill
Farm

5

Middle
Bickenhill

East Way

Coventry Road

BIRMINGHAM ROAD

COVENTRY ROAD

2283

National
Motorcycle Museum

E F G H

21 22

Ston Bridge 16

KENILWOR

Geary's
Heath

Pasture Farm

E   **6**   F   G   H

38   COVENTRY

MILE TREE LANE

Top   Road

The Fu
Farm

I

Coventry Way

39

85

Top   Road

Spring Rd

Park
Farm

Chapel
La

†

Barnacle

2

Lower   Road

Wood

Shilton   Lane

Chris Ln

M69

3

e Fields

Coventry   Way

84

4

Coventry   Way

Coventry   Way

Grove   Road

Ansty

Ma
Ha

Shilton Lane

Brookfield
Farm

Centenary Way

Meadow Close

The
Rw

B4065

owe
Common

Woodway Lane

Main
Rd

5

38

25

39

B4065

HINCKLEY ROAD

283

E   F   G   H

Lane

The Mill Farm

BIRMINGHAM

E F 1D G H Shepherds

22 23 83

A45

Maxstoke Lane W

Geary's Heath

Golf Course

I

Maxs

ROAD

Warwickshire County

Solihull

Somers Wood Caravan Park

Stonebridge Golf Club

The Somers

Forest Hall

Maxstoke

B410

Hampton Gra

2

BIRMINGHAM ROAD

Somers Road

Molands Bridge

A452

HAMPTON LANE

B4102

North Warwickshire Golf Club

Heath Farm

82

3

18

Golf Course

patrick ridge

Cornets End Lane

KENILWORTH ROAD

4

Hornbrook Farm

281

Cornets End

5

Mercote Mill Farm

E F G H

22 23

Park Farm

Green

18

Lane
Shepherds Lane
Maxstoke Lane
Whitestitch
A Lane
Old Hall Farm
B
Warwickshire County Solihull
C
B4102
D
Lodge Gr

424
83
25

A45

I
HAM ROAD

Forest Hall
Maxstoke Cl
Kittermaster Road
Kitchery Road
Meriden CE Primary School

FILLONGLEY ROAD

Highfield
Arden Cl
Alspath Road
Leymere Close

B4102
Walsh Lane

Eaves Green Lane

Meriden

2
B4104
Hampton Gra
82
Maxstoke Lane
W A

MAIN ROAD

PO
Fairfield Pl
The Croft
Clovers Cl
Waterfall Close
W A
Leys Lane

strawberry Fields
Innkeeper's Lodge
Manor Hotel

Old Road

BIRMINGHAM

Meriden House

3
Surgery

Church Lane

17

4

Berkswell Road

281

5
Cornets End

Heart of England

Cornets End Lane

A
424
B
26
Back Lane
C
25
D

Road

Four Oaks

rk Farm

1 grid square represents 500 metres

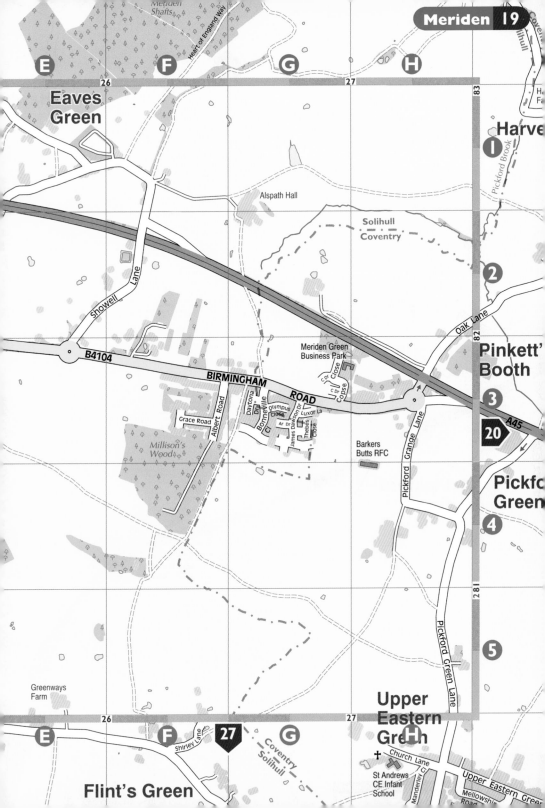

Meriden Shafts

Heart of England Way

E   26   F   G   27   H

Eaves Green

83

Harve

Solihull
Coventry

Alspath Hall

Snowell Lane

1

Pickford Brook

H F

2

Oak Lane

82

Pinkett' Booth

B4104

Meriden Green Business Park

3

A45

BIRMINGHAM ROAD

20

Albert Road

Grace Road

Daytona Dr

Bonneville Cl

Olympus Close

Ar Dr

James Dawton Dr

Thetles Close

Luxor La

C Dr

C Dr Copse

Close

Pickfo Green

Millison's Wood

Barkers Butts RFC

Pickford Grange Lane

4

281

5

Greenways Farm

Pickford Green Lane

Upper Eastern Gre n

H

E   26   F   27   G   27

Shirley Lane

Coventry
Solihull

Church Lane

St Andrews CE Infant School

Manderle

Upper Eastern

Mellows

Flint's Green

20

Coventry
Solihull

A 428 **B** **10** **C** 29 **D**

83

Hawke

Hill Fields
Farm

Harvest Hill Lane

Oak Lane

1 **Harvest Hill**

Hawkes

Pickford Brook

Washbrook Lane

Alton Hall
Farm

2

82

Oak Lane

Hill Lane

**Pinkett's
Booth**

Pickford
Farm

3 A45 Brick Hill

Pickford Grange Lane

19

Pickford

BIRMINGHAM ROAD

**Pickford
Green**

Windmill
Industrial
Estate

Birmingham Road

281

CV5

Brett Close
Worsfold Close
Harvey Close

4

Windmill Village
Golf & Leisure Club

The Windmill

Cameron Cl
Halifax Cl
Mackenzie Cl

Allesley
Croft

Pickford Green Lane

Ridge Ct

Fairways Cl
Berkett Cl

5

Golf Course

Oakford Drive

Birch Close

DUNCHURCH HIGHWAY

Woodridge Avenue

Larkfield Way

Rye Hill

A 428 **B** **28** **C** 29 **D**

Juniper Close
New Ash Dr
Cherrywood

Greenland Ct
Greenland Av
Greenland

P.H.
Peregrine Drive
Harpenden Drive

Debeck Drive
Park Hill Lane

Birch Lane

Manderley Cl
Upper Eastern Green
Mellowship Rd

Beaumaris Cl

Drive
Popperro Dr

1 grid square represents 500 metres

E F H G H

B4098

Sandpits Lane

Cardinal New
RC School &
Community

Ted Pitts Lane

Burton Cl

Freshfield Close

Carvell Close

Saunton Close

Lane

Marystow Close

Brown's Way

St Helen's Way

Brownshill Green

Wyevale Garden Centre

TAMWORTH ROAD

Brownshill

Waste

2 Keresley Grange Primary Sch

Green

Fairbourne W

Greno

Brownshill Ct

Kelmscot

Brn Rd

Jaguar Daimler Heritage Centre

Works

Allesley

North Brook Road

Staircase Lane

B4076

Northbrook Sports Club

North   Brook   Road

Coundon

Overslade Crescent

Birchfi

3

Brackley Close

22

Map

Hollyfast Primary School

Eversleigh Road

Normandy Place Road

4 Duncroft

Coundon

Northfield Farm

Staircase   Lane

Butt Lane

Northfield

Town Fields

Ramsay Crs

Anglesey Close

Whitelaw Crs

The Wardens

Ln C Av

Lion Fields Av

Lion Fields Av

Avenue

PO

gbey Clo

Packington Avenue

The Bridal Path

Allesley Hotel

Butcher's La

Rectory Lane

Church   Walk

Claremont Wk

River Sherbourne

COUNDON WEDGE DRIVE

Cem

Three Spires Special School

Hollyfast

Coundon Court School & Community College

Christ the King RC Junior Schoo

Rosslyn Av

Shorncliffe Road

Haynestone Road

William

Clipstone Road

Kendon Av

5

PO

Kingsbury Road

Tarlington Rd

Branksome

Dallington Rd

Gaveston Road

Welgarth Av

Westhill Road

Denham Av

KCKFORD WAY   A4114

Birmingham Rd

N Gra

E F 29 ooklands range Hotel

HOLYHEAD   ROAD

Sherbourne Fields School

G Tiverton Special School

Newington Cl

Rowington

ovecote Cl

Forfield

Donnington   Road

Bryfield Road

Chelveston Road

Clayton Road

H Coundon Primary School

Courtland

Evenlode

Avenue

Fedars Cres

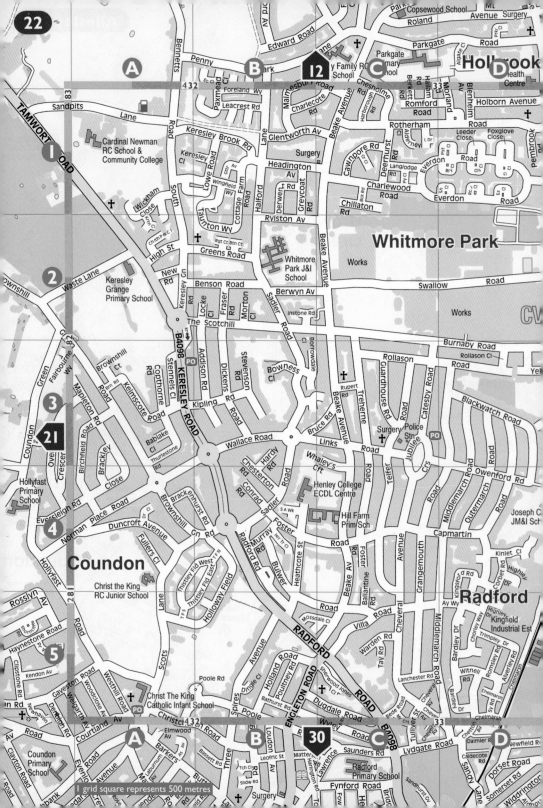

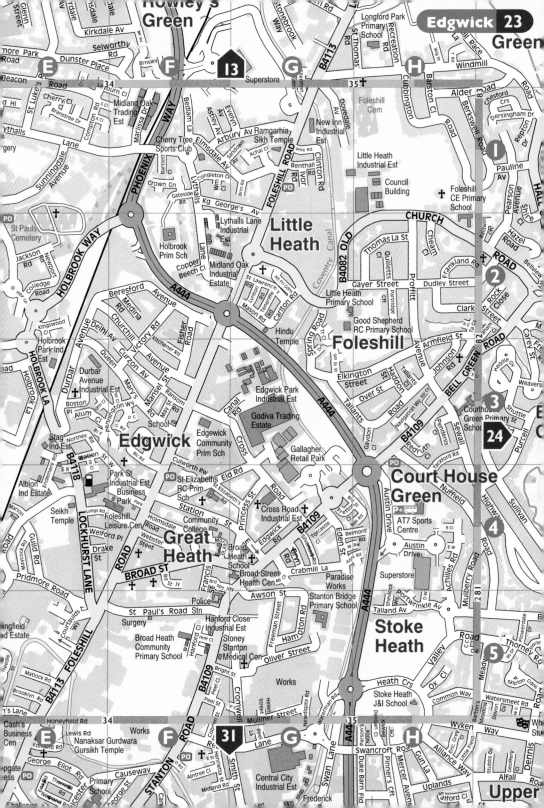

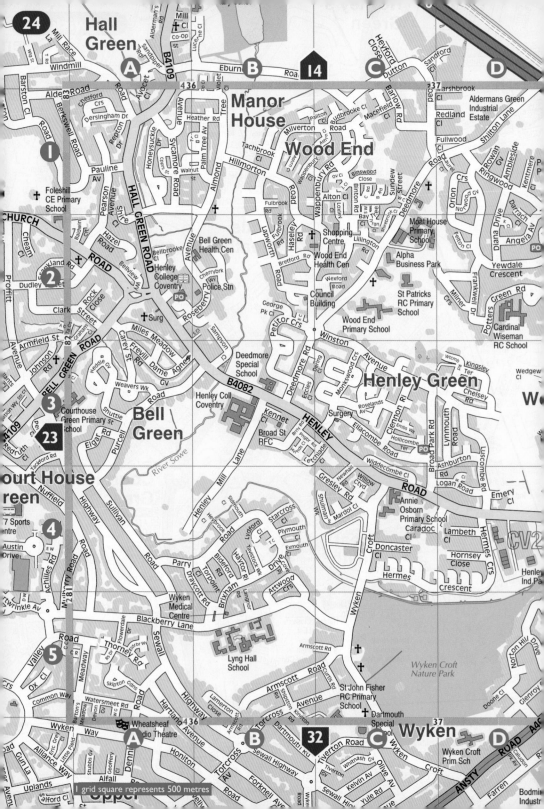

Brookfield Farm

Centenary Way

ay Lane

B4065

Main Rd

M6 Cl

E Sowe Common

F

15

G

H

HINCKLEY ROAD

83

I

38

39

Woodway Park Community School

Council Building

2 M6

M6

M69

Potter's Green

Merryfields Way

North Vw

Paradise Way

Showcase Cinemas

Junction 2

A46

Peacock Av

Hickory Cl

Norman Av

Wigston Rd

Beckfoot Dr

squirs Cft

Solent Drive

Walsgrave Triangle Business Park

Eden Rd

HINCKLEY ROAD

Olivier Way

Gielgud Way

Cross-Point Business Park

3

82

Southcot Wy

Linwood Dr

wvnd

Drt Pw Wy

Deanston Cft

Stoneywood Rd

Hemingford Rd

Ed Rd

D C

Leven Way

Stonefield

Lymore Croft

Mega Bowl

Redgrave Cl

Parkway

Ashcroft Way

Richardson Wy

Oakworth

Wigston Road

Denshaw Cft

Edgefield Rd

A4600

way Park

Dunsville Dr

Pilling Close

Lumsden Wy

Primary School

Boyd Cl

CWy

Gillians

Campanile

4

281

Anson Wy

Narberth Wy

Way

Calmere

Chaceley

Elizabeth Wy

Shirley Road

Regina Crs

HINCKLEY ROAD

Manfield Avenue

Blade Drive

Turlands Cl

Shuna Cft

The Kintyre

Walsgrave Retail Park

Walsgrave on Sowe

B4082

& St Paul RC School

WOODWAY LANE

A4600

PO

Boswell Drive

Walsgrave Gdns

Olaf Pl

Fronks Cl

Fairbanks

Lucian Cl

Osprey Drive

Brade Drive

The Close

Arkle Dr

Crowmere

Rd

Nrd Dr

Larkin

Walsgrave CE Primary School

Cress

Cape Road

Athol Rd

Feilding Cl

Field Cl

Beamish Cl

Barrow

Gibbs Cl

ANSTY ROAD

Hall Lane

Cloister Cft

House La

D Cl

Arne Rd

Ely Cl

H Cl

Fitzroy Cl

Farber Road

5

Caludon Centre

BMI Meriden Hospital

A&E

University Hospital

A46

E

F

33

G

H

38

39

River Sowe

Coventry

Warwickshire County

CLIFFOR

Dorchester

Tollard

Cranborne

Pearl Hyde Primary

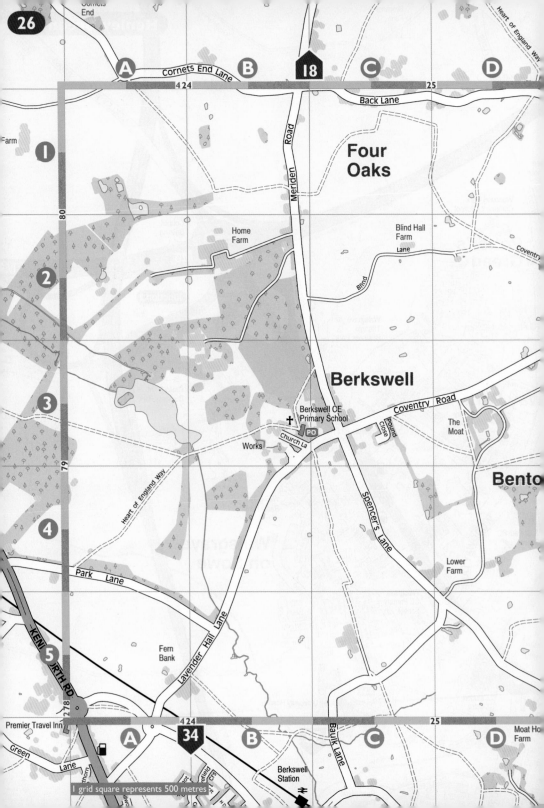

E F **19** G **H**

Upper Eastern Green

I

Greenways

Shirley Lane

Coventry Solihull

Flint's Green

Church Lane

St Andrews CE Infant School

Manderley

Hockley Lane

William Bree Road

Upper Eastern Gre

Mellowship Road

Holmes Dr

Despard

Eastern Green Junior Sch

Hockley

Morgans Rd

Orchard Dr

Garrick Close

Thm Cl

Kenthurst Cl

Frederick

Suttor

Hill House Farm

Broad Lane

Lyndhn Cl

Nova Cft

2

Oldthorn Cl

Broad Lane Trading Estate

Broad Lane

Coventry Solihull

Works

Banner Lane

B4

3

Peliam Bend

28

Placid Close

Hudson Av

Sycamore Cl

Manhattan

Wickmans Dr

Glendale Wy

4

Fow Pheasant Oak

Fein Bank Greenways

Oak

Milehurst Dr

Beec

Oak Wy

Tile Hurst Dr

Brck Dr

reen

Benton Green Lane

Victoria Farm

Rough Close

Cromes Wd

Ashfield

Asp

Maureen Cl

Dvrx Cl

Goodman Way

Ensign Cl

Edgehill Place

Wn Pl

Smmn Wy

5

Patricia Close

Stowe Pl

Ireton Cl

Tanyard

Grendon

B4101

Coventry Way

TANNERS' LANE

Nailcote Avenue

Conway Avenue

Station Avenue

Rex Cl

Trevor

Hathaway Rd

PO

Coventry Solihull

E **35** F G **36** H

Spencer's Lane

Coventry Way

well Lane

Reeves Green

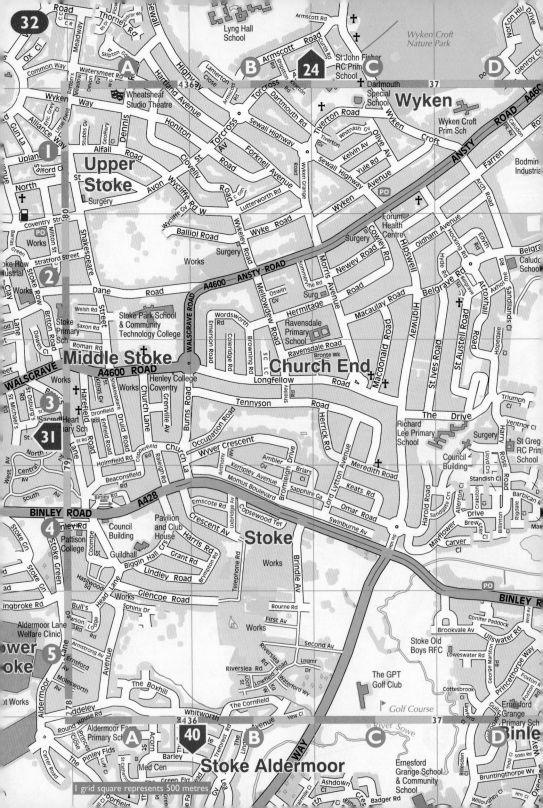

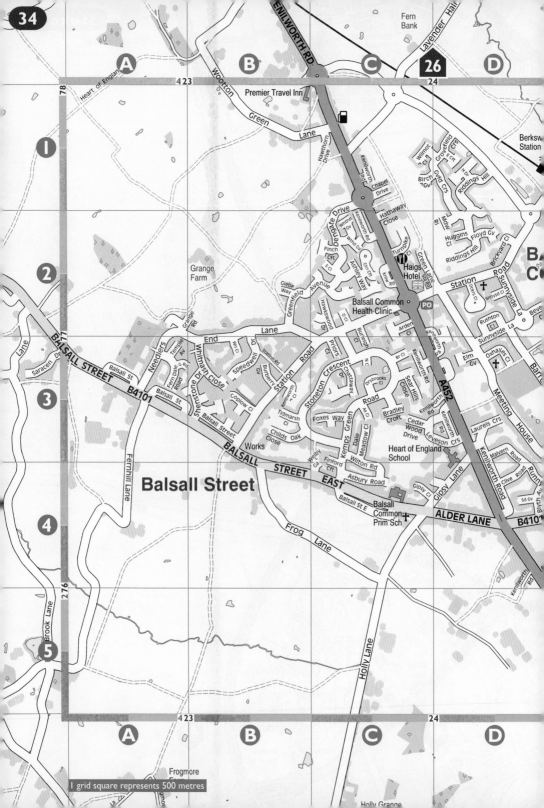

Balsall Street

E
F
G
27
26
H

Bauk Lane

Moat House Farm

Spencer's Lane

Coventry Way

Reeves G

I

Truggist Lane

Carol Green

Hodgett's Lane

Works
Lant Cl

SALL
MON

Nailcote Hall
Hotel

NAILCOTE LANE

2

77

Beechwood

B4101

3

36

Coventry Way

Old Waste Lane

WASTE LANE

Hodgett's Lane

ELSEY LANE

La

**Catchems
Corner**

4

Wellfield
Cl

Hob Lane

Berkswell
Windmill

Windmill Lane

Beanit
Farm

276

5

E
25
F
G
26
H

The Firs

Hob Lane

Bu
CE

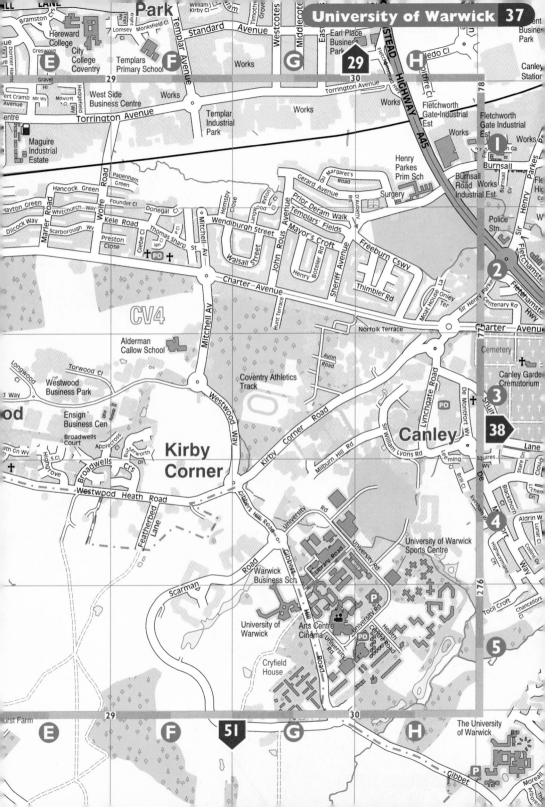

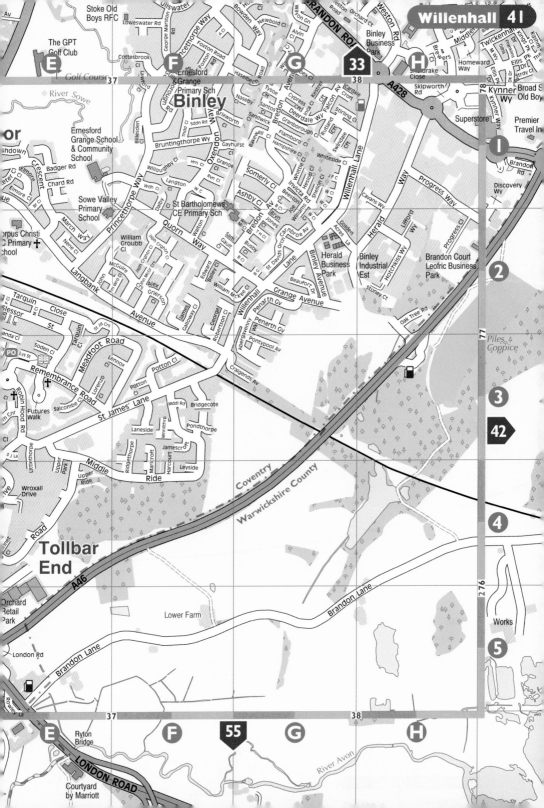

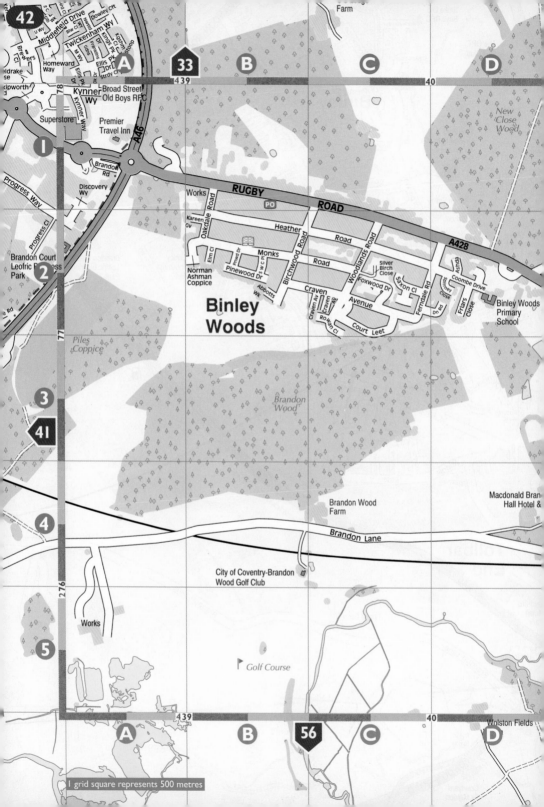

Binley Woods

42

33 439

A B C 40 D

Middlefield Drive
Twickenham Wy
Homeward Way
Brewers
Kipworth
Kynner Wy
Broad Street
Old Boys RFC
Superstore
Premier Travel Inn
Brandon Rd
Discovery Wy
Progress Way
Progress Cl
Brandon Court
Leofric Business Park

New Close Wood

Works
RUGBY ROAD
PO
Kareen Gv
Oakdale Road
Heather
Road
Elm Cl
Priest Dr
Pinewood Dr
Monks
Birchwood Road
Road
Woodlands Road
Silver Birch Close
Saxon Cl
Ferndale Rd
Ashda
Coombe Drive
Abbotts
Wk
Craven
Craven Av
Craven Av
Avenue
Foxwood Dr
Friars Close
Binley Woods Primary School
Norman Ashman Coppice
Rowan Cl
Court Leet

A428

2
Piles Coppice

3

41

Brandon Wood

4
Brandon Wood Farm
Brandon Lane
Macdonald Bran Hall Hotel &

City of Coventry-Brandon Wood Golf Club

Works

5
Golf Course

439 40
A B 56 C Wolston Fields D

1 grid square represents 500 metres

E 41 F G 42 H

Brinklow Heath

78

I

2

Gossett Lane

Speedway Lane

Brandon Grange Farm

77

BRANDON ROAD

A428

3

44

Works

RUGBY ROAD

Kirby Cl

The Close

Hallams Cl

Avondale Rd

Nicholas

Everton Close

brandon

Brandon La

River Avon

4

Marston

276

Wolston Business Park

Bluebells Dr

St Margarets Av

Hawthorne Close

Main

Meadow

Road

Priory Road

The Priory

Rugby Road

Road

5

Police Station

Wl B Rd

Elmdene Close

Larchfields

Surgery

St Margarets CE Primary School

Street

School Street

Coalpit Lane

New Far

E F 57 Wolston G 42 H

Coventry Wa

Manor Estate

PO

Brook Street

Dyer's Lane

Lammas

Cemetery

William Cree

Close

Salisbury

Mil Wy

Manor Est

Warwick Road

Chstnt Gv

Paddock Cl

E F G H

45 46

78

Fennis Fields Farm

I

Highfields

Little Lawford La

2

77

King's
Newnham

Lane

Newnham
Hall

Wyevale
Garden Centre

3

46

Dalton
Close

Kings Newnham Road School

House

Fitzalan Close

PO

Smithy
Lane

al Farm

Clayhill

4

Holly Gv

Church
Lawford

Green
La

Street

†

Church Road

Long

Coronation
Road

RUGBY ROAD

276

A428

COVENTRY

5

Livingsto

South View

ROAD

Mount
Pleasant

E F 59 G H

45 46

Fennis Fields Farm

Oxford Canal

Cathiron Lane

Oxford Canal Walk

Cathiron Lane

A 447 **B** 48 **C** **D**

78

1

Oxford Canal Walk

B4112

HARBOROUGH ROAD

Little Lawford Lane

Little Lawford Lane

2

47

Clayhill Lane

Little Lawford

River Avon

3

Holbrook Grange

45

Clayhill Farm

Clayhill Lane

Home Farm

Clayhill Lane

Cemetery

St John's La

Thomas Way

Hirst Cl

Ashman Avenue

Pr Cl

4

Long Lawford

Cross Street

The Spinney

Edric Wy

Boyce

Round Avenue

Grn

Holbrook Road

Tove Ct

Steeling

Judge Close

Street

Street

Long Lawford Primary School

Garratt Close

Anvil

W W

Thurnmill

C I Ms

Bailey's La

Elizabeth Way

Cherwell Wy

Cdr

Steeling Way

Rd

Weaver Dr

Rd

276

Chapel

West St Pl

Main Street

School Street

PO

Townsend

Cherwell Wy

Lane

Weaver Dr

Badger Close

Railway Street

Back

Tee

Redhill Rd

5

TRY

Livingstone Avenue

South View Road

The Green

Green

Lane

Tong Rd

ROAD

Briars Close

A 447 **B** **60** **C** 48 **D**

A428 RUGBY ROAD

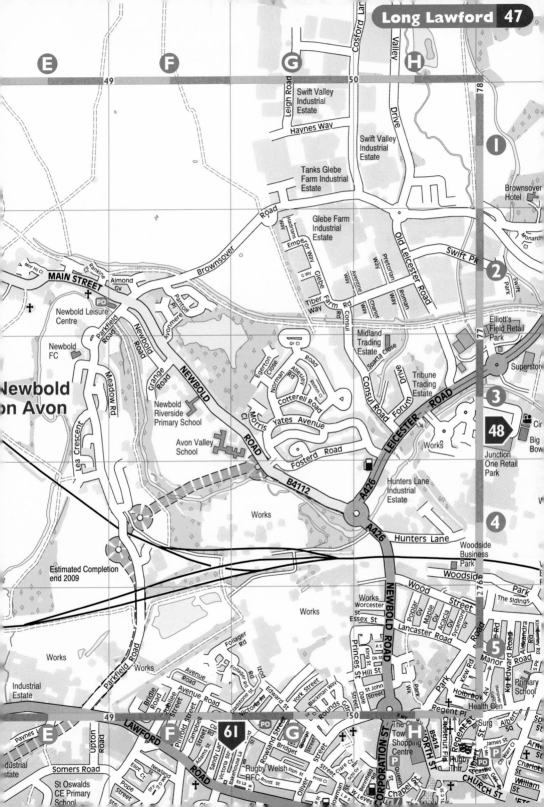

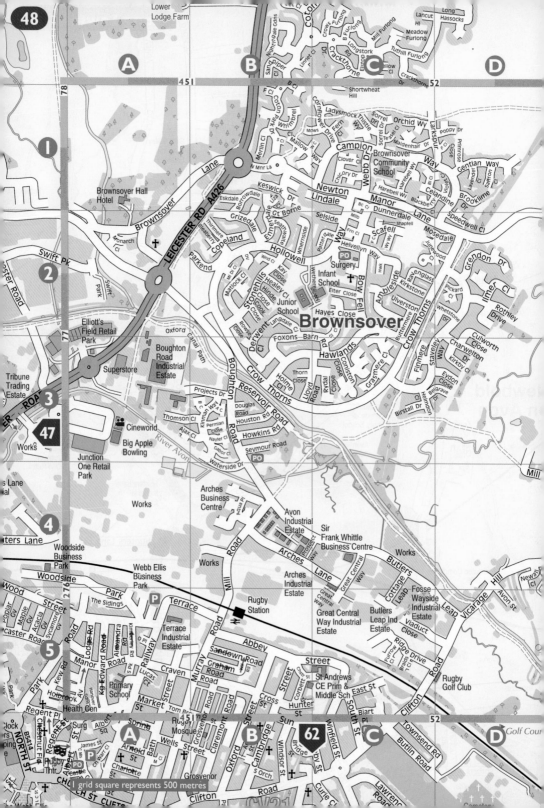

Newton

Leys

The Hollies
The Paddock
The Orchards
Pilgrims Lane

Main St
Shilton
Little London Lane

E **F** **G** **H**

54

78

River

I

Newton Road

...ton ...or House

...more Farm

77

2

Lane

Buckwell

3

Cemetery

Manor Farm

Buckwell Lane

Road
North Road
The Elms
Clifton upon Dunsmore CE Primary School
The Paddock
Church St
Robertson Cl
Hadfield Cl

Lilbourne Road

Dun

4

...ton Road
Main Street
Rugby Road
Whaley Cl
Allans La
Allans Cl
Orwell Cl
Everard Close
...C Cl

South Road
Shuttle
Worth Road

Clifton upon Dunsmore

276

Clifton Hall

5

The Kent

E **F** **63** **G** **H**

53 54

...ton Brook

Lane
Home Farm

50

A **B** **36** **C** **D**

Burton Green

427d Lane

Hob Lane

Burton Green
CE Primary

Coventry Way

1

75

2

Long Meadow
Barn Farm

Redfern
Manor

3

BIRMINGHAM

74

ROAD

South H
Farm

Crackley Lane

Rye

Dunns Pitts
Farm

4

se Farm

A452

Red Lane

Camp Farm

Hollis Lane

5

273

Chase Lane

East Chase
Farm

Priors Field
CP School

Clinton La

A452

B4103

St Augustines RC
Primary School

BEEHIVE HILL

A Pleasance Farm

28 427

B

64

C

Cobbs
Rd

CLINTON LANE

Woodcote
Avenue

De Montfort

Avenue

Priorsfld
Road

Quarry
Rd

Fernhill

Malthouse Lane

D

Amherst Road

Berkel

Bromley
Cl

Port

1 grid square represents 500 metres

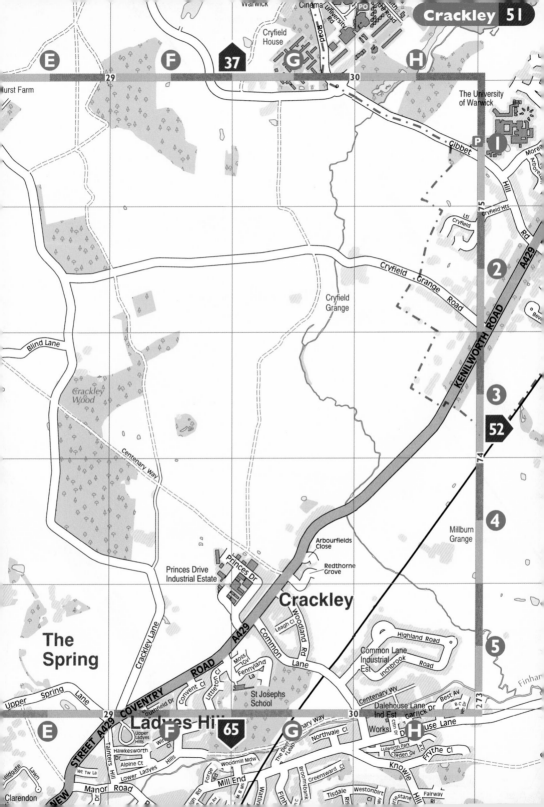

E 29 F 37 30 G H

P PO

Cinema University Rd Warwick

Cryfield House

The University of Warwick

P 1

Gibbet

Hill Rd A429

Cryfield Hts

Ltl Cryfield

2

Cryfield Grange Road

KENILWORTH ROAD

75

Cryfield Grange

Bev

Blind Lane

3

52

74

Crackley Wood

4

Millburn Grange

Centenary Way

Arbourfields Close

Redthorne Grove

Princes Dr

Princes Drive Industrial Estate

Crackley

Highland Road

5

Common Lane Industrial Est

Inchbrook Road

Leagh Cl

Woodland Rd

Common Lane

The Spring

Crackley Lane

A429 ROAD

COVENTRY

Moss Gv

Fennyland La

Convent Cl

Littleton Cl

St Josephs School

Highland Road

Centenary Wy

Best Av

Dalehouse Lane Ind Est

House Lane

Garlick Dr

Works

B C Dr

Finha

273

Finham

Upper Spring Lane

STREET A429

NEW

Manor Road

Southfield Dr

E 29 COVENTRY 30 G H

F 65

Ladyes Hill

Upper Ladyes Hills

Wil

Hills

Tainters Hill

Hawkesworth Dr

Alpine Ct

Lower Ladyes Hills

Forge

Mill End

Woodmill Mdw

nary Way

The Best Leasb

Watting St

Northvale Cl

Finh

Tisdale Ri

Broomsward Cl

Greensward Cl

Westonbirt

Knowle

Lulworth Park

Virden Gv

Frythe Cl

Fairway Ri

Limestone

Wt Tw La

Ieldgate Lawn

Clarendon

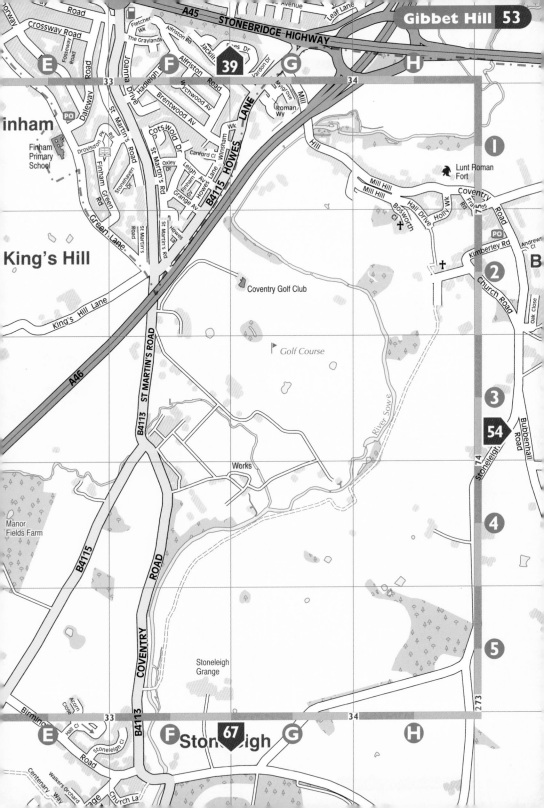

54

40

I

2

3

53

4

5

STONEBRIDGE HIGHWAY

River Sowe

A

A45

B

C

D

Sibree Road

Rowley Dr

Rowley Drive

435

36

Rowley Road

Stonebridge
Trading
Estate

Coventry

Warwickshire County

Middlemarch
Business
Park

Wood
Roa

Lunt Roman
Fort

Rowley Road

M Midland Air Museum

Coventry
Road

Hall Drive

Holly Wk

75

Rd

nces

Road

PO

Kimberley Rd

Andrews
Cl

Oak Close

Baginton

Church Road

74

Stoneleigh Road

Bubbenhall Road

Coventry
Airport

Coventry
Trading
Estate

Siskin Parkway West

Middlemarch
Business
Park

Coventry
Trading
Estate

Siskin Parkway
East

Siskin Pkwy East

Siskin Parkway East

Middlemarch
Business
Park

Rock Farm

River Avon

273

435

Bubbenhall
Bridge

A

B

C

D

36

End
Close

I grid square represents 500 metres

London Rd

Brandon Lane

Roxley La

E

F

41

G

H

37

38

Ryton
Bridge

LONDON ROAD

Courtyard
by Marriott

River Avon

I

75

Redland Lane

Church Road

Church Rd

2 Ryto
Duns

A45

LONDON ROAD

Glenfern
Gdns

Works

Chapel
La

Field
W

Bagshaw Cl

Crs

Fetherston Cl

PO

3

OXFORD ROAD

Centenary Way

Handley's
Cl

Soden's Av

Warren Field

High Street

Poplar

Xe
nk

56

Ryton
Lodge

Provost Williams
CE Primary School

Warren
Cl

Cedar
Av

Works

LEAMINGTON ROAD

Holly

ROAD

A423

Mann's Cl

Coppice

4

Works

Centenary Way

Works

5

273

OXFORD ROAD

37

38

E

F

G

H

LEAMINGTON ROAD

A445

Ryton
Pool

bbenhall

56

A   B   **42**   C   D

Golf Course

439   40

Wolston Fields Farm

I

75

Redland Lane

Church Rd

Works

Centenary Way

2

Church Road

Chapel La

Ryton-on-Dunsmore

Field VW

Ryton Organic Gardens

Bagshaw Cl

PO

Wolston Lane

C Cl

Fetherston Crs

Handley's Cl

B Cl

Crs

3

Soden's Av

High Street

Poplar GV

55

Holly Drive

Lea WK

Cedar Av

Warren Cl

Holly Dr

74

LONDON ROAD

A445

LONDON ROAD   A45

Grange Farm

LONDON ROAD A45

ROAD

Mann's Cl

Coppice Close

4

LEAMINGTON

Works

Freeboard Lane

5

273

Ryton Heath

439   40

Plott

A   B   C   D

OXFORD ROAD

Lane

I grid square represents 500 metres

Wolston

E

F

43

G

H

I

2

3

58

4

5

St Margarets
CE Primary
School

Police
Station

Wl B Rd

Main

Mead

Road

Elmdene
Close

Surgery

Larchfields

School St

Rugby

Coalpit Lane

New Farm

41

42

75

74

273

Coventry Way

Paddocks Cl

Manor Estate

William Cres

Salisbury

Manor Est

Mill Wy

Kelsey's Cl

Wolston Lane

Warwick Road

Stretton Road

John
Simpson
Close

Brook
Street

Chstnt Gv

PO

Lammas
Ct

Dyer's Lane

Cemetery

Coalpit Lane

Grounds Farm

Fosse Farm

Dyer's Lane

FOSSE WAY

Heath
Busine
Park

Heath
House

FOSSE WAY

Frog
Hall

Knightlow CE (Aided)
Primary School

Lane

School

Ferry
Farm

41

42

E

F

Squires Rd

Robert
Close

Hill

Moor
Farm
Close

FOSSE

Meadow Close

Surgery

rchard

ookside

G

H

Avenue
House

Rugby Lane

A45

LONDON ROAD

A 4 43 B 44 C 44 D

New 1

Limestone Hall

75

Coalpit Lane

2

Rookery Hall

Heath Business Park
Heath House
Heath Farm

3

57

74

Ling Lane

4

Coalpit Lane

5

Manor Farm

Ferry Farm

273

OAD 4 43 44 Wolston Grange

A Dunsmore Heath B Home Farm C D

Avenue House

by Lane A45

1 grid square represents 500 metres

ROAD

E   F   **45**   G   H

ount
Pleasant

I

2   Lawford
Farm

3

60 ▶ Completic

4

Lawford Lodge
Farm

ng Lane   Ling Lane

5

273

Lawford Heath
Industrial Estate

Works

Lawford Heath

The
Ryelands

E   **45**   F   **68**   G   H

Coalpit Lane

Lawford Heath

The
Crescent

Potford's Dam
Farm

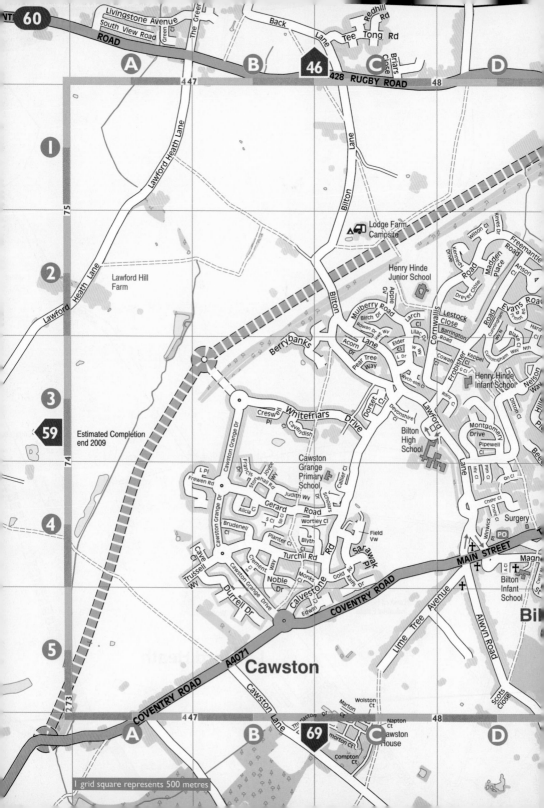

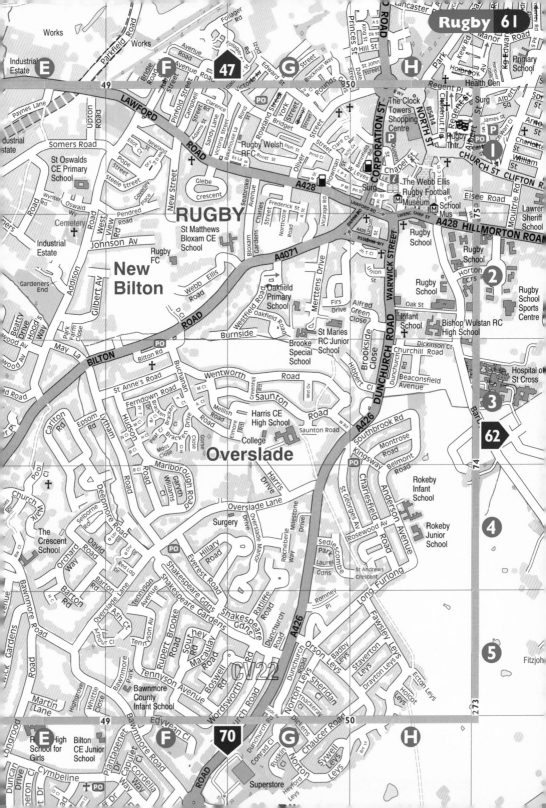

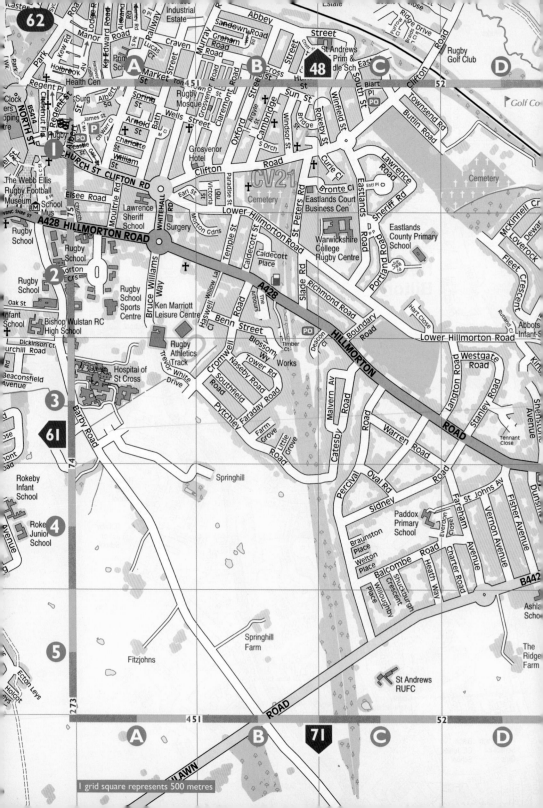

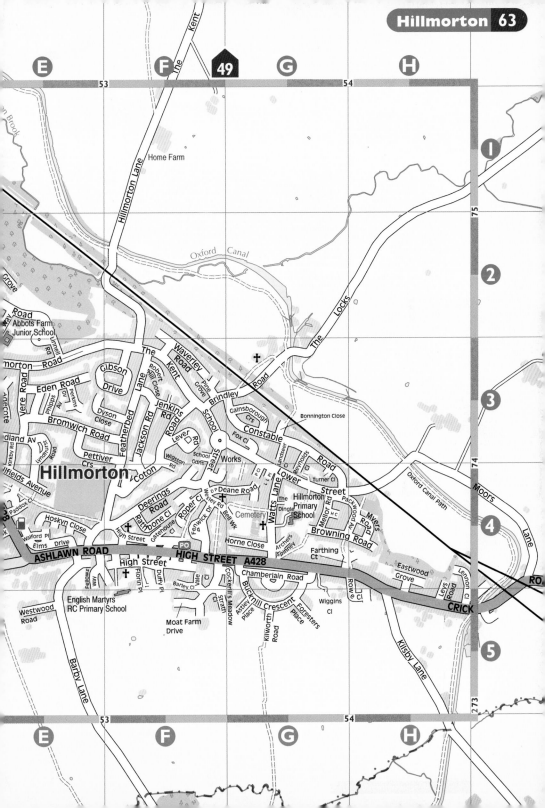

E F **53** G H

Stoneleigh
Grange

COVENTRY

Birmingham 33 B4113 34 73

Acorn
Close

Hall Cl

Stoneleigh Cl

Stoneleigh

Road

Walkers Orchard

Centenary Way

Vicarage Road

Church La

✝

I

STONELEIGH ROAD

Centenary Way

Stoneleigh Deer Park
Golf Club

Cloud Bridge

2

River Avon

Golf Course

72

3

Stoneleigh Deer Park
Business Village

Stareton

4

271

Stoneleigh Pk

STONELEIGH ROAD

5

A445

33 34

E F G H

Stone House
Farm

LEICEST LANE

Furzenhill
Farm

Lawford Heath

68

A   B   59   C   D
        46

COVENTRY

445
73

The Ryelands

Lawford Heath Lane

1

The Crescent

Potford's Dam Farm

A4071

72

LONDON ROAD

2

Lawford Heath Lane

Lawford Heath Lane

A45

Travelodge

Dunchurch Trading Estate

3

COVENTRY ROAD

B44

Junction 1

271

4

Stocks Lane

The Bch o

Street

Church walk

Lane

Biggin Hall

Main

Church

PdGn bg

Moat Close

Biggin Hall Lane

Thurlaston Grange

Grayso Orchard

5

445
73

46

A   B   46   C   D

Draycote Water

1 grid square represents 500 metres

70

Martin Lane

Bawnmore Park

Rupert Rd
Tennyson Avenue
South Rd
Macaulay Road
Boswell Rd
Wordsworth Rd

CV22

Orson Leys
Badby Leys
Staverton Leys
Ecton Leys
Sheridan
Dunchurch Rd

Fitzjohns

Bawnmore County Infant School

A

B

61

C

D

Rugby High School for Girls

Bilton CE Junior School

449

73

Edyvean Cl

Bawnmore Road

Plantagenet Dr

Capulet Cl

Cordella Cl

Dunchurch Road

Dunchurch Rd
Conrad Cl
Ruskin Rd
Norton Leys
Dickens Rd
Chaucer Road
Sywell Leys

Bri ly

50

Cymbeline

PO

Juliet Dr
Ariel Wy
Wolsey Road
Falstaff Dr
Macbeth Cl
Arden Close

Superstore

Hewford Leys

ASH

Othello
Montague

Road

DUNCHURCH

Bilton Fields

Ash Hou

Ash

2

ROAD   A426

72

The Drive

ASHLAWN ROAD

B4429

Inwoods Farm

Lane

Rugby Rd

RUGBY

3

field Lane

Homefield School

Bilton Grange School

69

arage Lane

GEC Management College

Dunchurch Lodge

4

Dunchurch

RY ROAD

B4429

271

5

A45

M45

Onley Grounds

449

50

A

B

C

D

DAVENTRY ROAD

1 grid square represents 500 metres

Springhill Farm

The Ridgeway Farm

E

F St Andrews RUFC

62

G

H

ROAD

52

53

73

I

Rains Brook

Warwickshire County

Northamptonshire County

2

72

Lower Rainsbrook Farm

Onley Lane

3

Oxford Canal Path

Whitehall Farm

Onley Farm

4

M45

271

5

Barby Lane

Barby Wood Farm

HM Young Offenders Institution

52

53

E

F

G

H

Alderman's Green 14 B4	Coalpit Field 6 A4	Kenilworth 64 D4
Allesley 21 E3	Collycroft 5 G1	Keresley 12 A4
Ansty 15 H5	Corley 11 E1	Keresley Newlands 12 C2
Ash Green 12 D2	Corley Moor 10 B1	Kings Hill 53 E2
Baginton 54 A2	Coundon 21 H4	King's Newnham 45 F2
Balsall Common 34 D2	Court House Green 23 H4	Kirby Corner 37 F3
Balsall Street 34 A4	Coventry 2 E7	Ladyes Hill 65 F1
Barnacle 15 G2	Crackley 51 G5	Lawford Heath 59 G5
Bedworth 5 G5	Dunchurch 69 H4	Lime Tree Park 28 D5
Bedworth Heath 4 C3	Earlsdon 30 B5	Little Heath 23 G2
Beechwood 35 G3	Eaves Green 19 E1	Little Lawford 46 B2
Bell Green 24 A3	Edgwick 23 F3	Little Packington 9 F2
Benton Green 26 D4	Exhall 14 A1	Longford 13 G4
Berkswell 26 C3	Finham 53 E1	Long Lawford 46 A4
Bilton 60 D5	Flint's Green 27 E1	Lower Eastern Green 28 B3
Bilton Fields 70 B1	Foleshill 23 G3	Lower Stoke 31 H5
Binley 41 F1	Four Oaks 26 C1	Manor House 24 B1
Binley Woods 42 B2	Foxford 13 G4	Marston 43 H4
Black Bank 5 F4	Gibbet Hill 52 B2	Meriden 18 C2
Brandon 43 E4	Goodyers End 4 B4	Middle Bickenhill 9 E5
Bretford 44 B2	Gosford Green 3 K4	Middle Stoke 31 H3
Brownshill Green 21 F2	Great Heath 23 F4	Mount Pleasant 5 F2
Brownsover 48 B2	Green Lane 38 D4	Neal's Green 13 E2
Bulkington 7 F4	Hall Green 14 A5	New Bilton 61 F2
Burton Green 36 B5	Hampton in Arden 16 A4	Newbold on Avon 47 E3
Canley 37 H3	Harvest Hill 20 A1	Overslade 61 F3
Carol Green 35 G1	Hawkes End 20 D1	Park Hill 65 H2
Catchems Corner 35 F4	Henley Green 24 C3	Pickford 20 B3
Cawston 60 B5	Hillfields 3 F1	Pickford Green 20 A4
Chapel Fields 29 H4	Hillmorton 63 E4	Pinkett's Booth 20 A3
Cheylesmore 39 H2	Hockley 27 G2	Pinley 40 B2
Church End 32 B3	Holbrooks 12 D5	Potter's Green 25 E2
Church Lawford 45 E4	Hollyberry End 10 A4	Radford 22 D5
Clifton upon Dunsmore 49 F4	Hollyhurst 6 B5	Reeves Green 35 H1
		Rowley's Green 13
		Rugby 61
		Ryton-on-Dunsmore 56
		St Johns 65
		Spon End 30
		The Spring 51
		Stareton 67
		Stivichall 39
		Stoke 32
		Stoke Aldermoor 40
		Stoke Heath 23
		Stonebridge 16
		Stoneleigh 67
		Thurlaston 68
		Tile Hill 28
		Toft 69
		Tollbar End 41
		Upper Eastern Green 19
		Upper Stoke 32
		Walsgrave on Sowe 25
		Weston in Arden 5
		Westwood Heath 36
		Whitemoor 65
		Whitley 40
		Whitmore Park 22
		Whoberley 29
		Willenhall 40
		Windy Arbour 65
		Wolston 57
		Wood End 24
		Woodway Park 24
		Wyken 32

USING THE STREET INDEX

Street names are listed alphabetically. Each street name is followed by its postal town or area locality, the Postcode District, the page number, and the reference to the square in which the name is found.

Standard index entries are shown as follows:

Abberton Wy *TLHL/CAN* CV4......... **52** A1

Street names and selected addresses not shown on the map due to scale restrictions are shown in the index with an asterisk:

Abbey Cottages *COVS* CV3 * **41** G2

GENERAL ABBREVIATIONS

ACC ...... ACCESS	CSWY ...... CAUSEWAY	GND ...... GROUND	MEM ...... MEMOR
ALY ...... ALLEY	CT ...... COURT	GRA ...... GRANGE	MI ...... M
AP ...... APPROACH	CTRL ...... CENTRAL	GRG ...... GARAGE	MKT ...... MARK
AR ...... ARCADE	CTS ...... COURTS	GT ...... GREAT	MKTS ...... MARKE
ASS ...... ASSOCIATION	CTYD ...... COURTYARD	GTWY ...... GATEWAY	ML ...... M
AV ...... AVENUE	CUTT ...... CUTTINGS	GV ...... GROVE	MNR ...... MAN
BCH ...... BEACH	CV ...... COVE	HGR ...... HIGHER	MS ...... ME
BLDS ...... BUILDINGS	CYN ...... CANYON	HL ...... HILL	MSN ...... MISSI
BND ...... BEND	DEPT ...... DEPARTMENT	HLS ...... HILLS	MT ...... MOU
BNK ...... BANK	DL ...... DALE	HO ...... HOUSE	MTN ...... MOUNTA
BR ...... BRIDGE	DM ...... DAM	HOL ...... HOLLOW	MTS ...... MOUNTAI
BRK ...... BROOK	DR ...... DRIVE	HOSP ...... HOSPITAL	MUS ...... MUSE
BTM ...... BOTTOM	DRO ...... DROVE	HRB ...... HARBOUR	MWY ...... MOTORW
BUS ...... BUSINESS	DRY ...... DRIVEWAY	HTH ...... HEATH	N ...... NOR
BVD ...... BOULEVARD	DWGS ...... DWELLINGS	HTS ...... HEIGHTS	NE ...... NORTH EA
BY ...... BYPASS	E ...... EAST	HVN ...... HAVEN	NW ...... NORTH WE
CATH ...... CATHEDRAL	EMB ...... EMBANKMENT	HWY ...... HIGHWAY	O/P ...... OVERPA
CEM ...... CEMETERY	EMBY ...... EMBASSY	IMP ...... IMPERIAL	OFF ...... OFFI
CEN ...... CENTRE	ESP ...... ESPLANADE	IN ...... INLET	ORCH ...... ORCHA
CFT ...... CROFT	EST ...... ESTATE	IND EST ...... INDUSTRIAL ESTATE	OV ...... O
CH ...... CHURCH	EX ...... EXCHANGE	INF ...... INFIRMARY	PAL ...... PALA
CHA ...... CHASE	EXPY ...... EXPRESSWAY	INFO ...... INFORMATION	PAS ...... PASSA
CHYD ...... CHURCHYARD	EXT ...... EXTENSION	INT ...... INTERCHANGE	PAV ...... PAVILI
CIR ...... CIRCLE	F/O ...... FLYOVER	IS ...... ISLAND	PDE ...... PARA
CIRC ...... CIRCUS	FC ...... FOOTBALL CLUB	JCT ...... JUNCTION	PH ...... PUBLIC HOU
CL ...... CLOSE	FK ...... FORK	JTY ...... JETTY	PK ...... PA
CLFS ...... CLIFFS	FLD ...... FIELD	KG ...... KING	PKWY ...... PARKW
CMP ...... CAMP	FLDS ...... FIELDS	KNL ...... KNOLL	PL ...... PLA
CNR ...... CORNER	FLS ...... FALLS	L ...... LAKE	PLN ...... PL
CO ...... COUNTY	FM ...... FARM	LA ...... LANE	PLNS ...... PLAI
COLL ...... COLLEGE	FT ...... FORT	LDG ...... LODGE	PLZ ...... PLA
COM ...... COMMON	FTS ...... FLATS	LGT ...... LIGHT	POL ...... POLICE STATI
COMM ...... COMMISSION	FWY ...... FREEWAY	LK ...... LOCK	PR ...... PRIN
CON ...... CONVENT	FY ...... FERRY	LKS ...... LAKES	PREC ...... PRECIN
COT ...... COTTAGE	GA ...... GATE	LNDG ...... LANDING	PREP ...... PREPARATO
COTS ...... COTTAGES	GAL ...... GALLERY	LTL ...... LITTLE	PRIM ...... PRIMA
CP ...... CAPE	GDN ...... GARDEN	LWR ...... LOWER	PROM ...... PROMENA
CPS ...... COPSE	GDNS ...... GARDENS	MAG ...... MAGISTRATES'	PRS ...... PRINCE
CR ...... CREEK	GLD ...... GLADE	MAN ...... MANSIONS	PRT ...... PA
CREM ...... CREMATORIUM	GLN ...... GLEN	MD ...... MEAD	PT ...... POI
CRS ...... CRESCENT	GN ...... GREEN	MDW ...... MEADOWS	PTH ...... PA

...PIAZZA	SCH...SCHOOL
...QUADRANT	SE...SOUTH EAST
...QUEEN	SER...SERVICE AREA
...QUAY	SH...SHORE
...RIVER	SHOP...SHOPPING
...ROUNDABOUT	SKY...SKYWAY
...ROAD	SMT...SUMMIT
...RIDGE	SOC...SOCIETY
...REPUBLIC	SP...SPUR
...RESERVOIR	SPR...SPRING
...RUGBY FOOTBALL CLUB	SQ...SQUARE
...RISE	ST...STREET
...RAMP	STN...STATION
...ROW	STR...STREAM
...SOUTH	STRD...STRAND

SW...SOUTH WEST	VIAD...VIADUCT
TDG...TRADING	VIL...VILLA
TER...TERRACE	VIS...VISTA
THWY...THROUGHWAY	VLG...VILLAGE
TNL...TUNNEL	VLS...VILLAS
TOLL...TOLLWAY	VW...VIEW
TPK...TURNPIKE	W...WEST
TR...TRACK	WD...WOOD
TRL...TRAIL	WHF...WHARF
TWR...TOWER	WK...WALK
U/P...UNDERPASS	WKS...WALKS
UNI...UNIVERSITY	WLS...WELLS
UPR...UPPER	WY...WAY
V...VALE	YD...YARD
VA...VALLEY	YHA...YOUTH HOSTEL

POSTCODE TOWNS AND AREA ABBREVIATIONS

WTH...Bedworth	COVN...Coventry north
AMNEC...Birmingham N.E.C.	COVS...Coventry south
WD/FDBR/MGN...Chelmsley Wood/ Fordbridge/ Marston Green	COVW...Coventry west
	CSHL/WTROR...Coleshill/Water Orton
	HIA/OLT...Hampton in Arden/ Olton
OV...Coventry	KNWTH...Kenilworth
OVE...Coventry east	

LGN/SDN/BHAMAIR...Lyndon Green/ Sheldon/Birmingham Airport	RLSN...Royal Leamington Spa north
LUTT...Lutterworth	RRUGBY...Rural Rugby
NUN...Nuneaton	RUGBYN/HIL...Rugby north/ Hillmorton
RCOVN/BALC/EX...Rural Coventry north/Balsall Common/ Exhall	RUGBYS/DCH...Rugby south/ Dunchurch
	TLHL/CAN...Tile Hill/Canley

A

berton Wy *TLHL/CAN* CV4.....52 A1
bbey Cottages *COVS* CV3 *.....41 G2
beydale CI *COVS* CV3.....33 E3
bbey End *KNWTH* CV8.....65 E3
bbey HI *KNWTH* CV8.....65 E3
bbey Rd *COVS* CV3.....40 A3
bbey St *RUGBYN/HIL* CV21.....48 B5
bbey Wy *COVS* CV3.....40 A3
botsbury CI *COVE* CV2.....33 F2
botts La *COV* CV1.....2 B2
botts Wk *COVS* CV3.....42 B2
botts Wy *RUGBYN/HIL* CV21.....63 E3
ercorn Rd *COVW* CV5.....29 H4
erdeen Rd *COVW* CV5.....28 D4
ergavenny Wk *COVS* CV3.....41 G3
acia Av *COV* CV1.....3 C6
acia Crs *BDWTH* CV12.....6 A2
acia Gv *RUGBYN/HIL* CV21.....47 H5
hal CI *COVN* CV6.....23 C1
chilles Rd *COVN* CV6.....23 H5
orn CI *BDWTH* CV12.....4 B5
KNWTH* CV8.....53 E5
orn Dr *RUGBYS/DCH* CV22.....60 C3
orn St *COVS* CV3.....40 C1
lam Rd *COVN* CV6.....23 G4
ams St *RUGBYN/HIL* CV21.....61 F1
are Dr *COVS* CV3.....39 F1
cock Dr *KNWTH* CV8.....65 G2
denbrooke Rd
RCOVN/BALC/EX CV7.....12 B1
derley St *COV* CV1.....31 F2
dison Rd *COVN* CV6.....22 B3
RUGBYS/DCH CV22.....61 E2
elaide St *COV* CV1.....31 F2
kinson Av *RUGBYS/DCH* CV22.....69 G4
miral Gdns *KNWTH* CV8.....65 H1
incourt Rd *COVS* CV3.....39 H1
nsbury Rd *COVW* CV5.....38 B1
sdale CI *COVN* CV6.....14 A4
ntree CI *BDWTH* CV12.....5 G1
COVN CV6.....21 G5
COVN CV6.....31 F1
rport Wy *HIA/OLT* B92.....8 A5
ax CI *RUGBYN/HIL* CV21.....48 A3
andale Av *COVW* CV5.....28 B2
an Higgs Wy *TLHL/CAN* CV4.....36 B2
pany Rd *COVW* CV5.....30 B5
ert Crs *COVN* CV6.....12 C5
ert Fearn Gdns *COVN* CV6.....23 E3
ert Rd *COVW* CV5.....19 F3
ert Sq *RUGBYN/HIL* CV21.....62 A1
ert St *COV* CV1.....3 G1
RUGBYN/HIL CV21.....61 H1
gion St *KNWTH* CV8.....65 F2
lbourne Rd *COV* CV1.....30 D1
lbury Ri *COVW* CV5.....29 F2
ler La *RCOVN/BALC/EX* CV7.....34 D4
derman's Green Rd *COVE* CV2.....14 A5
der Meadow CI *COVN* CV6.....13 E5
derminster Rd *COVW* CV5.....28 D2
dermoor La *COVS* CV3.....40 B1

Alderney CI *COVN* CV6.....22 C1
Alder Rd *COVN* CV6.....23 H1
The Alders *BDWTH* CV12.....4 D3
Aldrich Av *TLHL/CAN* CV4.....28 B4
Aldrin Wy *TLHL/CAN* CV4.....38 A4
Alexander Rd *BDWTH* CV12.....5 H1
Alexandra Rd *COV* CV1.....3 J1
RUGBYN/HIL CV21.....48 A5
Alfall Rd *COVE* CV2.....32 A1
Alfred Green CI
RUGBYS/DCH CV22.....61 H2
Alfred Rd *COV* CV1.....31 G2
Alfred St *RUGBYN/HIL* CV21.....61 G2
Alfriston Rd *COVS* CV3.....39 F5
Algate CI *COVN* CV6.....12 D5
Alice CI *BDWTH* CV12.....5 E4
Alicia CI *RUGBYS/DCH* CV22.....60 B4
Alison Sq *COVE* CV2.....14 A4
Allan Rd *COVN* CV6.....30 A2
Allansbury CI *RUGBY* CV23.....49 F4
Allans La *RRUGBY* CV23.....49 F4
Allard Wy *COVS* CV3.....40 D2
Allerton CI *COVE* CV2.....32 D4
Allesley Cft *COVW* CV5.....20 D5
Allesley Hall Dr *COVW* CV5.....29 F1
Allesley Old Rd *COV* CV1.....30 B3
COVW CV5.....29 G2
Allesley Rd *RUGBYN/HIL* CV21.....47 G3
Alliance Wy *COVE* CV2.....31 H1
Allied CI *COVN* CV6.....23 E1
Allitt Gv *KNWTH* CV8.....65 G2
All Saints La *COV* CV1.....3 J3
All Saints Rd *BDWTH* CV12.....5 E4
Alma St *COV* CV1.....3 G3
Almond Gv *RUGBYN/HIL* CV21.....47 F2
Almond Tree Av *COVE* CV2.....24 B1
Alpine Ct *KNWTH* CV8.....65 F1
Alspath La *COVW* CV5.....28 C2
Alspath Rd *RCOVN/BALC/EX* CV7.....18 B2
Alton CI *COVE* CV2.....24 C1
Alum CI *COVN* CV6.....23 E5
Alverley Rd *COVN* CV6.....22 D5
Alverstone Rd *COVE* CV2.....31 H2
Alvin CI *COVS* CV3.....33 E5
Alwyn Freeman Ct
RCOVN/BALC/EX CV7 *.....12 B1
Alwyn Rd *RUGBYS/DCH* CV22.....69 H2
Ambassador Rd
LGN/SDN/BHAMAIR B26.....8 A4
Amberley Av *BDWTH* CV12.....7 F2
Ambler Gv *COVE* CV2.....32 B3
Ambleside *COVE* CV2.....24 D1
RUGBYN/HIL CV21.....48 C2
Ambleside Rd *BDWTH* CV12.....5 F3
Ambrose CI *RUGBYN/HIL* CV21.....48 B3
Amelia CI *BDWTH* CV12.....7 F2
Amersham CI *COVW* CV5.....29 E2
Amherst Rd *KNWTH* CV8.....64 D1
Amos Jacques Rd *BDWTH* CV12.....5 F1
Amy CI *COVN* CV6.....13 G4
Anchorway Rd *COVS* CV3.....39 E5
Anderson Av *RUGBYS/DCH* CV22.....61 H4
Anderton Rd *BDWTH* CV12.....4 B4

COVN CV6.....14 A4
Andrews CI *KNWTH* CV8.....54 A2
Angela Av *COVE* CV2.....24 D2
Anglesey CI *COVW* CV5.....21 E4
Angless Wy *KNWTH* CV8.....65 E4
Angus CI *COVW* CV5.....28 D4
Anker Dr *RRUGBY* CV23.....46 C4
Anley Wy *COVN* CV6.....22 D5
Anne Crs *COVS* CV3.....40 D4
Ansell Dr *COVN* CV6.....13 H3
Anson CI *RUGBYS/DCH* CV22.....60 D2
Anson Wy *COVE* CV2.....25 E3
Ansty Rd *COVE* CV2.....32 B2
Anthony Wy *COVE* CV2.....32 B4
Antrim CI *COVW* CV5.....20 D4
Applecross CI *TLHL/CAN* CV4.....37 E3
Appledore Dr *COVW* CV5.....28 C1
Apple Gv *RUGBYS/DCH* CV22.....60 C2
Appleyard CI *BDWTH* CV12.....5 G3
Aqua PI *RUGBYN/HIL* CV21.....48 B4
The Arboretum *TLHL/CAN* CV4.....52 A1
Arbour CI *KNWTH* CV8.....65 G4
RUGBYS/DCH CV22.....61 E5
Arbourfields CI *KNWTH* CV8.....51 E4
The Arbours *RUGBYS/DCH* CV22.....62 B2
Arbury Av *BDWTH* CV12.....5 F2
COVN CV6.....23 F1
Archer Rd *KNWTH* CV8.....64 D4
Archers Spinney
RUGBYN/HIL CV21.....63 G4
Archery Rd
RCOVN/BALC/EX CV7.....18 A2
Arches La *RUGBYN/HIL* CV21.....48 B4
Arch Rd *COVE* CV2.....32 D1
Arden CI *RCOVN/BALC/EX* CV7.....18 B2
RCOVN/BALC/EX CV7.....34 C2
RUGBYS/DCH CV22.....69 E4
Arden Ct *HIA/OLT* B92 *.....16 B4
Arden Rd *BDWTH* CV12.....7 F3
KNWTH CV8.....65 G4
Arden St *COVW* CV5.....30 A5
Argyle St *RUGBYN/HIL* CV21.....62 B1
Argyll St *COVE* CV2.....31 H3
Ariel Wy *RUGBYS/DCH* CV22.....69 H1
Arkle Dr *COVE* CV2.....25 E4
Arlidge Crs *KNWTH* CV8.....65 H2
Armarna Dr *COVW* CV5.....19 G3
Armfield St *COVN* CV6.....23 H3
Armorial Rd *COVS* CV3.....39 E3
Armscott Rd *COVE* CV2.....24 B5
COVE CV2.....32 B1
Armson Rd *RCOVN/BALC/EX* CV7.....5 F4
Armstrong Av *COVS* CV3.....31 H5
Armstrong CI
RUGBYS/DCH CV22.....61 F3
Arne Rd *COVE* CV2.....25 F5
Arnhem Cnr *COVS* CV3.....41 E3
Arnold Av *COVS* CV3.....39 F4
Arnold St *RUGBYN/HIL* CV21.....62 A1
Arnside CI *COV* CV1.....3 G1
Arthingworth CI *COVS* CV3.....32 D5
Arthur St *COV* CV1.....31 E2
KNWTH CV8.....65 F2
Arundel Rd *BDWTH* CV12.....7 F2
COVS CV3.....39 G3

Asbury Rd *RCOVN/BALC/EX* CV7.....34 C4
Ascot CI *BDWTH* CV12.....5 C1
COVS CV3.....40 D3
Ashbridge Rd *COVW* CV5.....29 F2
Ashburton Rd *COVE* CV2.....24 D4
Ashby CI *COVS* CV3.....41 G1
Ashcombe Dr *TLHL/CAN* CV4.....28 C3
Ash Ct *RUGBYS/DCH* CV22.....61 F5
Ashcroft CI *COVE* CV2.....25 F3
Ashcroft Wy *COVE* CV2.....25 G3
Ashdale CI *COVS* CV3.....42 D2
Ashdene Gdns *KNWTH* CV8.....65 G3
Ashdown CI *COVS* CV3.....41 E1
Ash Dr *KNWTH* CV8.....65 F3
Ashfield Av *TLHL/CAN* CV4.....28 A5
Ashfield Rd *KNWTH* CV8.....65 G4
Ashford Dr *BDWTH* CV12.....5 F2
Ashfurlong CI
RCOVN/BALC/EX CV7.....34 C3
Ash Green La
RCOVN/BALC/EX CV7.....12 D2
Ash Gv *RCOVN/BALC/EX* CV7.....12 D1
Ashington Gv *COVS* CV3.....40 B4
Ashington Rd *BDWTH* CV12.....4 B4
Ashlawn Rd *RUGBYS/DCH* CV22.....70 A2
Ashley Wy *RCOVN/BALC/EX* CV7.....34 C2
Ashman Av *RRUGBY* CV23.....46 C4
Ashmore Rd *COVN* CV6.....30 C2
Ashorne CI *COVE* CV2.....24 C1
Ashow CI *KNWTH* CV8.....65 G3
Ash Priors CI *TLHL/CAN* CV4.....29 E4
Ash Tree Av *TLHL/CAN* CV4.....28 D4
Ashurst CI *COVN* CV6.....14 A3
Ashwood Av *COVN* CV6.....30 A1
Ashwood Ct
RUGBYN/HIL CV21 *.....47 G5
Aspen CI *TLHL/CAN* CV4.....28 A5
Aspen Dr *COVN* CV6.....14 B2
Asplen Ct *KNWTH* CV8.....65 H3
Asra CI *COVE* CV2.....31 G2
Assheton CI *RUGBYS/DCH* CV22.....60 D4
Asthill Cft *COVS* CV3.....2 C7
Asthill Gv *COVS* CV3.....39 F1
Astley Av *COVN* CV6.....23 F1
Astley La *BDWTH* CV12.....4 A1
Astley PI *RUGBYN/HIL* CV21.....63 C5
Aston Rd *COVW* CV5.....30 A5
Athena Gdns *COVN* CV6.....23 H2
Atherston PI *TLHL/CAN* CV4.....38 A3
Athol Rd *COVE* CV2.....25 F5
Attoxhall Rd *COVE* CV2.....32 D2
Attwood Crs *COVE* CV2.....24 B5
Augustus Rd *COVN* CV1.....3 J1
Austin Dr *COVN* CV6.....23 H4
Aventine Wy
RUGBYN/HIL CV21.....47 G2
Avenue Rd *KNWTH* CV8.....64 C1
RUGBYN/HIL CV21.....47 F5
The Avenue *COVS* CV3.....40 B3
Avocet CI *COVN* CV6.....24 A1
Avondale Rd *COVW* CV5.....38 D1
KNWTH CV8.....43 E4
Avonmere *RUGBYN/HIL* CV21.....47 F3
Avon Rd *KNWTH* CV8.....64 D4
TLHL/CAN CV4.....37 G3

Avon St COVE CV2.....32 A1
   RRUGBY CV23.....48 D5
   RUGBY/HIL CV21.....47 H5
Awson St COV CV6.....23 G5
Axholme Rd COVE CV2.....32 D2
Aylesford St COV CV1.....31 F2
Aynho Cl COVW CV5.....28 D3

B

Babbacombe Rd COVS CV3.....39 G4
Bablake Cl COVN CV6.....22 A3
Back La RCOVN/BALC/EX CV7.....26 C1
   RRUGBY CV23.....46 B5
Badby Leys RUGBYS/DCH CV22.....61 G5
Badger Cl RRUGBY CV23.....46 A5
Badger Rd COVS CV3.....41 E1
Baffin Cl RUGBYS/DCH CV21 F3
Baginton Rd COVS CV3.....39 F4
Bagshaw Cl KNWTH CV8.....55 H3
Bailey's La RRUGBY CV23.....46 B5
Bakehouse La
   RUGBYN/HIL CV21.....61 G1
Bakers La COVW CV5.....29 H4
Baker St COVN CV6.....14 A2
Bakewell Cl COVS CV3.....41 G1
Balcombe Rd
   RUGBYS/DCH CV22.....62 C4
Baldwin Cft COVN CV6.....24 D4
Ballantine Rd COVN CV6.....22 C5
Ballingham Cl TLHL/CAN CV4.....28 D4
Balliol Rd COVE CV2.....32 A2
Balmoral Cl COVE CV2.....24 D5
Balsall St RCOVN/BALC/EX CV7.....34 B3
Balsall St East
   RCOVN/BALC/EX CV7.....34 C4
Bankside Cl COVS CV3.....40 A3
Banks Rd COVN CV6.....30 B1
Bank St RUGBYN/HIL CV21 *.....61 H1
Banner La TLHL/CAN CV4.....28 A3
Bantam Gv COVN CV6.....12 B5
Bantock Rd TLHL/CAN CV4.....28 B4
Barbican Ri COVE CV2.....32 D4
Barbridge Cl BDWTH CV12.....7 F3
Barbridge Rd BDWTH CV12.....7 E3
Barby La RUGBYS/DCH CV22.....63 E5
Barby Rd RUGBYS/DCH CV22.....61 H5
Bardley Dr COVN CV6.....22 D5
Barford Cl COVS CV3.....41 E1
Barford Rd KNWTH CV8.....65 E4
Barker's Butts La COVN CV6.....30 B2
Barley Cl RUGBYN/HIL CV21.....63 F4
The Barley Lea COVS CV3.....40 C1
Barley Pl COVS CV3 *.....40 C1
Barlow Rd COVE CV2.....14 C5
Barnack Av COVS CV3.....39 G4
Barnacle La BDWTH CV7.....7 F4
Barnfield Av COVW CV5.....21 E4
Barnstaple Cl COVW CV5 *.....28 C1
Barnwell Cl RUGBYS/DCH CV22.....69 G3
Baron Leigh Dr
   TLHL/CAN CV4 *.....36 C3
Baron's Cft COVS CV3.....39 H2
Baron's Field Rd COVS CV3.....39 G2
Barracks Wy COV CV1 *.....2 D4
Barras Gn COVE CV2.....31 H2
Barras La COV CV1.....2 A3
Barretts La
   RCOVN/BALC/EX CV7.....34 D3
Barrington Rd
   RUGBYS/DCH CV22.....60 D2
Bar Rd COVS CV3.....40 A1
Barrow Cl COVE CV2.....25 G5
Barrowfield La KNWTH CV8.....65 E3
Barrow Rd KNWTH CV8.....65 E3
Barston Cl COVN CV6.....13 H5
Bartholomew Ct COVS CV3 *.....40 B3
Bartlett Cl COVN CV6.....23 F1
Barton Rd BDWTH CV12.....5 G1
   COVN CV6.....23 G1
   RUGBYS/DCH CV22.....61 H2
Bartons Ct COVE CV2 *.....31 H2
Barton's Meadow COVE CV2.....32 A1
Basford Brook Dr COVN CV6.....13 G3
Basley Wy COVN CV6.....13 E4
Bassett Rd COVN CV6.....30 B1
Bateman's Acre South
   COVN CV6.....30 B2
Bates Rd COVW CV5.....38 B4
Bath St COV CV1.....3 F1
   RUGBYN/HIL CV21.....62 A1
Bathurst Cl RUGBYS/DCH CV22.....61 F4
Bathurst Rd COVN CV6.....22 B5
Bathway Rd COVS CV3.....38 D5
Batsford Rd COVS CV3.....30 A2
Battalion Ct COVN CV6.....22 B2
Baulk La RCOVN/BALC/EX CV7.....35 E1

Bawnmore Ct
   RUGBYS/DCH CV22.....61 E4
Bawnmore Pk
   RUGBYS/DCH CV22.....61 F5
Bawnmore Rd
   RUGBYS/DCH CV22.....61 F5
Baxter Cl TLHL/CAN CV4.....28 D4
Bayley La COV CV1.....2 E4
Bayliss Av COVN CV6.....13 H4
Bayton Rd RCOVN/BALC/EX CV7.....13 H1
Bayton Wy
   RCOVN/BALC/EX CV7.....14 B1
Bay Tree Cl COVE CV2.....24 C2
Beacon Rd COVN CV6.....13 E5
Beaconsfield Av
   RUGBYS/DCH CV22.....61 H3
Beaconsfield Rd COVE CV2.....32 A4
Beake Av COVN CV6.....22 C5
Beamish Cl RUGBYS/DCH CV22.....61 F5
Beanfield Av COVS CV3.....38 C5
Beatty Dr RUGBYS/DCH CV22.....61 E2
Beauchamp House COV CV1.....2 C1
Beauchamp Rd KNWTH CV8.....64 D5
Beaudesert Rd COVW CV5.....30 B5
Beaufort Dr COVS CV3.....41 G2
Beaumaris Cl COVW CV5.....28 C1
Beaumont Crs COVN CV6.....30 B2
Beaumont Rd
   RCOVN/BALC/EX CV7.....12 B2
Beausale Cft COVW CV5.....28 D3
Beckbury Rd COVE CV2.....25 E5
Beckfoot Cl RUGBYN/HIL CV21.....48 C1
Beckfoot Dr COVE CV2.....25 E2
Bede Rd BDWTH CV12.....5 F1
   COVN CV6.....30 C1
Bede Village BDWTH CV12 *.....4 B5
Bedford St COVW CV5.....30 B4
Bedlam La COVN CV6.....23 F1
Bedworth La BDWTH CV12.....4 B1
Bedworth Rd BDWTH CV12.....6 D3
   COVN CV6.....13 H3
Beechcroft BDWTH CV12.....5 E4
Beech Cl KNWTH CV8.....65 G2
   RRUGBY CV23.....68 D4
   RUGBYS/DCH CV22.....60 D3
The Beeches BDWTH CV12.....4 D3
Beechnut Cl TLHL/CAN CV4.....28 A4
Beech Rd COVN CV6.....30 C1
Beech Tree Av TLHL/CAN CV4.....29 E4
Beechwood Av COVW CV5.....38 C1
Beechwood Ct
   RUGBYN/HIL CV21 *.....47 G5
Beechwood Cft KNWTH CV8.....65 E5
Beechwood Rd BDWTH CV12.....5 H1
Beehive HI KNWTH CV8.....50 C5
Beeston Cl COVS CV3.....41 G1
Belgrade Sq COV CV1 *.....2 C1
Belgrave Dr RUGBYN/HIL CV21.....48 C3
Belgrave Rd COVE CV2.....32 D2
Belgrave Sq COVE CV2.....32 D2
Bellairs Av BDWTH CV12.....4 D4
Bellbrooke Cl COVN CV6.....24 A2
Bell Dr RCOVN/BALC/EX CV7.....13 F1
Belle Vue Ter HIA/OLT B92.....16 B5
Bell Green Rd COVN CV6.....23 H3
Bellview Wy COVN CV6.....24 A2
Bell Wk RUGBYN/HIL CV21.....63 F4
Belmont Rd COVE CV2.....23 G4
   RUGBYS/DCH CV22.....61 H4
Belvedere Rd COVS CV3.....39 F2
Benedictine Ct COVS CV3.....39 F2
Bennett Ct KNWTH CV8 *.....57 E1
Bennetts Rd
   RCOVN/BALC/EX CV7.....12 A3
Bennetts Rd North
   RCOVN/BALC/EX CV7.....11 H1
Bennetts Rd South COVN CV6.....12 A5
Bennett St RUGBYN/HIL CV21.....61 G1
Bennfield Rd RUGBYN/HIL CV21.....61 H1
Benn Rd BDWTH CV12.....7 E3
Benn St RUGBYS/DCH CV22.....62 B2
Benson Rd COVN CV6.....22 B2
Benthall Rd COVN CV6.....23 G1
Bentley Ct COVN CV6.....12 B2
Bentley Rd RCOVN/BALC/EX CV7.....5 H4
Benton Green La
   RCOVN/BALC/EX CV7.....27 E4
The Bentree COVS CV3.....40 C1
Beresford Av COVN CV6.....23 F2
Berkeley Rd KNWTH CV8.....64 D1
Berkeley Rd North COVW CV5.....30 B5
Berkeley Rd South COVW CV5.....38 C1
Berkett Rd COVN CV6.....22 C1
Berkswell Rd COVN CV6.....23 H1
   RCOVN/BALC/EX CV7.....18 B3
Berners Cl TLHL/CAN CV4.....28 A4
Berrybanks RUGBYS/DCH CV22.....60 B3
Berry St COV CV1.....3 H1

Bertie Ct KNWTH CV8 *.....65 F3
Bertie Rd KNWTH CV8.....65 F3
Berwick Cl COVW CV5.....29 E2
Berwyn Av COVN CV6.....22 C2
Best Av KNWTH CV8.....51 H5
Beswick Gdns
   RUGBYS/DCH CV22.....61 E5
Bettman Cl COVS CV3.....39 H3
Beverley Cl
   RCOVN/BALC/EX CV7.....34 D2
Beverly Dr TLHL/CAN CV4.....52 A2
Bevington Crs COVN CV6.....29 H1
Bewick Cft COVE CV2.....31 H1
Bexfield Cl COVW CV5.....20 D5
Biart Pl RUGBYN/HIL CV21.....62 C1
Bickenhill La
   LGN/SDN/BHAMAIR B26.....8 A4
Bickenhill Pkwy
   CHWD/FDBR/MGN B37.....8 B2
Bideford Rd COVE CV2.....24 B4
Bigbury Cl COVS CV3.....39 H4
Biggin Hall Crs COVS CV3.....32 A4
Biggin Hall La RRUGBY CV23.....68 C5
Bilberry Rd COVE CV2.....24 C1
Billesden Cl COVS CV3.....41 F1
Billing Rd COVW CV5.....29 G3
Billinton Cl COVE CV2.....32 A4
Bilton La RRUGBY CV23.....60 C1
Bilton Rd RUGBYS/DCH CV22.....61 E3
Binley Av COVS CV3.....41 G2
Binley Gv COVS CV3.....41 G2
Binley Rd COV CV1.....3 J4
   COVS CV3.....3 K4
Binns Cl TLHL/CAN CV4.....37 E1
Binswood Cl COVE CV2.....24 C1
Binton Rd COVE CV2.....24 C1
Birch Cl BDWTH CV12.....6 A1
   COVW CV5.....20 C5
Birch Dr RUGBYS/DCH CV22.....60 C2
Birches La KNWTH CV8.....65 F4
The Birches BDWTH CV12.....7 E1
Birchfield Rd COVN CV6.....22 A4
Birchgrave Cl COVN CV6.....23 H1
Birch Gv RCOVN/BALC/EX CV7.....34 C1
Birchwood Rd COVS CV3.....42 B2
Bird Grove Ct COV CV1.....31 E1
Bird St COV CV1.....2 E1
Birkdale Cl COVN CV6.....12 C4
Birmingham Rd COVW CV5.....19 F3
   KNWTH CV8.....50 A3
   RCOVN/BALC/EX CV7.....9 H5
Birstall Dr RUGBYN/HIL CV21.....48 C3
Bishop St COV CV1.....2 D2
Bishops Wk COVW CV5.....39 E1
Bishopton Cl COVW CV5.....29 E3
Black Bank RCOVN/BALC/EX CV7.....5 G4
Blackberry Cl RRUGBY CV23.....48 C2
Blackberry La COVE CV2.....24 A5
   COVN CV6.....12 D3
Blackburn Rd COVN CV6.....13 G5
Blackfirs La BHAMNEC B40.....8 C1
Black Horse Rd COVN CV6.....14 A3
   RCOVN/BALC/EX CV7.....13 H2
Blackman Wy
   RUGBYN/HIL CV21.....47 G5
Black Pad COVN CV6.....22 D3
Black Prince Av COVS CV3.....39 H3
Blackshaw Dr COVE CV2.....25 F3
Blackthorn Cl TLHL/CAN CV4.....38 A4
Blackthorne Rd KNWTH CV8.....65 F4
Blackwatch Rd COVN CV6.....22 D3
Blackwell Rd COVN CV6.....23 F3
Blackwood Av
   RUGBYN/HIL CV21.....61 E2
Blair Dr BDWTH CV12.....4 C4
Blake Cl RUGBYS/DCH CV22.....60 D2
Blandford Dr COVE CV2.....33 E1
Bleaberry RUGBYN/HIL CV21.....48 B2
Blenheim Av COVN CV6.....12 D5
Bletchley Dr COVW CV5.....29 E2
Blind La KNWTH CV8.....51 E3
   RCOVN/BALC/EX CV7.....26 C1
Blockley Rd BDWTH CV12.....5 H1
Blondvil St COVS CV3.....39 F2
Blossom Wy RUGBYS/DCH CV22.....62 B3
Bloxam Gdns
   RUGBYS/DCH CV22.....61 G1
Bloxam Pl RUGBYN/HIL CV21.....61 H1
Bluebell Cl RRUGBY CV23.....48 C1
Bluebell Dr BDWTH CV12.....4 D3
Bluebell Wk TLHL/CAN CV4.....28 C5
Bluemels Dr COVW CV5.....43 F5
The Blundells KNWTH CV8.....65 E2
Blyth Av RCOVN/BALC/EX CV7.....34 D4
Blyth Cl BDWTH CV12.....4 B4
   RUGBYS/DCH CV22.....60 B4
Blythe Rd COV CV1.....31 F2
Blythe Vw KNWTH CV8 *.....53
Boar Cft TLHL/CAN CV4.....28 C4
Bockendon Rd TLHL/CAN CV4.....36 C5

Bodmin Rd COVE CV2.....33
Bodnant Wy KNWTH CV8.....65
Bohun St TLHL/CAN CV4.....28
Bolingbroke Rd COVS CV3.....31
Bolton Cl COVS CV3.....39
Bond St RUGBYN/HIL CV21.....61
Bonington Dr BDWTH CV12.....5
Bonneville Cl COVW CV5.....19
Bonnington Cl
   RUGBYN/HIL CV21.....63
Borrowdale RUGBYN/HIL CV21.....48
Borrowdale Cl COVN CV6.....22
Boston Pl COVN CV6.....23
Boswell Dr COVE CV2.....25
Boswell Rd RUGBYS/DCH CV22.....61
Bosworth Cl KNWTH CV8.....53
Botoner Rd COV CV1.....3
Bott Rd COVW CV5.....38
Boughton Rd RUGBYN/HIL CV21.....21
Boundary Rd
   RUGBYS/DCH CV22.....62
Bourne Rd COVS CV3.....32
Bowater Ct COVS CV3 *.....40
Bowden Wy COVS CV3.....32
Bow Fell RUGBYN/HIL CV21.....48
Bowfell Cl COVW CV5.....29
Bowling Green La
   RCOVN/BALC/EX CV7.....13
Bowls Ct COVW CV5.....30
Bowness Cl COVN CV6.....22
The Boxhill COVS CV3.....32
Boyce Wy RRUGBY CV23.....46
Boyd Cl COVE CV2.....25
Bracadale Cl COVS CV3.....33
Bracebridge Cl
   RCOVN/BALC/EX CV7.....34
Bracken Cl RUGBYS/DCH CV22.....61
Bracken Dr RUGBYS/DCH CV22.....61
Brackenhurst Rd COVN CV6.....22
Brackley Cl COVN CV6.....22
Braddock Cl COVS CV3.....33
Brade Dr COVE CV2.....25
Bradley Cft
   RCOVN/BALC/EX CV7.....34
Bradney Gn TLHL/CAN CV4.....36
Bradnick Pl TLHL/CAN CV4.....28
Braemar Cl COVE CV2.....24
Brafield Leys
   RUGBYS/DCH CV22.....70
Braids Cl RUGBYN/HIL CV21.....48
Bramble St COV CV1.....3
Bramcote Cl BDWTH CV12.....7
Brampton Wy BDWTH CV12.....7
Bramston Crs TLHL/CAN CV4.....28
Bramwell Gdns COVN CV6.....13
Brandfield Rd COVN CV6.....22
Brandon La COVS CV3.....41
   KNWTH CV8
Brandon Rd COVS CV3.....42
   RRUGBY CV23.....43
Branksome Rd COVN CV6.....21
Bransdale Av COVN CV6.....13
Bransford Av TLHL/CAN CV4.....38
Branstree Dr COVN CV6.....23
Brathay Cl COVS CV3.....39
Braunston Pl
   RUGBYS/DCH CV22.....62
Brayford Av COVS CV3.....39
Bray's La COVE CV2.....32
Braytoft Cl COVN CV6.....22
Brazil St TLHL/CAN CV4.....28
Bredon Av COVS CV3.....41
Bree Cl COVW CV5.....20
Brentwood Av COVS CV3.....53
Bretford Rd COVE CV2.....24
Bretts Cl COV CV1.....31
Brewer Rd BDWTH CV12.....7
Brewers Cl COVS CV3.....33
Brewster Cl COVE CV2.....32
Briansway COVN CV6.....13
Briardene Av BDWTH CV12
Briars Cl COVE CV2.....32
   RRUGBY CV23.....46
Brick Hill La COVW CV5
Brick Kiln Wy BDWTH CV12
Brickyard Cft
   RCOVN/BALC/EX CV7.....34
The Bridal Pth COVW CV5.....21
Bridgeacre Gdns COVS CV3.....33
Bridgecote COVS CV3.....41
Bridgeman Rd COVN CV6.....30
Bridge St COVN CV6.....23
   KNWTH CV8
   RUGBYN/HIL CV21.....61
Bridget St RUGBYN/HIL CV21.....61
Bridge Vw KNWTH CV8 *.....53
Bridle Brook La
   RCOVN/BALC/EX CV7.....10
Bridle Rd RUGBYN/HIL CV21

idport Cl COVE CV2 ...... 33 F2
erley Rd COV CV2 ...... 24 B3
ghtmere Rd COVN CV6 ...... 30 C2
ghton St COV CV2 ...... 3 K2
ight St COVN CV6 ...... 23 F5
ghtwalton Rd COVS CV3 ...... 39 G3
ill Cl TLHL/CAN CV4 ...... 37 H4
indle Av COVS CV3 ...... 32 B4
indley Paddocks COV CV1 ...... 2 C2
indley Rd
  RCOVN/BALC/EX CV7 ...... 14 A1
  RUGBYN/HIL CV21 ...... 63 F3
inklow Rd COVS CV3 ...... 33 F4
isbane Cl COVS CV3 ...... 39 H3
iscoe Rd COVN CV6 ...... 12 D4
istol Rd COVW CV5 ...... 30 C4
itannia St COV CV1 ...... 3 J2
iton Rd COVE CV2 ...... 31 H2
ixham Dr COVE CV2 ...... 24 B5
ixworth Cl COVS CV3 ...... 41 F1
oadgate COV CV1 ...... 2 D4
oadlands Cl COVW CV5 ...... 29 F4
oad La COVW CV5 ...... 28 A2
  RCOVN/BALC/EX CV7 ...... 27 F2
oadmere Ri COVW CV5 ...... 28 D4
oad Park Rd COVE CV2 ...... 24 C4
oad St COVN 23 F4
oad St Jetty COVN CV6 ...... 23 F4
oadwater COVW 38 D1
oadway COVW CV5 ...... 30 B5
oadway Man COVW CV5 * 30 B5
oadwells Ct TLHL/CAN CV4 ...... 37 E4
oadwells Crs TLHL/CAN CV4 ...... 37 E4
ockenhurst Wy COVN CV6 ...... 14 A2
ockhurst Dr TLHL/CAN CV4 ...... 28 A4
omleigh Dr COVE CV2 ...... 32 B4
omley Cl KNWTH CV8 ...... 64 D1
omwich Cl COVS CV3 ...... 41 G1
omwich Rd RUGBYN/HIL CV21 ...... 63 E3
onte Cl RUGBYN/HIL CV21 ...... 62 C1
onte Wk COVE CV2 ...... 32 C3
ook Cl COV CV1 ...... 3 H1
ooke Rd KNWTH CV8 ...... 65 G3
ookford Av COVN CV6 ...... 12 B5
ooklea BDWTH CV12 ...... 5 F2
ooklime Dr RRUGBY CV23 ...... 48 D1
ooklyn Rd COV CV1 ...... 23 E5
ookshaw Wy COVE CV2 ...... 25 E3
ookside Av COVW CV5 ...... 29 F3
  KNWTH CV8 ...... 64 D3
ookside Cl RUGBYS/DCH CV22 ...61 H4
ook St KNWTH CV8 ...... 57 F1
ookvale Av COVS CV3 ...... 32 D5
ook Vw RUGBYS/DCH CV22 ...... 69 E4
oome Cl RUGBYS/DCH CV22 ...... 61 F3
oome Cft COVN CV6 ...... 12 C5
oomfield Pl COVW CV5 ...... 30 B4
oomfield Rd COVW CV5 ...... 30 A5
oomybank KNWTH CV8 ...... 65 G1
owett Rd COVN CV6 ...... 30 A2
owning Rd COVE CV2 ...... 32 B2
  RUGBYN/HIL CV21 ...... 63 G4
ownshill Ct COVN CV6 ...... 22 A4
ownshill Green Rd COVN CV6 ...21 H3
own's La COVW CV5 ...... 21 E3
ownsover La
  RUGBYN/HIL CV21 ...... 48 A2
ownsover Rd
  RUGBYN/HIL CV21 ...... 47 F2
uce Rd COVN CV6 ...... 22 B3
  RCOVN/BALC/EX CV7 ...... 13 G1
uce Williams Wy
  RUGBYS/DCH CV22 ...... 62 A2
udenell Cl RUGBYS/DCH CV22...60 B4
unel Cl COV CV1 ...... 3 J3
unswick Cl RUGBYN/HIL CV21..48 B3
unswick Rd COV CV1 ...... 2 A5
untingthorpe Wy COVS CV3 ...41 F1
unton Cl COVS CV3 ...... 33 G5
yanston Cl COVE CV2 ...... 33 F2
yant Rd RCOVN/BALC/EX CV7 ...13 H1
ympton Rd COVS CV3 ...... 32 B4
yn Jones Cl COVS CV3 ...... 41 G2
yn Rd COVN CV6 ...... 23 G4
yony Cl BDWTH CV12 ...... 4 D4
bbenhall Rd KNWTH CV8 ...... 54 C1
ccleuch Cl RUGBYS/DCH CV22..69 G3
chanan Rd
  RUGBYS/DCH CV22 ...... 61 F3
ckfast Cl COVS CV3 ...... 39 H4
ckhold Dr COVW CV5 ...... 29 H1
ckingham Ri COVW CV5 ...... 29 E2
ckland Rd COVN CV6 ...... 22 C1
cknill Crs RUGBYN/HIL CV21 ...63 G4
ckwell La RRUGBY CV23 ...... 49 E3
dbrooke Cl COVE CV2 ...... 24 C1
ilkington Rd BDWTH CV12 ...... 6 A3
illfield Av TLHL/CAN CV4 ...... 28 B5
illimore Gv KNWTH CV8 ...... 65 F5

Bull's Head La COVS CV3 ...... 31 H5
Bull Yd COV CV1 ...... 2 D3
Bulwer Rd COVN CV6 ...... 22 B4
Bulwick Cl COVS CV3 ...... 33 G5
Bungalow Est COVN CV6 * 13 G4
Burbages La COVN CV6 ...... 13 E3
Burberry Gv
  RCOVN/BALC/EX CV7 ...... 34 B3
Burbury Cl BDWTH CV12 ...... 5 H1
Burges COV CV1 ...... 2 D2
Burleigh Cl
  RCOVN/BALC/EX CV7 ...... 34 C2
Burlington Rd COVE CV2 ...... 31 H2
Burnaby Rd COVN CV6 ...... 22 D3
Burnham Rd COVS CV3 ...... 40 B3
Burnsall Gv COVW CV5 ...... 38 A1
Burnsall Rd COVW CV5 ...... 38 A1
Burnside COVS CV3 ...... 33 F4
  RUGBYS/DCH CV22 ...... 61 F2
Burns Rd COVE CV2 ...... 32 A3
Burns Wk BDWTH CV12 ...... 5 H4
Burrow Hill La
  RCOVN/BALC/EX CV7 ...... 11 F1
Burton Cl COVW CV5 ...... 21 F2
Busby Cl COVS CV3 ...... 41 G2
Bushbery Av TLHL/CAN CV4 ...28 C5
Bush Cl TLHL/CAN CV4 ...... 28 C3
Bushelton Cl COV CV1 ...... 3 F7
Butcher's La COVW CV5 ...... 21 F5
Butchers Rd HIA/OLT B92 ...... 16 B5
Butler Cl KNWTH CV8 ...... 51 H5
Butlers Crs RCOVN/BALC/EX CV7 ...5 F4
Butlers Leap RUGBYN/HIL CV21...48 C4
Butlin Rd COVN CV6 ...... 12 D4
  RUGBYN/HIL CV21 ...... 62 C1
Buttercup Wy BDWTH CV12 ...... 4 D3
Buttermere RUGBYN/HIL CV21 ...48 C3
Buttermere Cl COVS CV3 ...... 41 G2
Butterworth Dr TLHL/CAN CV4 ...37 F3
Butt La COVW CV5 ...... 21 E4
Butts COV CV1 ...... 2 A4
Butts Rd COVS CV3 ...... 2 A5
Byfield Rd COVN CV6 ...... 29 H1
Byron Av BDWTH CV12 ...... 6 A3
Byron St COV CV1 ...... 2 E1
Bywater Cl COVS CV3 ...... 39 E4

C

Cadden Dr TLHL/CAN CV4 ...... 29 E4
Cadman Cl BDWTH CV12 ...... 5 H1
Caesar Rd KNWTH CV8 ...... 64 D4
Caithness Cl COVW CV5 ...... 28 D2
Caldecote Rd COVN CV6 ...... 30 D1
Caldecott Pl RUGBYN/HIL CV21...62 B2
Caldecott St RUGBYS/DCH CV22...62 B2
Calder Cl BDWTH CV12 ...... 7 E3
  COVS CV3 ...... 39 H1
Calgary Cl COVS CV3 ...... 33 F4
Callier Cl RUGBYS/DCH CV22 ...60 C4
Calmere Cl COVE CV2 ...... 25 E3
Caludon Park Av COVE CV2 ...32 D1
Caludon Rd COVE CV2 ...... 31 H2
Calvert Cl COVS CV3 ...... 39 G3
Calvestone Pl
  RUGBYS/DCH CV22 * 60 B5
Calvestone Rd
  RUGBYS/DCH CV22 ...... 60 B5
Calvestone Sq
  RUGBYS/DCH CV22 * 60 C4
Cambridge St COV CV1 ...... 31 F1
  RUGBYN/HIL CV21 ...... 62 B1
Camden St COVE CV2 ...... 31 H2
Cameron Cl COVW CV5 ...... 20 D4
Campbell St RUGBYN/HIL CV21 ...61 F1
Campion Cl COVS CV3 ...... 39 G3
Campion Wy RRUGBY CV23 ...... 48 C1
Campling Cl BDWTH CV12 ...... 7 E3
Camville COVS CV3 ...... 33 F4
Canal Rd COVN CV6 ...... 23 G3
Canalside COVN CV6 ...... 14 A2
Canberra Rd COVE CV2 ...... 14 B4
Canford Cl COVS CV3 ...... 53 F1
Canley Ford COVW CV5 ...... 38 B2
Canley Rd COVW CV5 ...... 38 A1
Cannas Ct TLHL/CAN CV4 * 38 A3
Cannocks La TLHL/CAN CV4 ...38 A3
Cannon Cl TLHL/CAN CV4 ...... 38 A3
Cannon Hill Rd TLHL/CAN CV4 ...38 A3
Cannon Pk Centre
  TLHL/CAN CV4 * 37 H3
Cannon Park Rd TLHL/CAN CV4...38 A4
Canon Dr RCOVN/BALC/EX CV7 ...13 G2
Canon Hudson Cl COVS CV3 ...40 D4
Canterbury St COV CV1 ...... 3 G1
Cantlow Cl COVW CV5 ...... 28 D3
Capmartin Rd COVN CV6 ...... 22 C4

Capulet Cl COVS CV3 ...... 40 D3
  RUGBYS/DCH CV22 ...... 70 A1
Caradoc Cl COVE CV2 ...... 24 C4
Cardale Cft COVS CV3 ...... 41 G1
Cardigan La BDWTH CV12 ...... 4 B4
Carding Cl COVW CV5 ...... 28 C2
Carey St COVN CV6 ...... 24 A2
Cargill Cl COVS CV3 ...... 13 G3
Carlton Cl BDWTH CV12 ...... 7 E2
Carlton Gdns COVW CV5 * 38 D1
Carlton Rd COVN CV6 ...... 23 G2
  RUGBYS/DCH CV22 ...... 61 E3
Carmelite Rd COV CV1 ...... 3 H4
Carnbroe Av COVS CV3 ...... 41 G2
Carnegie Cl COVS CV3 ...... 40 C4
Carpenter Rd COVE CV2 ...... 23 H5
Carroll Crs COVE CV2 ...... 25 F3
Carsal Cl RCOVN/BALC/EX CV7 ...13 E3
Carter Rd COVS CV3 ...... 40 B1
Carthusian Rd COVS CV3 ...... 39 F1
Cartmel Cl COVW CV5 ...... 28 D2
Carvell Cl COVW CV5 ...... 21 E2
Carver Cl COVE CV2 ...... 32 D4
Cascade Cl COVS CV3 ...... 39 H3
Cashmore Rd BDWTH CV12 ...... 4 D5
  KNWTH CV8 ...... 65 H3
Cash's La COVN CV6 ...... 23 E5
Casita Gv KNWTH CV8 ...... 65 H3
Caspian Wy COVE CV2 ...... 25 F3
Cassandra Cl TLHL/CAN CV4 ...52 A1
Castle Cl COVS CV3 ...... 39 G3
Castle Gn KNWTH CV8 ...... 64 C2
Castle Hl KNWTH CV8 ...... 64 D2
Castle Ms RUGBYN/HIL CV21 ...61 H1
Castle Pl COV CV1 * 31 F2
Castle Rd KNWTH CV8 ...... 64 D2
Castle St COV CV1 ...... 3 G1
  RUGBYN/HIL CV21 ...... 61 H1
Catesby Rd COVN CV6 ...... 22 D4
  RUGBYS/DCH CV22 ...... 62 C3
Catherine De Barnes La
  HIA/OLT B92 ...... 8 A5
Catherine St COVE CV2 ...... 3 J2
Cavans Wy COVS CV3 ...... 41 H3
Cave Cl RUGBYS/DCH CV22 ...... 60 B4
Cavendish Cl RUGBYS/DCH CV22...60 B3
Cavendish Rd TLHL/CAN CV4 ...28 B4
Cawnpore Rd COVN CV6 ...... 22 C1
Cawston Grange Dr
  RUGBYS/DCH CV22 ...... 60 B4
Cawston La RUGBYS/DCH CV22...69 F1
Cawston Wy RUGBYS/DCH CV22...60 D4
Cawthorne Cl COV CV1 ...... 31 F2
Cecily Rd COVS CV3 ...... 39 G2
Cedar Av KNWTH CV8 ...... 56 A3
Cedars Av COVN CV6 ...... 29 H1
Cedars Rd RCOVN/BALC/EX CV7 ...5 G5
Cedar Wood Dr
  RCOVN/BALC/EX CV7 ...... 34 C3
Cedric Cl COVS CV3 ...... 40 D4
Celandine RRUGBY CV23 ...... 48 C1
Celandine Rd COVE CV2 ...... 24 C1
Celandine Wy BDWTH CV12 ...... 4 D3
Centaur Rd COVW CV5 ...... 30 A4
Centenary Rd TLHL/CAN CV4 ...38 A2
Centenary Wy BDWTH CV12 ...... 6 B2
  COVE CV2 ...... 14 C2
  KNWTH CV8 ...... 64 C4
  RCOVN/BALC/EX CV7 ...... 5 H5
Centernary Wy KNWTH CV8 ...... 43 E1
Central Av COVE CV2 ...... 31 H4
Central Bvd
  RCOVN/BALC/EX CV7 ...... 12 A3
Chace Av COVS CV3 ...... 40 C4
Chaceley Cl COVE CV2 ...... 25 F3
Chadwick Cl COVW CV5 ...... 29 E4
Chalfont Cl BDWTH CV12 ...... 5 H1
  COVW CV5 ...... 29 E2
Challenge Cl COV CV1 ...... 31 E2
Chamberlaine St BDWTH CV12 ...5 G1
Chamberlain Rd
  RUGBYN/HIL CV21 ...... 63 G4
Chancellors Cl TLHL/CAN CV4 ...28 A4
Chandos St COVE CV2 ...... 31 H3
Channel Wy COVN CV6 ...... 14 A2
The Chantries COV CV1 ...... 31 F1
Chapel Dr RCOVN/BALC/EX CV7 ...34 C1
Chapel Farm Cl COVS CV3 ...... 40 D3
Chapel La KNWTH CV8 ...... 55 H2
  RCOVN/BALC/EX CV7 ...... 15 G1
Chapel St BDWTH CV12 ...... 5 G1
  COV CV1 ...... 2 C2
  RRUGBY CV23 ...... 46 B5
  RUGBYN/HIL CV21 ...... 61 H1
Chapel Yd COVE CV2 * 14 C3
Chard Rd COVS CV3 ...... 41 E1
Chariot Wy RUGBYN/HIL CV21 ...47 H2
Charity Rd RCOVN/BALC/EX CV7 ...12 A1
Charlecote Rd COVN CV6 ...... 22 B1

Charles Eaton Rd BDWTH CV12...5 E2
Charlesfield Rd
  RUGBYS/DCH CV22 ...... 61 H4
Charles Lakin Cl
  RCOVN/BALC/EX CV7 ...... 15 H3
Charles St COV CV1 ...... 3 G1
  RUGBYS/DCH CV22 ...... 61 G2
Charles Warren Cl
  RUGBYN/HIL CV21 ...... 62 A1
Charlewood Rd COVN CV6 ...... 22 C1
Charlotte St RUGBYN/HIL CV21 ...62 A1
Charminster Dr COVS CV3 ...... 39 G5
Charter Av TLHL/CAN CV4 ...... 36 C2
Charterhouse Rd COV CV1 ...... 3 H4
Charter Rd RUGBYS/DCH CV22 ...62 D4
Charwelton Dr
  RUGBYN/HIL CV21 ...... 48 D3
Chase La KNWTH CV8 ...... 50 B5
Chatham Cl COVS CV3 * 40 D1
Chatsworth Gv KNWTH CV8 ...65 H2
Chatsworth Ri COVS CV3 ...... 39 H4
Chattaway Dr
  RCOVN/BALC/EX CV7 ...... 34 C3
Chaucer Rd RUGBYS/DCH CV22...70 A1
Chauntry Pl COV CV1 ...... 2 E2
Cheadle Cl COVN CV6 ...... 13 H4
Cheam Cl COVN CV6 ...... 23 H2
Cheetah Rd COV CV1 ...... 3 F6
Chelmarsh Cl COVN CV6 ...... 30 D1
Chelney Wk COVS CV3 ...... 33 F5
Chelsey Rd COVE CV2 ...... 24 D3
Cheltenham Cl BDWTH CV12 ...... 5 C1
Chelveston Rd COVN CV6 ...... 29 H1
Chelwood Gv COVE CV2 ...... 25 E2
Chenies Cl COVW CV5 ...... 29 E3
Chepstow Cl COVS CV3 ...... 40 D4
Chequer St BDWTH CV12 ...... 7 F3
Cheriton Cl COVW CV5 ...... 29 C2
Cherrybrook Wy COVE CV2 ...... 24 B2
Cherry Cl COVN CV6 ...... 23 E1
Cherry Gv RUGBYS/DCH CV22 ...61 H4
Cherry Orch KNWTH CV8 ...... 65 F2
Cherry Wy KNWTH CV8 ...... 65 F2
Cherrywood Gv COVW CV5 ...... 28 C1
Cherwell Wy RRUGBY CV23 ...... 46 C5
Chesford Crs COVN CV6 ...... 24 A1
Cheshire Cl RUGBYS/DCH CV22 ...60 D4
Chesholme Rd COVN CV6 ...... 12 C5
The Chesils COVS CV3 ...... 39 F3
Chester Rd HIA/OLT B92 ...... 9 F4
Chester St COV CV1 ...... 2 A2
  RUGBYN/HIL CV21 ...... 48 B5
Chesterton Rd COVN CV6 ...... 22 B3
Chestnut Av KNWTH CV8 ...... 65 E4
Chestnut Fld RUGBYN/HIL CV21 ...61 H1
Chestnut Gv KNWTH CV8 ...... 57 F1
  TLHL/CAN CV4 ...... 28 D4
Chestnut Rd BDWTH CV12 ...... 6 A1
The Chestnuts BDWTH CV12 ...... 4 D3
Chestnut Tree Av TLHL/CAN CV4...28 D4
Cheswick Cl COVN CV6 * 23 H4
Chetton Av COVN CV6 ...... 30 D1
Chetwode Cl COVW CV5 ...... 29 E2
Cheveral Av COVN CV6 ...... 30 C1
Cheveral Rd BDWTH CV12 ...... 5 F2
Cheylesmore COV CV1 ...... 2 D5
Chicory Dr RRUGBY CV23 ...... 48 C1
Chideock Hl COVS CV3 ...... 38 D3
Chiel Cl COVW CV5 ...... 28 C2
Childs Oak Cl
  RCOVN/BALC/EX CV7 ...... 34 B3
Chillaton Rd COVN CV6 ...... 22 C1
Chiltern Leys COVN CV6 ...... 30 B5
The Chilterns COVN CV6 ...... 29 E2
Chingford Rd COVN CV6 ...... 13 H4
Chorley Wy COVN CV6 ...... 22 D5
Christchurch Rd COVN CV6 ...... 22 A5
Church Cl KNWTH CV8 ...... 56 A4
Church Dr KNWTH CV8 ...... 65 E2
Churchill Av COVN CV6 ...... 23 F2
  KNWTH CV8 ...... 65 F1
Churchill Rd RUGBYS/DCH CV22...61 H1
Church La COVE CV2 ...... 32 A3
  COVW CV5 ...... 27 H1
  KNWTH CV8 ...... 67 E1
  RCOVN/BALC/EX CV7 ...... 13 F1
  RCOVN/BALC/EX CV7 ...... 26 B3
  RRUGBY CV23 ...... 68 D4
Church Park Cl COVN CV6 ...... 22 A2
Church Rd KNWTH CV8 ...... 54 A2
  RRUGBY CV23 ...... 45 F4
Church St BDWTH CV12 ...... 7 E3
  COV CV1 ...... 31 E2
  RRUGBY CV23 ...... 49 F4
  RUGBYN/HIL CV21 ...... 61 H1
Church Vw KNWTH CV8 * 56 A3
Church Wk COVW CV5 ...... 21 F5
  RRUGBY CV23 ...... 68 D4
  RUGBYN/HIL CV21 ...... 62 A1

RUGBYS/DCH CV22......**61** E4
Church Wy *BDWTH* CV12......**5** G2
Chylds Ct *COWW* CV5......**28** D1
Clara St *COV* CV1......**31** H4
Clare Ct *RUGBYN/HIL* CV21......**61** G1
Claremont Cl *BDWTH* CV12......**7** E1
Claremont Rd
   RUGBYN/HIL CV21......**62** B1
Claremont Wk *COWW* CV5......**21** F5
Clarence Rd *RUGBYN/HIL* CV21......**61** H1
Clarence St *COV* CV1......**3** H1
Clarendon Rd *KNWTH* CV8......**65** F4
Clarendon St *COWW* CV5......**30** A5
Clarke's Av *KNWTH* CV8......**65** F4
Clark St *COVN* CV6......**23** H2
Claverdon Av *COWW* CV5......**29** E3
Clayhill La *RUGBY* CV23......**46** A4
Clay La *COVE* CV2......**31** H2
   COVW CV5......**10** B4
Clayton Rd *COVN* CV6......**29** H1
Clements Cl *KNWTH* CV8......**65** F2
Clements St *COVE* CV2......**31** H5
Clement Wy *RUGBYS/DCH* CV22......**60** B4
Clennon Ri *COVE* CV2......**24** C3
Cleveland Rd *BDWTH* CV12......**7** E2
   COVE CV2......**31** H2
Clifden Gv *KNWTH* CV8......**65** H1
Clifford Bridge Rd *COVE* CV2......**25** E5
   COVS CV3......**33** E4
Clifton Rd *RUGBYN/HIL* CV21......**62** A1
Clifton St *COV* CV1......**31** F2
Clinton Av *KNWTH* CV8......**64** C1
Clinton La *KNWTH* CV8......**64** C1
Clinton Rd *COVN* CV6......**23** G1
Clipstone Rd *COVN* CV6......**21** H5
Clive Rd *RCOVN/BALC/EX* CV7......**34** D4
Cloister Cft *COVE* CV2......**25** E5
The Close *KNWTH* CV8......**43** E4
Cloud Br *KNWTH* CV8......**67** H2
Cloud Gn *TLHL/CAN* CV4......**38** A4
Clovelly Gdns *COVE* CV2......**32** B1
Clovelly Rd *COVE* CV2......**32** A1
Clover Cl *RRUGBY* CV23......**48** C1
Cloverdale Cl *COVN* CV6......**12** C4
Clyde Rd *BDWTH* CV12......**6** D2
Coalpit Fields Rd *BDWTH* CV12......**5** H3
Coalpit La *KNWTH* CV8......**58** A2
Coat of Arms Bridge Rd
   COVS CV3......**38** D3
Cobb Cl *COVE* CV2......**3** K1
Cobbs Rd *KNWTH* CV8......**64** C1
Cobden St *COVN* CV6......**31** F1
Cockerill's Meadow
   RUGBYN/HIL CV21......**63** F4
Colchester St *COV* CV1......**3** G2
Colebrook Cl *COVS* CV3......**33** E4
Coleby Cl *TLHL/CAN* CV4......**36** C3
Cole Ct *COVN* CV6......**30** B2
Coleman St *TLHL/CAN* CV4......**28** C3
Coleridge Rd *COVE* CV2......**32** B2
Coleshill Heath Rd
   CHWD/FDBR/MGN B37......**8** B1
Colina Cl *COVS* CV3......**40** D4
Colledge Rd *COVN* CV6......**23** E2
Collett Wk *COV* CV1......**2** A1
   KNWTH CV8 *......**65** E3
Colliery La (North)
   RCOVN/BALC/EX CV7......**5** G4
Collingwood Av
   RUGBYS/DCH CV22......**60** D3
Collingwood Rd *COWW* CV5......**30** B4
Collins Gv *TLHL/CAN* CV4......**38** A4
Columbia Gdns *BDWTH* CV12......**6** A3
Columbine Wy *BDWTH* CV12......**4** D4
Colyere Cl *RCOVN/BALC/EX* CV7......**12** B2
Comet Rd
   LGN/SDN/BHAMAIR B26......**8** A4
Common La *KNWTH* CV8......**51** G5
   RCOVN/BALC/EX CV7......**10** B1
Common Wy *COVE* CV2......**23** H5
Compton Cl *RUGBYS/DCH* CV22......**69** F1
Compton Rd *COVN* CV6......**23** E1
Comrie Cl *COVE* CV2......**25** E5
Concorde Rd
   LGN/SDN/BHAMAIR B26......**8** A4
Coney La *COVN* CV6......**14** B2
Congleton Cl *COVN* CV6......**23** F1
Conifer Cl *BDWTH* CV12......**5** H1
Conifer Paddock *COVS* CV3......**32** D5
The Conifers *KNWTH* CV8......**65** G4
Coniston Cl *BDWTH* CV12......**7** F2
   RUGBYN/HIL CV21......**48** C3
Coniston Dr *COVW* CV5......**28** A3
Coniston Rd *COVW* CV5......**30** A5
Conrad Cl *RUGBYS/DCH* CV22......**70** B1
Conrad Rd *COVN* CV6......**22** B4
Constable Rd *RUGBYN/HIL* CV21......**63** G3
Constance Cl *BDWTH* CV12......**5** E5
Consul Rd *RUGBYN/HIL* CV21......**47** H3

Convent Cl *KNWTH* CV8......**51** F5
Conway Av *TLHL/CAN* CV4......**36** C1
Cook Cl *COVN* CV6......**13** H4
   RUGBYN/HIL CV21......**48** B2
Cook St *COV* CV1......**2** D2
Coombe Cl *COVS* CV3......**33** F4
Coombe Dr *COVS* CV3......**42** D2
Coombe Park Rd *COVS* CV3......**33** E4
Coombe St *COVS* CV3......**32** A4
Co-operative St *COVE* CV2......**14** A5
Cope Arnolds Cl *COVN* CV6......**13** G4
Copeland *RUGBYN/HIL* CV21......**48** B2
Cope St *COV* CV1......**2** D1
Copland Pl *TLHL/CAN* CV4......**28** B5
Coplow St *RCOVN/BALC/EX* CV7......**34** B3
Copperas St *COVE* CV2......**24** A1
Copper Beech Cl *COVN* CV6......**23** F2
Copperfield Rd *COVE* CV2......**32** A3
Coppice Cl *KNWTH* CV8......**56** A4
The Coppice *COVS* CV3......**40** C1
Copse Cl *COVW* CV5......**19** G3
Copse Dr *COVW* CV5......**19** G3
The Copse *RCOVN/BALC/EX* CV7......**5** F5
Copsewood Ter *COVS* CV3......**32** B4
Copthorne Rd *COVN* CV6......**22** A3
Copt Oak Cl *TLHL/CAN* CV4......**36** B2
Coral Cl *COVS* CV3......**29** F4
Corbet Rd *COVN* CV6......**22** D4
Corbetts Cl *HIA/OLT* B92......**16** C4
Corbett St *RUGBYN/HIL* CV21......**48** B5
Cordelia Wy *RUGBYS/DCH* CV22......**70** A1
Corfe Cl *COVE* CV2......**33** E1
Corinthian Pl *COVE* CV2 *......**24** C4
Corley Vw *RCOVN/BALC/EX* CV7......**12** D1
Cornelius St *COVS* CV3......**39** G1
Cornets End La
   RCOVN/BALC/EX CV7......**17** F4
Cornflower Dr *RRUGBY* CV23......**48** B1
Cornhill Gv *KNWTH* CV8......**65** H2
Corn Mdw *BDWTH* CV12......**5** H3
Cornwallis Rd
   RUGBYS/DCH CV22......**60** C3
Cornwall Rd *COV* CV1......**3** G6
Coronation Rd *COV* CV1......**3** J1
   RRUGBY CV23......**45** E4
Coronel Av *COVN* CV6......**13** F4
Corporation St *COV* CV1......**2** C4
   RUGBYN/HIL CV21......**61** H1
Cotman Cl *BDWTH* CV12......**5** F1
Coton Park Dr *RRUGBY* CV23......**48** B1
Coton Rd *RUGBYN/HIL* CV21......**63** F4
Cotswold Dr *COVS* CV3......**53** F1
Cottage Farm Rd *COVN* CV6......**22** B2
Cottage Leap *RUGBYN/HIL* CV21......**48** C5
Cotterell Rd *RUGBYN/HIL* CV21......**47** G3
Cottesbrook Cl *COVS* CV3......**32** D5
Cotton Dr *KNWTH* CV8......**65** H1
Coundon Gn *COVN* CV6......**21** H3
Coundon Rd *COV* CV1......**2** A1
Coundon St *COV* CV1......**2** A2
Coundon Wedge Dr *COVW* CV5......**21** F5
The Countess's Cft *COVS* CV3......**39** G2
Country Inn Ms *RRUGBY* CV23......**46** B4
Courtaulds Wy *COVN* CV6......**23** E5
Courthouse Cft *KNWTH* CV8......**65** H5
Courtland Av *COVN* CV6......**30** A1
Court Leet *COVS* CV3......**42** C2
Court Leet Rd *COVS* CV3......**39** H2
Coventry Point *COV* CV1 *......**2** D4
Coventry Rd *BDWTH* CV12......**5** E4
   HIA/OLT B92......**9** F5
   KNWTH CV8......**53** F5
   KNWTH CV8......**65** F1
   RCOVN/BALC/EX CV7......**26** C3
   RRUGBY CV23......**68** B3
Coventry Rd Exhall
   RCOVN/BALC/EX CV7......**13** H1
Coventry St *COVE* CV2......**31** H2
Coventry Wy *BDWTH* CV12......**5** E5
   COVE CV2......**15** E1
   KNWTH CV8......**50** B1
   KNWTH CV8......**57** E1
   RCOVN/BALC/EX CV7......**5** G4
   RCOVN/BALC/EX CV7......**35** G1
Cove Pl *COVE* CV2......**24** B4
Coverley Pl *RUGBYS/DCH* CV22......**61** F1
Cowan Cl *RUGBYS/DCH* CV22......**60** C3
Cowley Rd *COVE* CV2......**32** C2
Cox Crs *RUGBYS/DCH* CV22......**69** G3
Cox St *COV* CV1......**3** F4
Cozens Cl *BDWTH* CV12......**5** F1
Crabmill La *COVN* CV6......**23** G4
Crackley Cottages
   KNWTH CV8 *......**51** G4
Crackley Hl *KNWTH* CV8 *......**51** G4
Crackley La *KNWTH* CV8......**36** D5
Craigends Av *COVS* CV3......**41** G3
Crakston Cl *COVE* CV2......**32** D4

Cramper's Fld *COVN* CV6......**30** B1
Cranborne Cha *COVE* CV2......**33** E1
Craner's Rd *COV* CV1......**31** G2
Cranford Rd *COVW* CV5......**29** G2
Crathie Cl *COVE* CV2......**25** E5
Craven Av *COVS* CV3......**42** C2
Craven Rd *RUGBYN/HIL* CV21......**48** A5
Craven St *COVW* CV5......**30** A4
Crecy Rd *COVS* CV3......**39** H2
Crediton Cl *COVN* CV6......**39** H4
Crescent Av *COVS* CV3......**32** A4
The Crescent *HIA/OLT* B92......**16** C4
   RCOVN/BALC/EX CV7......**12** A2
   RRUGBY CV23......**68** A1
Cressage Rd *COVE* CV2......**25** F5
Creswell Pl *RUGBYS/DCH* CV22......**60** B3
Crew La *KNWTH* CV8......**66** B2
Cricket Cl *COVW* CV5......**30** A3
Crick Rd *RUGBYN/HIL* CV21......**63** H5
Critchley Dr *RUGBYS/DCH* CV22......**69** H4
Croft Flds *BDWTH* CV12......**5** E3
Croft Pool *BDWTH* CV12......**5** E3
Croft Rd *BDWTH* CV12......**5** E3
   COV CV1......**2** B4
The Croft *BDWTH* CV12......**7** E3
   COVN CV6......**13** G4
   RCOVN/BALC/EX CV7......**18** B2
   RUGBYN/HIL CV21 *......**63** F4
Crondal Rd
   RCOVN/BALC/EX CV7......**14** A1
Croome Cl *COVN* CV6......**30** A2
Crosbie Rd *COVW* CV5......**29** H3
Cross Cheaping *COV* CV1......**2** D3
Cross Rd *COVN* CV6......**23** G3
   RCOVN/BALC/EX CV7......**12** A2
Cross St *COV* CV1......**3** F1
   RRUGBY CV23......**46** B4
   RUGBYN/HIL CV21......**48** B5
Crossway Rd *COVS* CV3......**39** E5
Crowmere Rd *COVE* CV2......**25** E4
Crown Gn *COVN* CV6......**23** F1
Crow Thorns *RUGBYN/HIL* CV21......**48** C3
Croxhall St *BDWTH* CV12......**5** H3
Croydon Cl *COVS* CV3......**39** H3
Crummock Cl *COVN* CV6......**13** E5
Cryfield Grange Rd *KNWTH* CV8......**51** H2
Cryfield Hts *TLHL/CAN* CV4......**52** A2
Cubbington Rd *COVN* CV6......**23** F1
Cuckoo La *COV* CV1......**2** E3
Culworth Cl *RUGBYN/HIL* CV21......**48** D3
Culworth Rw *COVN* CV6......**23** F3
Cumbria Cl *COV* CV1......**30** B3
The Cunnery *KNWTH* CV8......**66** D4
Cunningham Wy North
   RUGBYS/DCH CV22......**60** D3
Curie Cl *RUGBYN/HIL* CV21......**62** C1
Curriers Cl *TLHL/CAN* CV4......**36** C2
Curtis Rd *COVE* CV2......**24** C5
Curzon Av *COVN* CV6......**23** F3
Cymbeline Wy
   RUGBYS/DCH CV22......**69** H1
Cypress Cft *COVS* CV3......**41** G1

D

Dadleys Wd
   RCOVN/BALC/EX CV7 *......**10** C3
Daffern Rd *RCOVN/BALC/EX* CV7......**5** F4
Daffodil Dr *BDWTH* CV12......**4** C3
Daimler Rd *COVN* CV6......**30** D1
Daintree Cft *COVS* CV3......**39** F2
Daisy Cft *BDWTH* CV12......**4** C3
Dalby Cl *COVS* CV3......**41** F2
Dalehouse La *KNWTH* CV8......**65** H1
Dale Meadow Cl
   RCOVN/BALC/EX CV7......**34** C3
Dale St *RUGBYN/HIL* CV21......**47** H5
Daleway Rd *COVS* CV3......**53** E1
Dalkeith Av *RUGBYS/DCH* CV22......**61** E5
Dallington Rd *COVN* CV6......**21** H5
Dalmeny Rd *TLHL/CAN* CV4......**36** C2
Dalton Cl *RRUGBY* CV23......**45** E3
Dalton Gdns *COVE* CV2......**33** E2
Dalton Rd *BDWTH* CV12......**6** D2
   COVW CV5......**39** E1
Dame Agnes Gv *COVN* CV6......**24** A3
Dane Rd *COVE* CV2......**32** A2
Daneswood Rd *COVS* CV3......**42** D2
Daphne Cl *COVE* CV2......**24** B1
Dark La *BDWTH* CV12......**4** C4
   COV CV1......**30** D2
Darnford Cl *COVE* CV2......**25** E4

Darrach Cl *COVE* CV2......**24** D
Dartmouth Rd *COVE* CV2......**32** A
Darwin Cl *COVE* CV2......**25** F
Datchet Cl *COVN* CV6......**29** F
D'Aubeny Rd *TLHL/CAN* CV4......**37** C
Davenport Rd *COVW* CV5......**39** E
Daventry Rd *COVS* CV3......**39** C
   RRUGBY CV23......**70** A
   RUGBYS/DCH CV22......**69** H
David Rd *COV* CV1......**3** H
   RCOVN/BALC/EX CV7......**13** C
   RUGBYS/DCH CV22......**61** E
Davies Rd *RCOVN/BALC/EX* CV7......**13** C
Dawes Cl *COVE* CV2......**31** H
Dawlish Dr *COVS* CV3......**39** C
Dawson Rd *COVS* CV3......**31** H
Days Cl *COV* CV1......**3** H
Day's La *COV* CV1......**3** H
Daytona Dr *COVW* CV5......**19** C
Deacon Cl *RUGBYS/DCH* CV22......**62** B
Deane Pde *RUGBYN/HIL* CV21......**63** H
Deane Rd *RUGBYN/HIL* CV21......**63** H
Deanston Cft *COVE* CV2......**25** C
Dean St *COVE* CV2......**31** H
Deans Wy *RCOVN/BALC/EX* CV7......**13** C
Deasy Rd *COV* CV1......**3** H
De-Compton Cl
   RCOVN/BALC/EX CV7......**12** C
Deedmore Rd *COVE* CV2......**24** C
Deegan Cl *COVE* CV2......**31** C
Deepmore Rd
   RUGBYS/DCH CV22......**61** C
Deerdale Wy *COVS* CV3......**41** C
Deerhurst Rd *COVN* CV6......**22** C
Deerings Rd *RUGBYN/HIL* CV21......**63** H
The Deer Leap *KNWTH* CV8......**65** C
Deighton Gv *COVS* CV3......**40** C
Delage Cl *COVN* CV6......**14** C
Delamere Rd *BDWTH* CV12......**5** E
Delaware Rd *COVS* CV3......**39** C
Delhi Av *COVN* CV6......**23** C
Delius St *TLHL/CAN* CV4......**28** C
Dell Cl *COVS* CV3......**40** C
De Montfort Rd *KNWTH* CV8......**64** C
De Montfort Wy *TLHL/CAN* CV4......**37** C
Dempster Rd *BDWTH* CV12......**5** C
Denbigh Rd *COVN* CV6......**29** C
Dencer Dr *KNWTH* CV8......**65** C
Denewood Wy *KNWTH* CV8......**65** C
Dengate Dr
   RCOVN/BALC/EX CV7......**34** C
Denham Av *COVW* CV5......**29** C
Dennis Rd *COVE* CV2......**32** C
Denshaw Cft *COVE* CV2......**25** C
Denton Cl *KNWTH* CV8......**64** C
Dering Cl *COVE* CV2......**24** C
Deronda Cl *BDWTH* CV12......**5** C
Derry Cl *KNWTH* CV8......**64** C
Dersingham Dr *COVN* CV6......**24** C
Derwent Cl *COVW* CV5......**29** C
   RUGBYN/HIL CV21......**48** C
Derwent Rd *BDWTH* CV12......**5** C
   COVN CV6......**22** C
Despard Rd *COVW* CV5......**28** C
Devereux Cl *TLHL/CAN* CV4......**27** C
Devon Gv *COVE* CV2......**32** C
Devonshire Cl
   RUGBYS/DCH CV22......**60** C
Devoran Cl *RCOVN/BALC/EX* CV7......**5** C
Dewar Gv *RUGBYN/HIL* CV21......**62** C
Dew Cl *RUGBYS/DCH* CV22......**69** C
Dewsbury Av *COVS* CV3......**39** C
Dial House La *COVW* CV5......**28** C
Diana Dr *COVE* CV2......**24** C
Dickens Rd *COVN* CV6......**22** C
   RUGBYS/DCH CV22......**70** C
Dickinson Ct *RUGBYS/DCH* CV22......**69** C
Diddington La *HIA/OLT* B92......**17** C
Didsbury Rd
   RCOVN/BALC/EX CV7......**5** C
Digbey Cl *COVW* CV5......**21** C
Dilcock Wy *TLHL/CAN* CV4......**36** C
Dillam Cl *COVN* CV6......**13** C
Dillotford Av *COVS* CV3......**38** C
Dingle Cl *COVN* CV6......**13** C
The Dingle *RUGBYN/HIL* CV21......**63** C
Dingley Rd *BDWTH* CV12......**7** C
Discovery Wy *COVS* CV3......**23** C
Ditton Cl *RUGBYS/DCH* CV22......**60** C
Dockers Cl *RCOVN/BALC/EX* CV7......**5** C
Dodgson Cl *COVN* CV6......**13** C
Doe Bank La *COV* CV1......**30** C
Dogberry Cl *COVS* CV3......**40** C
Dolomite Av *COVW* CV5......**29** C
Dolomite La *TLHL/CAN* CV4 *......**29** C
Doncaster Cl *COVE* CV2......**33** C
Done Cerce Cl
   RUGBYS/DCH CV22......**69** C
Donegal Cl *TLHL/CAN* CV4......**37** C

nnington Av COVN CV6.............29 H1
nnybrook Dr COVS CV3.............42 A1
one Cl COVE CV2.............24 D5
rchester Wy COVE CV2.............33 E2
rmer Harris Av TLHL/CAN CV4..28 C5
rney Cl COVS CV3.............38 B1
rothy Powell Wy COVE CV2.....25 E2
rset's Flds COV CV1.............2 D1
rset Rd COV CV1.............30 D1
uglas Rd RUGBYN/HIL CV21...48 B3
ulton Cl COVE CV2 *.............24 D2
ve Cl BDWTH CV12.............4 D2
vecote Cl COVS CV3.............29 G1
vedale RUGBYN/HIL CV21.......48 B2
vedale Av COVN CV6.............23 G1
ver St COV CV1 *.............2 B3
wley Cft COVS CV3.............33 G5
wnderry Wy COVN CV6.............23 H5
wning Crs BDWTH CV12.............5 H1
wnton Cl COVE CV2.............25 F3
yle Dr COVN CV6.............13 G5
ake St COVN CV6.............23 E4
ayton Crs COVW CV5.............28 A1
aper Cl KNWTH CV8.............65 H3
aper's Flds COV CV1.............2 D1
aycott Rd COVE CV2.............24 A4
ayton Leys RUGBYS/DCH CV22.............61 H5
ayton Rd BDWTH CV12.............5 H3
ew Crs KNWTH CV8.............65 F3
eyer Cl RUGBYS/DCH CV22....60 D2
e Drive COVE CV2.............32 C3
iggots Cl RUGBYN/HIL CV21...69 H5
onfield Rd COVE CV2.............32 A3
oylsdon Park Rd COVS CV3....53 E1
uid Rd COVE CV2.............32 A3
ummond Cl COVN CV6.............22 A4
ury La RUGBYN/HIL CV21 *....61 H1
ybrooks Cl RCOVN/BALC/EX CV7.............34 C3
yden Cl KNWTH CV8.............65 E4
yden Pl RUGBYS/DCH CV22....61 F1
yden Wk RUGBYS/DCH CV22....61 F1
ckham Ct COVN CV6.............30 E2
dley Rd KNWTH CV8.............65 E5
dley St COVN CV6.............23 H2
ffy Pl RUGBYN/HIL CV21.......63 F4
gdale Rd COVN CV6.............22 B5
ggins La TLHL/CAN CV4.........36 A1
ke Barn Fld COVE CV2.............31 H1
ke St COVW CV5.............30 A4
RUGBYN/HIL CV21.............47 H5
verton Av COVW CV5.............29 G2
verton St COVW CV5.............29 G2
ncan Dr RUGBYS/DCH CV22....69 H1
nchurch Cl RCOVN/BALC/EX CV7.............34 C2
nchurch Hwy COVW CV5.......28 D2
nchurch Rd RUGBYS/DCH CV22.............70 B1
ncroft Av COVN CV6.............22 A4
nhill Av TLHL/CAN CV4.........28 B3
nnerdale RUGBYN/HIL CV21...48 C1
nnose Cl COVN CV6.............23 F3
nrose Cl COVE CV2.............32 D4
nsmore Av COVS CV3.............40 D3
RUGBYS/DCH CV22.............62 D4
nsmore Heath RUGBYS/DCH CV22.............69 G4
nster Cl RUGBYS/DCH CV22...61 F2
nster Pl COVN CV6.............13 C5
nsville Dr COVE CV2.............25 E3
nvegan Dr COVS CV3.............33 F4
NWTH CV8.............65 H3
rbar Av COVN CV6.............23 E3
rham Cl RCOVN/BALC/EX CV7..12 A4
rham Crs COVW CV5.............21 E4
rrell Dr RUGBYS/DCH CV22....60 B4
cton Rd COVE CV2.............14 C5
er's La KNWTH CV8.............57 G2
mond Rd COVN CV6.............12 D5
art Cl COV CV1.............3 G1
on Cl RUGBYN/HIL CV21.......63 E3
on St TLHL/CAN CV4.............28 B3

E

ott Cl COVN CV6.............12 B5
le La KNWTH CV8.............65 E4
le St COVN CV6.............31 E1
le St East COV CV1.............31 E1
Earl's Cft COVS CV3.............39 G2
sdon Av North COVW CV5.....30 A5
sdon Av South COVW CV5.....38 C1
sdon St COVW CV5.............38 C1
St BDWTH CV12.............5 H3

COV CV1.............2 E4
RUGBYN/HIL CV21.............62 A1
Easedale Cl COVS CV3.............39 E3
East Av BDWTH CV12.............5 G4
COVE CV2.............31 H3
Eastbourne Cl COVN CV6.......31 H5
East Car Park Rd BHAMNEC B40....8 D4
Eastcotes TLHL/CAN CV4........29 E5
Eastern Green Rd COVW CV5...28 C3
Eastfield Pl RUGBYN/HIL CV21...61 H1
Eastlands Gv COVW CV5.........29 H2
Eastlands Pl RUGBYN/HIL CV21...62 C1
Eastlands Rd RUGBYN/HIL CV21...62 C1
Eastleigh Av COVW CV5.........38 C2
East St COV CV1.............3 H3
RUGBYN/HIL CV21.............48 C5
East Union St RUGBYS/DCH CV22.............61 H2
East Wy BHAMNEC B40.............8 C5
HIA/OLT B92.............9 E5
Eastwood Gv RUGBYN/HIL CV21..63 H4
Easy La RUGBYN/HIL CV21.......61 H1
Eathorpe Cl COVE CV2.............24 B2
Eaton Rd COV CV1.............2 C6
Eaves Green La RCOVN/BALC/EX CV7.............18 D2
Ebbw Vale Ter COVS CV3.........39 G2
Eborne Cft RCOVN/BALC/EX CV7..34 D1
Ebourne Cl KNWTH CV8.............65 F3
Ebro Crs COVS CV3.............33 E5
Eburne Rd COVE CV2.............14 B5
Eccles Cl COVE CV2.............24 B1
Edale Wy COVN CV6.............23 H4
Eddie Miller Ct BDWTH CV12 *.....5 F3
Eden Cft KNWTH CV8.............65 G3
Eden Rd COVE CV2.............25 F2
RUGBYN/HIL CV21.............48 C5
Eden St COVN CV6.............23 G4
Edgecote Cl RUGBYN/HIL CV21..63 E3
Edgefield Rd COVE CV2.............25 E3
Edgehill Pl TLHL/CAN CV4.......27 H5
Edgwick Rd COVN CV6.............23 G4
Edinburgh Vls KNWTH CV8......54 A2
Edinburgh Wy RRUGBY CV23....46 C4
Edingale Rd COVE CV2.............25 E3
Edmund Rd COV CV1.............31 F1
Edward Bailey Cl COVS CV3.....41 F2
Edward Rd BDWTH CV12.............5 H3
COVN CV6.............12 B5
Edwards Gv KNWTH CV8.............65 F3
Edward St COVN CV6.............31 F1
COV CV1.............47 G5
Edward Tyler Rd RCOVN/BALC/EX CV7.............5 F4
Edwin Cl RUGBYS/DCH CV22.....60 B5
Edyth Rd COVE CV2.............32 D2
Edyvean Cl RUGBYS/DCH CV22..70 A1
Egerton Cl RUGBYN/HIL CV21...47 G3
Elborow St RUGBYN/HIL CV21...61 H1
Elderberry Wy COVE CV2.........24 A5
Elder Cl RUGBYS/DCH CV22.....60 C3
Eld Rd COVN CV6.............23 F4
Electric Whf COV CV1.............30 D1
Elgar Rd COVN CV6.............24 A3
Eliot Cl RUGBYS/DCH CV22.....61 F1
Elizabeth Wy COVE CV2.............25 E4
KNWTH CV8.............64 C4
RRUGBY CV23.............46 C4
Elkington St COVN CV6.............23 G3
Ellacombe Rd COVE CV2.............24 C3
Ellerman Gdns COVN CV6........13 G5
Ellesmere Rd BDWTH CV12........5 F3
Ellis Park Dr COVS CV3.............33 F4
Ellys Rd COV CV1.............30 D1
Elm Cl COVS CV3.............42 B2
Elmdene Cl KNWTH CV8.............43 F5
Elmdene Rd KNWTH CV8.............65 F3
Elm Gv RCOVN/BALC/EX CV7....34 D3
Elmhurst Rd COVN CV6.............13 H4
Elm Ldg HIA/OLT B92 *.............16 B4
Elmore Cl COVS CV3.............41 E1
Elmore Rd RUGBYS/DCH CV22...61 E1
Elmsdale Av COVN CV6.............23 F1
Elms Dr RUGBYS/DCH CV22.....63 H1
The Elms Paddock RRUGBY CV23.............49 E4
The Elms BDWTH CV12.............4 D3
Elm Tree Av TLHL/CAN CV4.....28 B4
Elm Tree Ri HIA/OLT B92.........16 C5
Elm Tree Rd BDWTH CV12.........7 G3
Elmwood Av COVN CV6.............30 A1
Elphin Cl COVN CV6.............22 D1
Elsee Rd RUGBYN/HIL CV21.....61 H1
Elter Cl RUGBYN/HIL CV21.......48 C2
Eltham Rd COVS CV3.............39 H2
Elwy Cir RCOVN/BALC/EX CV7...12 D1
Ely Cl COVE CV2.............25 F5

Embassy Wk COVE CV2.............24 C3
Emerson Rd COVE CV2.............32 B2
Emery Rd COVE CV2.............24 D4
Emperor Wy RUGBYN/HIL CV21...47 G2
Empire Rd TLHL/CAN CV4.........27 H5
Empress Ar COVS CV3 *.............32 A4
Emscote Rd COVS CV3.............32 B4
Ena Rd COV CV1.............31 E1
Endemere Rd COVN CV6.............23 E4
Enfield Rd COVE CV2.............32 A3
Engleton Rd COVN CV6.............30 B1
Ennerdale RUGBYN/HIL CV21...48 B2
Ennerdale La COVE CV2.............33 E2
Ensign Cl TLHL/CAN CV4.........27 H5
Epsom Cl BDWTH CV12.............5 G1
Epsom Dr COVS CV3.............40 D3
Epsom Rd RUGBYS/DCH CV22...61 E3
Erica Av BDWTH CV12.............4 D3
Eric Grey Cl COVE CV2.............31 H1
Erithway Rd COVS CV3.............39 E5
Ernest Richards Rd BDWTH CV12.............5 G1
Ernsford Av COVS CV3.............31 H5
Esher Dr COVS CV3.............39 H2
Eskdale RUGBYN/HIL CV21.......48 B1
Essex Cl COVW CV5.............29 E3
KNWTH CV8.............64 D5
Essex St RUGBYN/HIL CV21.....47 G5
Esterton Cl COVN CV6.............22 D1
Ethelfield Rd COVE CV2.............32 A3
Ettington Rd COVW CV5.............28 D3
Eustace Rd BDWTH CV12.............7 G4
Euston Crs COVS CV3.............40 D3
Evans Cl BDWTH CV12.............5 H2
Evans Rd RUGBYS/DCH CV22...60 D2
Evelyn Av COVN CV6.............23 F1
Evenlode Crs COVN CV6.............30 A1
Everard Cl RRUGBY CV23.............49 F4
Everdon Cl RUGBYS/DCH CV22..62 D4
Everdon Rd COVN CV6.............22 C1
Everest Rd RUGBYS/DCH CV22..61 E4
Eversleigh Rd COVN CV6.............21 H4
Evesham Wk TLHL/CAN CV4.....37 H4
Evreux Wy RUGBYN/HIL CV21...61 H1
Exeter Cl COVS CV3.............41 E1
Exhall Basin COVN CV6 *.............14 A3
Exhall Gn RCOVN/BALC/EX CV7..13 G1
Exhall Rd RCOVN/BALC/EX CV7..12 A2
Exhibition Wy BHAMNEC B40...8 B4
Exminster Rd COVS CV3.............39 H4
Exmouth Cl COVE CV2.............24 B4
Exton Cl RCOVN/BALC/EX CV7...12 D1
Eydon Cl RUGBYN/HIL CV21.....48 C3

F

Fabian Cl COVS CV3.............41 E2
Fairbanks Cl COVE CV2.............25 F4
Fairbourne Wy COVN CV6.........21 H3
Faircroft KNWTH CV8.............65 E4
Fairfax St COV CV1.............2 E3
Fairfield Ct COVS CV3.............40 B2
Fairfield Ri RCOVN/BALC/EX CV7..18 B2
Fairlands Pk TLHL/CAN CV4.....38 B4
Fairmile Cl COVS CV3.............40 D1
Fairway Ri KNWTH CV8.............65 H1
Fairways Cl COVW CV5.............20 D5
Falcon Av COVS CV3.............41 C1
Falkland Cl TLHL/CAN CV4.......36 C2
Fallowfields COVN CV6.............12 D4
Falstaff Dr RUGBYS/DCH CV22..69 H1
Falstaff Rd TLHL/CAN CV4.......28 B4
Fancott Dr KNWTH CV8.............64 D1
Faraday Rd RUGBYS/DCH CV22..62 B3
Farber Rd COVE CV2.............25 F5
Farcroft Av COVW CV5.............28 A2
Fareham Av RUGBYS/DCH CV22.............62 D4
Far Gosford St COV CV1.............3 H4
Farlow Cl COVE CV6 *.............23 H5
Farman Rd COVW CV5.............30 A4
Farm Cl COVN CV6.............12 C5
Farmcote Rd COVE CV2.............14 A4
Farmer Ward Rd KNWTH CV8...65 F4
Farm Gv RUGBYS/DCH CV22.....62 B3
Farm Pl COVS CV3 *.............40 C1
Farm Rd KNWTH CV8.............65 F5
The Farmstead COVS CV3.............40 C1
Farndale Av COVN CV6.............13 C5
Farndon Cl BDWTH CV12.............7 G3
Farr Dr TLHL/CAN CV4.............29 E4
Farren Rd COVE CV2.............32 D1
Farthing Ct RUGBYS/DCH CV22..63 G4
Farthing Wk TLHL/CAN CV4.....36 C3
Faseman Av TLHL/CAN CV4.....28 C4
Faulconbridge Av COVW CV5...28 B2
Fawley Cl COVS CV3.............40 D3

Fawsley Leys RUGBYS/DCH CV22.............61 H5
Faygate Cl COVS CV3.............33 F3
Featherbed La RUGBYN/HIL CV21.............63 F3
TLHL/CAN CV4.............37 F4
Feilding Cl COVE CV2.............25 F5
Fein Bank TLHL/CAN CV4.........27 H4
Fellows Wy RUGBYN/HIL CV21...63 E4
Felton Cl COVE CV2.............24 D2
Fennyland La KNWTH CV8.........51 G5
Fenside Av COVS CV3.............39 G5
Fentham Cl HIA/OLT B92.........16 B4
Fentham Gn HIA/OLT B92.........16 B4
Fentham Rd HIA/OLT B92.........16 B4
Fenwick Dr RUGBYN/HIL CV21...63 F4
Fern Cl COVE CV2.............24 B1
RRUGBY CV23.............48 C1
Ferndale Dr KNWTH CV8.............65 H6
Ferndale Rd COVS CV3.............42 C2
Fern Dale Rd RCOVN/BALC/EX CV7.............34 A3
Ferndown Cl TLHL/CAN CV4.....28 C3
Ferndown Ct RUGBYS/DCH CV22.............61 F3
Ferndown Rd RUGBYS/DCH CV22.............61 F3
Ferndown Ter RUGBYS/DCH CV22.............61 F3
Fern Gv BDWTH CV12.............4 D3
Fernhill Cl KNWTH CV8.............64 D1
Fernhill La RCOVN/BALC/EX CV7..34 A3
Ferrers Cl TLHL/CAN CV4.........28 C4
Ferrieres Cl RUGBYS/DCH CV22..69 G4
Fetherston Crs KNWTH CV8......55 H3
Fiddlers Gn HIA/OLT B92.........16 B4
Field Cl KNWTH CV8.............65 G2
Field Cottages COVS CV3 *.............40 D4
Fieldfare Cl RRUGBY CV23.............48 B1
Fieldgate La KNWTH CV8.............50 D5
Fieldgate Lawn KNWTH CV8.....65 F3
Fieldside La COVS CV3.............33 E3
Field Vw KNWTH CV8.............55 H2
RUGBYS/DCH CV22.............60 C4
Field View Cl RCOVN/BALC/EX CV7.............5 F5
Fife Rd COVW CV5.............30 A4
Fillongley Rd RCOVN/BALC/EX CV7.............18 B2
Finch Cft RCOVN/BALC/EX CV7..34 C2
Findon Cl BDWTH CV12.............7 F3
Finford Cft RCOVN/BALC/EX CV7.............34 C3
Fingal Cl COVS CV3.............40 D3
Fingest Cl COVW CV5.............29 E2
Finham Crs KNWTH CV8.............65 G1
Finham Green Rd COVS CV3.....53 F1
Finham Gv COVS CV3.............53 F1
Finham Rd KNWTH CV8.............65 G2
Finmere RUGBYN/HIL CV21.......48 C3
Finnemore Cl COVS CV3.............39 E4
Firedrake Cft COV CV1.............3 J5
Fir Gv TLHL/CAN CV4.............28 D4
Firleigh Dr BDWTH CV12.............7 G3
Firs Dr RUGBYS/DCH CV22.....61 G2
First Av COVS CV3.............32 B5
First Exhibition Av BHAMNEC B40.............8 B4
The Firs BDWTH CV12.............4 D3
COVW CV5.............39 E1
RCOVN/BALC/EX CV7 *.............18 A2
Fir Tree Av TLHL/CAN CV4.......28 D4
Fisher Av RUGBYS/DCH CV22...62 D4
Fisher Rd COVN CV6.............23 F4
Fishponds Rd KNWTH CV8.........64 D1
Fishpool La RCOVN/BALC/EX CV7..9 F2
Fitzalan Cl RRUGBY CV23.............45 E3
Fitzroy Cl COVE CV2.............25 G5
Fivefield Rd RCOVN/BALC/EX CV7.............11 H3
Flamboro' Cl COVS CV3.............40 D4
Flaunden Cl COVW CV5.............29 E3
Flecknose St COVS CV3.............40 D3
Fleet Crs RUGBYN/HIL CV21.....62 D2
Fleet St COV CV1.............2 D2
Fletchamstead Hwy COVW CV5..38 A2
TLHL/CAN CV4.............29 F5
Fletcher Wk COVS CV3.............39 F5
Fletchworth Ga COVW CV5.......38 A1
Florence Cl BDWTH CV12.............5 E5
Florence Rd COVS CV3.............33 E3
Florin Cl TLHL/CAN CV4.............36 D3
Florin Pl RUGBYN/HIL CV21.....63 H1
Flowerdale Dr COVE CV2.............24 A5
Floyd Gv RCOVN/BALC/EX CV7..34 D2
Flude Rd RCOVN/BALC/EX CV7...12 D2
Flynt Av COVW CV5.............20 D5
Foleshill Rd COV CV1.............2 D1
Follager Rd RUGBYN/HIL CV21...47 F5

Follis Wk TLHL/CAN CV4 36 C3
Fontmell Cl COVE CV2 33 F2
Ford St COV CV1 3 F3
Fordwell Cl COVW CV5 30 A3
Foreland Wy COVN CV6 22 B1
Foresters Pl RUGBYN/HIL CV21 63 G5
Forester's Rd COVS CV3 39 H3
Forfield Rd COVN CV6 29 H1
Forge Rd KNWTH CV8 65 F1
Forge Wy COVN CV6 12 D5
Forknell Av COVE CV2 32 B1
Fornside Cl RUGBYN/HIL CV21 48 C2
Forum Dr RUGBYN/HIL CV21 47 H3
Fosse Wy KNWTH CV8 57 G4
Fosseway Rd COVS CV3 39 E5
Fosterd Rd RUGBYN/HIL CV21 47 G4
Foster Rd COVN CV6 22 C4
Founder Cl TLHL/CAN CV4 37 E1
Four Pounds Av COVW CV5 30 A3
Fowler Rd COVN CV6 30 C1
Fow Oak TLHL/CAN CV4 27 H4
Fox Cl RUGBYN/HIL CV21 63 G3
Foxes Wy RCOVN/BALC/EX CV7 34 C3
Foxfield Pl RRUGBY CV23 46 B5
Foxford Crs COVE CV2 14 A4
Foxglove Cl BDWTH CV12 4 D4
COVN CV6 22 D1
RRUGBY CV23 48 D1
Foxons Barn Rd
RUGBYN/HIL CV21 48 B3
Foxton Rd COVS CV3 32 D5
Foxwood Dr COVS CV3 42 C2
Framlingham Gv KNWTH CV8 65 H1
Frampton Wk COVE CV2 33 E2
Frances Crs BDWTH CV12 5 F2
Frances Rd KNWTH CV8 53 H1
Franciscan Rd COVS CV3 39 F1
Francis Dr RUGBYS/DCH CV22 60 B3
Francis St COVN CV6 23 F5
Frankland Rd COVN CV6 23 H2
Franklin Gv TLHL/CAN CV4 28 B5
Franklins Gdns COVS CV3 33 G5
Frankpledge Rd COVS CV3 39 H1
Frankton Av COVS CV3 39 G4
Frankwell Dr COVE CV2 24 D2
Fraser Rd COVN CV6 22 B2
Frederick Neal Av COVW CV5 28 A2
Frederick St RUGBYN/HIL CV21 61 G1
Fred Lee Gv COVS CV3 39 G5
Freeboard La RRUGBY CV23 56 D5
Freeburn Cswy TLHL/CAN CV4 37 H2
Freehold St COV CV1 31 G2
Freeman St COVN CV6 23 G5
Freemantle Rd
RUGBYS/DCH CV22 60 D2
Freshfield Cl COVW CV5 21 F2
Fretton Cl COVN CV6 23 G4
Frevill Rd COVN CV6 24 A3
Frewen Rd RUGBYS/DCH CV22 60 A4
Friars Cl COVS CV3 42 D2
Friars' Rd COV CV1 2 D6
Frilsham Wy COVW CV5 29 E2
Frisby Rd TLHL/CAN CV4 28 B4
Friswell Dr COVN CV6 23 G3
Frobisher Rd COVS CV3 39 F4
RUGBYS/DCH CV22 60 D3
Frog La RCOVN/BALC/EX CV7 34 B4
Frogmere Cl COVW CV5 21 F5
Frythe Cl KNWTH CV8 65 H1
Fulbrook Rd COVE CV2 24 B2
Fullers Cl COVN CV6 22 A4
Fullwood Cl COVE CV2 24 D1
Furlong Rd COV CV1 3 F7
Furnace Cl BDWTH CV12 5 H2
Furnace Rd BDWTH CV12 6 A2
Furness Cl RUGBYN/HIL CV21 48 C2
Furrow Cl RUGBYN/HIL CV21 48 C5
Futures Wk COVS CV3 41 E3
Fynford Rd COVN CV6 30 C1

G

Gables Cl RUGBYS/DCH CV22 61 E4
Gabor Cl RUGBYN/HIL CV21 48 B3
Gainford Ri COVS CV3 33 E3
Gainsborough Crs
RUGBYN/HIL CV21 63 G3
Gainsborough Dr BDWTH CV12 5 F1
Galey's Rd COVS CV3 39 G1
Gallagher Rd BDWTH CV12 5 F3
The Galliards TLHL/CAN CV4 38 A5
Galmington Dr COVS CV3 39 E4
Gardeners End
RUGBYS/DCH CV22 61 E2
Gardenia Dr COVW CV5 20 D5
The Gardens KNWTH CV8 65 F4
RRUGBY CV23 68 D4
Gardner Wy KNWTH CV8 65 F5
Garlands Cft
RCOVN/BALC/EX CV7 12 B2
Garlick Dr KNWTH CV8 65 H1
Garratt Cl RRUGBY CV23 46 C4
Garrick Cl COVW CV5 27 H2
Garth Crs COVS CV3 40 D1
Garyth Williams Cl
RUGBYS/DCH CV22 61 F4
Gas St RUGBYN/HIL CV21 62 A1
Gatehouse Cl RUGBYN/HIL CV21 63 F4
Gatehouse La BDWTH CV12 5 F3
Gateside Rd COVN CV6 23 F1
Gaulby Wk COVS CV3 33 F5
Gaveston Rd COVN CV6 21 H5
Gaydon Cl COVN CV6 23 H3
Gayer St COVN CV6 23 G2
Gayhurst Cl COVS CV3 41 F1
Gaza Cl TLHL/CAN CV4 28 D5
Gazelle Cl COV CV1 3 G2
Gentian Wy RRUGBY CV23 48 D1
Geoffery Cl COVE CV2 32 A1
George Eliot Av BDWTH CV12 6 A3
George Eliot Rd COV CV1 31 E1
George Hodgkinson Cl
TLHL/CAN CV4 28 C3
George Marston Rd COVS CV3 32 D5
George Park Cl COVE CV2 24 B2
George Robertson Cl COVS CV3 41 F2
George St COV CV1 31 F1
RUGBYN/HIL CV21 61 G1
George St Ringway BDWTH CV12 5 G2
Gerard Av TLHL/CAN CV4 37 G1
Gerard Rd RUGBYS/DCH CV22 60 B4
Gerard Rw RUGBYS/DCH CV22 * 60 B4
Gibbert Hill Rd TLHL/CAN CV4 37 G4
Gibbet Hill Rd TLHL/CAN CV4 51 H1
Gibbons Cl TLHL/CAN CV4 28 C4
Gibbs Cl COVE CV2 25 G5
Gibson Crs BDWTH CV12 5 G4
Gibson Dr RUGBYN/HIL CV21 63 E3
Gielgud Wy COVE CV2 25 G3
Gilbert Av RUGBYS/DCH CV22 61 E2
Gilbert Cl BDWTH CV12 5 G4
COV CV1 3 H2
Giles Cl COVN CV6 22 D1
Gillians Wk COVE CV2 25 F3
Gilquart Rd COV CV1 3 F7
Gilquart Wy COV CV1 3 F7
Gipsy Cl RCOVN/BALC/EX CV7 34 C4
Gipsy La RCOVN/BALC/EX CV7 34 D4
Girdlers Cl COVS CV3 39 E4
Girtin Cl BDWTH CV12 5 F1
The Glade TLHL/CAN CV4 28 C3
Gladiator Wy RUGBYN/HIL CV21 47 G2
Gladstone St RUGBYN/HIL CV21 61 G1
Glaisdale Av COVN CV6 13 F5
Glaramara Cl RUGBYN/HIL CV21 48 C3
Glasshouse La KNWTH CV8 65 H4
Glebe Av BDWTH CV12 4 D4
Glebe Cl TLHL/CAN CV4 37 F2
Glebe Crs KNWTH CV8 65 F4
RUGBYN/HIL CV21 61 F1
Glebefarm Gv COVS CV3 33 E3
Glebe Farm Rd
RUGBYN/HIL CV21 47 G2
The Glebe RCOVN/BALC/EX CV7 11 F1
Glebe Wy RCOVN/BALC/EX CV7 34 B2
Glencoe Rd COVS CV3 32 A5
Glendale Av KNWTH CV8 65 F2
Glendale Wy TLHL/CAN CV4 27 H4
Glendon Gdns BDWTH CV12 7 F2
Glendower Av COVW CV5 29 G4
Gleneagles Rd COVE CV2 24 D5
Glenfern Gdns KNWTH CV8 55 F2
Glenmore Dr COVN CV6 13 G3
Glenmount Av COVN CV6 13 G3
Glenn St COVN CV6 13 E5
Glenridding Cl COVN CV6 13 G3
Glenroy Cl COVE CV2 24 D5
Glentworth Av COVN CV6 22 B1
Gloster Dr KNWTH CV8 65 E1
Gloucester St COV CV1 2 A3
Glovers Cl RCOVN/BALC/EX CV7 18 B2
Glover St COVS CV3 39 G1
Godiva Pl COV CV1 3 G3
Gold Av RUGBYS/DCH CV22 60 C4
Golden Acres La COVS CV3 41 G2
Goldsmith Av
RUGBYS/DCH CV22 61 G5
Goldthorn Cl COVW CV5 28 A2
Goodacre Cl RRUGBY CV23 49 F4
Goode Cft TLHL/CAN CV4 28 C4
Goodman Wy TLHL/CAN CV4 27 H5
Goodwood Cl COVS CV3 40 D3
Goodyers End La BDWTH CV12 4 C5
Gordon Cl BDWTH CV12 5 G1
Gordon St COV CV1 2 A6
Goring Rd COVE CV2 31 H2
Gorse Cl RUGBYS/DCH CV22 61 F3
Gorseway COVW CV5 29 F3
Gorton Cft RCOVN/BALC/EX CV7 34 C2
Gosford St COV CV1 3 G4
Gospel Oak Rd COVN CV6 12 C4
Gosport Rd COVN CV6 23 F3
Gossett La KNWTH CV8 43 E2
Grace Rd COVW CV5 19 F3
Grafton Cl KNWTH CV8 65 F4
Grafton Ct TLHL/CAN CV4 * 37 G2
Grafton St COV CV1 3 H4
Graham Cl COVN CV6 24 A3
Graham Rd RUGBYN/HIL CV21 48 B5
Granborough Cl COVS CV3 41 G1
Grange Av COVS CV3 41 G2
COVS CV3 53 F1
KNWTH CV8 64 D1
Grangemouth Rd COVN CV6 22 C5
Grange Rd COVN CV6 14 A4
RCOVN/BALC/EX CV7 34 A2
RUGBYN/HIL CV21 47 F3
Grange Wk COVN CV6 * 14 A3
Granoe Cl COVS CV3 41 F1
Grantham St COVE CV2 3 K3
Grant Rd COVS CV3 32 A4
RCOVN/BALC/EX CV7 5 F5
Grasmere Av COVS CV3 38 C3
Grasmere Cl RUGBYN/HIL CV21 48 C3
Grasmere Rd BDWTH CV12 5 F3
Grasscroft Dr COVS CV3 39 H3
Gratton Ct COVS CV3 38 C3
Gravel Hl TLHL/CAN CV4 28 C5
The Graylands COVS CV3 39 F5
Grays Orch RRUGBY CV23 68 D5
Grayswood Av COVW CV5 29 G2
Great Borne RUGBYN/HIL CV21 48 B2
Great Central Wy
RUGBYN/HIL CV21 48 C5
Greenbank Rd
RCOVN/BALC/EX CV7 34 A3
Green Cl RRUGBY CV23 46 A5
Greendale Rd COVW CV5 29 G3
Greenfield Av
RCOVN/BALC/EX CV7 34 B2
The Green Fld COVS CV3 40 C1
Greenhill Rd RUGBYS/DCH CV22 61 G3
Greenland Av COVW CV5 28 C1
Greenland Ct COVW CV5 28 C1
Green La COVS CV3 53 E2
RCOVN/BALC/EX CV7 10 A2
RCOVN/BALC/EX CV7 34 C2
RRUGBY CV23 45 E4
Green La North COVS CV3 38 D3
Greenleaf Cl COVW CV5 28 D3
Greenodd Dr COVN CV6 13 G3
Greensleeves Cl COVN CV6 22 C1
Greens Rd COVN CV6 22 B2
Greensward Cl KNWTH CV8 65 G1
The Greensward COVS CV3 33 F4
Greens Yd BDWTH CV12 * 5 H2
The Green RRUGBY CV23 46 B5
RUGBYS/DCH CV22 60 D4
Greenways TLHL/CAN CV4 27 H4
Greenwood Cl RRUGBY CV23 46 B4
Gregory Av COVS CV3 38 D3
Gregory Hood Rd COVS CV3 39 G4
Grendon Cl TLHL/CAN CV4 27 H5
Grendon Dr RUGBYN/HIL CV21 48 D2
Grenville Av COVE CV2 32 A3
Grenville Cl RUGBYS/DCH CV22 60 D3
Gresham St COVE CV2 31 H4
Gresley Rd COVE CV2 24 C4
Greswold Cl TLHL/CAN CV4 28 C5
Gretna Rd COVS CV3 38 C5
Greville Rd KNWTH CV8 64 D3
Greycoat Rd COVN CV6 22 B1
Greyfriars La COV CV1 2 D4
Greyfriars Rd COV CV1 2 C5
Grimston Cl COVS CV3 33 F4
Grizebeck Dr COVW CV5 28 D1
Grizedale RUGBYN/HIL CV21 48 B2
Grosvenor Rd COVS CV3 2 B6
RUGBYN/HIL CV21 62 B1
Grovefield Crs
RCOVN/BALC/EX CV7 34 D1
Grovehurst Pk KNWTH CV8 67 E5
Grove La RCOVN/BALC/EX CV7 12 A1
Grove Rd RCOVN/BALC/EX CV7 15 H4
Grove St COV CV1 3 F3
The Grove BDWTH CV12 5 G2
HIA/OLT B92 16 B3
Guardhouse Rd COVN CV6 22 C3
Guild Rd COVN CV6 23 E4
Guilsborough Rd COVS CV3 32 D5
Guinea Crs TLHL/CAN CV4 36 C3
Gulson Rd COV CV1 3 J4
Gun La COVE CV2 31 H1
Gunton Av COVS CV3 40 D4
Guphill Av COVW CV5 29 G4
Gutteridge Av COVN CV6 22
Guy Rd KNWTH CV8 65

H

Haddon End COVS CV3 39
Haddon St COVN CV6 23
Hadfield Cl RRUGBY CV23 49
Hadleigh Rd COVS CV3 53
Hadrians Wy RUGBYN/HIL CV21 47
Hales St COV CV1 2
Halford La COVN CV6 22
Halfway La RUGBYS/DCH CV22 69
Halifax Cl COVW CV5 20
Hallam Rd COVN CV6 12
Hallams Cl KNWTH CV8 43
Hall Brook Rd COVN CV6 12
Hall Cl KNWTH CV8 67
The Hall Cl RUGBYS/DCH CV22 69
Hall Dr KNWTH CV8 53
Hall Green Rd COVN CV6 24
Hall La COVE CV2 25
Hamilton Cl BDWTH CV12 4
Hamilton Rd COVE CV2 31
Hamlet Cl RUGBYS/DCH CV22 69
Hammersley St BDWTH CV12 4
Hammond Rd COVE CV2 31
Hampden Wy
RUGBYS/DCH CV22 60
Hampshire Cl COVS CV3 41
Hampton Gra
RCOVN/BALC/EX CV7 18
Hampton La
RCOVN/BALC/EX CV7 17
Hampton Rd COVN CV6 23
Hanbury Rd BDWTH CV12 5
Hancock Gn TLHL/CAN CV4 37
Handcross Gv COVS CV3 38
Handley's Cl KNWTH CV8 55
Handsworth Crs COVW CV5 28
Hanford Cl COVN CV6 23
Hanover Gdns
RUGBYN/HIL CV21 48
Hans Cl COVE CV2 31
Hanson Wy COVN CV6 13
Hanwood Cl COVW CV5 28
Harbet Dr BHAMNEC B40 8
Harborough Rd COVN CV6 22
RRUGBY CV23 46
Harbourne Cl KNWTH CV8 65
Harcourt COVS CV3 41
Hardwick Cl COVW CV5 28
Hardwyn Cl COVS CV3 33
Hardy Cl RUGBYS/DCH CV22 60
Hardy Rd COVN CV6 22
Harebell Wy RRUGBY CV23 48
Harefield Rd COVE CV2 32
Harewood Rd COVW CV5 29
Harger Ct KNWTH CV8 65
Harger Ms KNWTH CV8 65
Hargrave Cl COVS CV3 33
Harington Rd COVN CV6 30
Harlech Cl KNWTH CV8 65
Harley St COVE CV2 31
Harmer Cl COVE CV2 25
Harnall La COV CV1 31
Harnall La East COV CV1 31
Harnall La West COV CV1 30
Harnall Rw COV CV1 3
Harold Rd COVE CV2 32
Harpenden Dr COVW CV5 28
Harper Rd COV CV1 3
Harris Dr RUGBYS/DCH CV22 61
Harrison Cl RUGBYN/HIL CV21 63
Harrison Crs BDWTH CV12 5
Harris Rd COVS CV3 32
Harrow Cl COVN CV6 13
Harry Rose Rd COVE CV2 32
Harry Truslove Cl COVN CV6 22
Harry Weston Rd COVS CV3 33
Hart Cl RUGBYN/HIL CV21 62
Hartington Crs COVW CV5 29
Hartland Av COVE CV2 24
Hartlepool Rd COV CV1 31
Hartridge Wk COVW CV5 29
Harvesters Cl COVS CV3 33
Harvest Hill La COVW CV5 20
Harvey Cl COVW CV5 20
Haselbech Rd COVS CV3 33
Haseley Rd COVE CV2 24
Hasilwood Sq COVS CV3 32
Hastings Rd COVE CV2 31
Haswell Cl RUGBYS/DCH CV22 62
Hathaway Cl
RCOVN/BALC/EX CV7 34
Hathaway Rd TLHL/CAN CV4 28
Hatters Ct BDWTH CV12 5

ven Ct *RUGBYS/DCH* CV22 *......61 F1
vendale Cl *COVN* CV6.........30 C1
kesbury La *COVE* CV2.........14 C3
kkeshead *RUGBYN/HIL* CV21...48 C2
kes Mill La *COVW* CV5.........20 D1
kksworth Dr *KNWTH* CV8.....65 F1
kkins Cl *RUGBYS/HIL* CV21.....61 F3
kkins Rd *COVW* CV5.........30 D5
kkswood Dr
  RCOVN/BALC/EX CV7.........34 C5
kksworth Dr *COV* CV1.........30 B3
wlands *RUGBYS/HIL* CV21.....48 C3
wthorn Dr
  RCOVN/BALC/EX CV7.........34 C1
wthorne Cl *KNWTH* CV8.......43 F5
wthorn La *TLHL/CAN* CV4.....28 B4
wthorn Wy
  RUGBYS/DCH CV22.........60 C3
ydock Cl *COVN* CV6.........14 A4
yes Cl *RUGBYS/HIL* CV21.....48 C2
yes Green Rd *BDWTH* CV12 *...5 F5
yes La *RCOVN/BALC/EX* CV7...5 E5
y La *COV* CV1.........2 E4
nestone Rd *COVN* CV6.........21 H5
nes Wy *RUGBYS/HIL* CV21.....47 G1
yton Gn *TLHL/CAN* CV4.........37 E2
ytor Ri *COVE* CV2.........24 B4
zel Gv *BDWTH* CV12.........6 A2
zel Rd *COVN* CV6.........24 A2
zelwood Cl
  RUGBYS/DCH CV22.........69 H4
zlemere Cl *COVW* CV5.........29 E2
adborough Rd *COVE* CV2.......31 H1
adington Av *COVN* CV6.........22 B1
e Headlands *COVW* CV5.........29 C2
aley Cl *RUGBYS/HIL* CV21.....48 B2
alth Centre Rd *TLHL/CAN* CV4.37 H5
arsall Common *COVW* CV5 ...29 H4
arsall La *COVE* CV2.........30 A4
art of England Wy
  RCOVN/BALC/EX CV7.........34 A1
ath Av *BDWTH* CV12.........4 D4
athcote St *COVN* CV6.........22 B4
ath Crs *COVE* CV2 *.........31 G1
ather Cl *RUGBYS/DCH* CV22...61 F3
ather Dr *BDWTH* CV12.........4 C2
ather Rd *COVE* CV2.........24 A1
  COVS CV3.........42 B2
athfield Rd *COVW* CV5.........29 F4
ath Green Wy *TLHL/CAN* CV4..37 E3
e Heathlands *RRUGBY* CV23 *..49 F4
ath Rd *BDWTH* CV12.........4 C5
e Heath *RUGBYS/DCH* CV22...69 G4
ath Wy *RUGBYS/DCH* CV22.....62 C4
ckley Rd
  RCOVN/BALC/EX CV7.........13 H1
ddle Cl *COVN* CV6.........24 A3
dgefield Wy *TLHL/CAN* CV4....37 E1
dgerow Wk *COVN* CV6.........12 C4
era Cl *COVE* CV2.........23 E3
en St *COVN* CV6.........23 G5
e Rd *COVS* CV3.........39 G3
mdon Cl *RUGBYN/HIL* CV21...48 C3
vellyn Wy *RUGBYN/HIL* CV21..48 C2
mingford Rd *COVE* CV2.........25 E3
msby Cl *TLHL/CAN* CV4.........37 F2
nsworth Dr *BDWTH* CV12.......7 E3
ndre Cl *COVW* CV5.........29 C4
n La *COVN* CV6.........13 E5
nley Mill La *COVE* CV2.........24 B4
nley Rd *COVE* CV2.........24 B3
nley Wk *COVE* CV2 *.........24 B1
nrietta St *COVN* CV6.........31 G1
ry Boteler Rd
  TLHL/CAN CV4.........37 G2
ry St *COV* CV1.........2 D2
  KNWTH CV8.........65 F2
  RUGBYS/HIL CV21 *.........61 H1
nson Rd *BDWTH* CV12.........4 D4
pworth Rd *COVS* CV3.........33 F5
rald Av *COVW* CV5.........29 G5
rald Wy *COVS* CV3.........41 G3
rbert's La *COVE* CV2.........65 F2
ritage Ct *TLHL/CAN* CV4.......52 A1
ritage Dr *COVN* CV6.........14 B2
rmes Crs *COVE* CV2.........24 D4
rmes Rd
  LGN/SDN/BHAMAIR B26.......8 A4
rmitage Rd *COVE* CV2.........32 B2
rmitage Wy *KNWTH* CV8.......65 H4
rmit's Cft *COVS* CV3.........39 G1
ronbank *TLHL/CAN* CV4.........27 H4
rrick Rd *COVE* CV2.........32 C3
rtford Pl *COV* CV1.........2 D4
rtford St *COV* CV1.........2 D4
slop Cl *COVS* CV3.........41 G1
witt Av *COVN* CV6.........2 A1
xby Cl *COVE* CV2.........25 F5
xworthy Av *COVS* CV3.........39 E4

Heybrook Cl *COVE* CV2.........24 B4
Heycroft *TLHL/CAN* CV4.........38 A5
Heyford Cl *COVE* CV2.........14 C5
Heyford Leys
  RUGBYS/DCH CV22.........70 B1
Heyville Cft *KNWTH* CV8.........64 D3
Heywood Rd *COVN* CV6 *.......23 H4
Hibberd Ct *KNWTH* CV8.........65 H3
Hibbert Rd *RUGBYS/DCH* CV22..61 G3
Hickory Cl *COVE* CV2.........25 E2
Hidcote Rd *KNWTH* CV8.........65 H1
High Ash Cl
  RCOVN/BALC/EX CV7.........13 G1
High Beech *COVW* CV5.........20 D5
Highfield *RCOVN/BALC/EX* CV7..18 B2
Highfield Cl *KNWTH* CV8.........64 D3
Highfield Rd *COVE* CV2.........3 K1
Highgrove *RUGBYS/DCH* CV22...61 E5
  TLHL/CAN CV4.........37 E3
Highland Rd *COVW* CV5.........30 A5
  KNWTH CV8.........51 H5
Highley Dr *COVN* CV6.........22 D5
High Park Cl *COVE* CV2.........28 C3
High St *BDWTH* CV12.........5 G3
  COV CV1.........2 D4
  COVN CV6.........22 A2
  HIA/OLT B92.........16 B5
  KNWTH CV8.........65 H4
  KNWTH CV8.........64 D2
  RUGBYN/HIL CV21.........63 F4
High View Dr
  RCOVN/BALC/EX CV7.........12 D1
Highwaymans Cft
  TLHL/CAN CV4.........38 A3
Hilary Rd *TLHL/CAN* CV4.........38 A3
Hillary Rd *RUGBYS/DCH* CV22...60 D3
Hillfield *RUGBYS/DCH* CV22.....60 D3
Hill Fray Dr *COVS* CV3.........40 B4
Hilliard Cl *BDWTH* CV12.........5 F1
Hillmorton La *RRUGBY* CV23....63 F2
Hillmorton Rd *COVE* CV2.........24 B1
  RUGBYS/DCH CV22.........61 H2
Hill Rd *RCOVN/BALC/EX* CV7....12 A2
Hill St *COV* CV1.........2 B3
  RUGBYN/HIL CV21.........63 F4
Hilton Ct *COVW* CV5 *.........30 A4
Himley Rd *BDWTH* CV12.........4 C3
Hinckley Rd *COVE* CV2.........25 C3
Hinde Cl *RUGBYN/HIL* CV21.....48 B2
Hipswell Hwy *COVE* CV2.........32 C4
Hiron Cft *COVS* CV3.........39 F1
The Hiron *COVS* CV3.........39 F1
Hirst Cl *RRUGBY* CV23.........46 B4
Hob La *KNWTH* CV8.........50 A1
  RCOVN/BALC/EX CV7.........35 H1
Hobley Cl *RUGBYS/DCH* CV22...61 E5
Hockett St *COVS* CV3.........39 G1
Hocking Rd *COVE* CV2.........32 D2
Hockley La *COVW* CV5.........27 H1
Hodgett's La *KNWTH* CV8.......36 A4
  RCOVN/BALC/EX CV7.........35 C1
Hodnet Cl *KNWTH* CV8.........65 G2
Hogarth Cl *BDWTH* CV12.........5 F1
Holbein Cl *BDWTH* CV12.........5 F1
Holborn Av *COVN* CV6.........22 D1
Holbrook Av
  RUGBYN/HIL CV21.........47 H5
Holbrook La *COVN* CV6.........22 D1
Holbrook La *COVW* CV5.........22 D1
Holbrook Wy *COVN* CV6.........23 E2
Holcot Leys *RUGBYS/DCH* CV22.61 H5
Holland Rd *COVN* CV6.........22 B5
Hollicombe Ter *COVE* CV2.......24 C3
Hollis La *KNWTH* CV8.........50 D4
Hollis Rd *COVS* CV3.........31 H4
Holloway Fld *COVN* CV6.........22 B5
Hollow Crs *COVN* CV6.........30 C1
Hollowell Wy *RUGBYN/HIL* CV21.48 B2
Holly Bank *COVW* CV5 *.........38 D1
Hollybush La *COVN* CV6.........13 H4
Holly Dr *KNWTH* CV8.........56 A3
Hollyfast La
  RCOVN/BALC/EX CV7.........11 F4
Hollyfast Rd *COVN* CV6.........21 H4
Holly Gv *RRUGBY* CV23.........45 E4
  TLHL/CAN CV4.........29 F4
Hollyhurst *BDWTH* CV12.........5 E4
Holly La *RCOVN/BALC/EX* CV7...34 C5
Holly Wk *KNWTH* CV8.........53 H2
Holmcroft *COVE* CV2.........25 E3
Holme Cl *RUGBYS/HIL* CV21.....48 B3
Holmes Dr *COVW* CV5.........28 A1
Holmewood Cl *KNWTH* CV8.....65 G2
Holmfield Rd *COVE* CV2.........32 A4
Holmsdale Rd *COVN* CV6.........23 H4
Holyhead Chambers *COV* CV1 *..2 B2
Holyhead Rd *COVN* CV6.........30 B3
  COVW CV5.........29 G1
  COVW CV5.........29 H2

Holyoak Cl *BDWTH* CV12.........5 E4
  RUGBYS/DCH CV22.........60 D4
Holywell Cl *TLHL/CAN* CV4.......28 A5
Homefield La
  RUGBYS/DCH CV22.........69 H3
Homeward Wy *COVS* CV3.........33 F5
Honeybourne Cl *COVW* CV5.....29 E3
Honeyfield Rd *COV* CV1.........31 E1
Honeysuckle Dr *COVE* CV2.......24 A1
Honiley Wy *COVE* CV2 *.........24 C2
Honiton Rd *COVE* CV2.........32 A1
Hood St *COV* CV1.........3 G3
Hood's Wy *RUGBYS/DCH* CV22...61 E5
Hope Cl *RCOVN/BALC/EX* CV7...12 B1
Hopedale Cl *COVE* CV2.........32 D3
Hope St *COV* CV1.........2 A4
Hopkins Rd *COVS* CV3.........30 B2
Hopton Cl *COVW* CV5.........28 D2
Hornbeam Dr *TLHL/CAN* CV4....28 A5
Hornchurch Cl *COV* CV1.........2 D7
Horndean Cl *COVN* CV6.........23 F3
Horne Cl *RUGBYN/HIL* CV21.....63 F4
Horninghold Cl *COVS* CV3.......41 F1
Hornsey Cl *COVE* CV2.........24 D4
Horobins Yd *BDWTH* CV12 *......5 J1
Horse Shoe Rd *COVN* CV6.......13 H4
Horsford Rd *COVS* CV3.........39 H3
Horton Cl *RCOVN/BALC/EX* CV7..13 C1
Horton Crs *RUGBYS/DCH* CV22..61 H2
Hosiery St *BDWTH* CV12.........5 G2
Hoskyn Cl *RUGBYN/HIL* CV21....63 E4
Hospital La *BDWTH* CV12.........4 A4
Hotchkiss Wy *COVS* CV3.........41 H2
Hothorpe Cl *COVS* CV3.........33 E5
Houldsworth Crs *COVN* CV6.....12 D4
Houston Rd *RUGBYN/HIL* CV21..48 B3
Hove Av *COVW* CV5.........28 B2
Hovelands Cl *COVE* CV2.........24 B3
Howard Cl *COVW* CV5.........28 C2
  RUGBYS/DCH CV22.........69 H3
Howard St *COV* CV1.........31 E2
Howat Rd *RCOVN/BALC/EX* CV7..12 A1
Howcotte Gn *TLHL/CAN* CV4....36 D2
Howells Cl *BDWTH* CV12.........4 C5
Howes La *COVS* CV3.........53 F2
Howkins Rd *RUGBYN/HIL* CV21..48 B3
Howlette Rd *TLHL/CAN* CV4.....28 B4
Huddesford Dr
  RCOVN/BALC/EX CV7.........34 D1
Hudson Rd *RUGBYS/DCH* CV22..61 F3
Hudson V *TLHL/CAN* CV4.........27 H3
Huggins Cl *RCOVN/BALC/EX* CV7.34 D2
Hugh Rd *COVS* CV3.........31 H4
Hulme Cl *COVS* CV3.........33 G5
Humber Av *COV* CV1.........3 H5
Humber Rd *COVS* CV3.........3 K5
Humphrey Burton's Rd
  COVS CV3.........39 F1
Humphrey-Davy Rd
  BDWTH CV12.........4 C5
Hunters Cl *COVS* CV3.........33 F4
Hunters La *RUGBYN/HIL* CV21...47 H4
Hunter St *RUGBYN/HIL* CV21....48 B5
Hunter Ter *COVW* CV5.........37 H1
Huntingdon Rd *COVW* CV5.......30 B5
Hunt Ter *TLHL/CAN* CV4.........37 G2
Hurn Wy *COVN* CV6.........14 A4
Hurst Rd *BDWTH* CV12.........5 G2
  COVN CV6.........13 H4
Hyde Rd *COVE* CV2.........32 D2
  KNWTH CV8.........65 G2
Hypericum Gdns *COVE* CV2.....32 B2

I

Ibex Cl *COVS* CV3.........33 E5
Ibstock Rd *COVN* CV6.........13 H3
Iden Rd *COV* CV1.........31 F1
Ilam Pk *KNWTH* CV8.........65 H2
Ilford Cl *BDWTH* CV12.........5 E2
Ilford Dr *COVS* CV3.........39 E4
Ilfracombe Gv *COVS* CV3.........38 D4
Ilmer Cl *RUGBYN/HIL* CV21.....48 D2
Ilmington Cl *COVS* CV3.........39 E4
Inca Cl *COVS* CV3.........41 G1
Inchbrook Rd *KNWTH* CV8.......51 H5
Ingram Rd *COVW* CV5.........38 A1
Innis Rd *COVW* CV5.........38 B2
Instone Rd *COVN* CV6.........22 B4
International Dr
  LGN/SDN/BHAMAIR B26.......8 A4
International Sq
  CHWD/FDBR/MGN B37 *.......8 A3
Inveraray Cl *KNWTH* CV8.........65 H3
Inverness Cl *COVW* CV5.........28 D2
Invicta Rd *COVS* CV3.........41 G1
Ireton Cl *TLHL/CAN* CV4.........27 H5

Ironbridge Wy *COVN* CV6.........14 A2
Ironmonger Rw *COV* CV1.........2 D3
Irving Rd *COVS* CV3.........3 H6
Isambard Dr *COVN* CV6.........13 C3
Ivor Rd *COVN* CV6.........23 G1
Ivybridge Rd *COVS* CV3.........39 G4
Ivy Farm La *TLHL/CAN* CV4.....38 A3
Izod Rd *RUGBYN/HIL* CV21.......47 G5

J

Jacker's Rd *COVE* CV2.........14 A4
Jacklin Dr *COVS* CV3.........39 F5
Jackson Cl *RCOVN/BALC/EX* CV7..12 B1
Jackson Gv *KNWTH* CV8.........65 H3
Jackson Rd *COVN* CV6.........23 H3
  RUGBYN/HIL CV21.........63 F3
Jacob Dr *TLHL/CAN* CV4.........38 A3
Jacox Crs *KNWTH* CV8.........65 H2
Jade Cl *COV* CV1.........31 E2
Jamescroft *COVS* CV3.........41 F3
James Dawson Dr *COVW* CV5...19 C3
James Galloway Cl *COVS* CV3...41 F2
James Green Rd *TLHL/CAN* CV4.28 C4
James St *RUGBYN/HIL* CV21.....62 A1
Jardine Crs *TLHL/CAN* CV4.......28 C4
Jasmine Gv *COVS* CV3.........40 D1
Jasmine Pl *COVS* CV3 *.........40 D1
Jedburgh Gv *COVS* CV3.........38 D5
Jeffrey Cl *BDWTH* CV12.........4 C5
Jeliff St *TLHL/CAN* CV4.........28 C5
Jenkins Av *COVW* CV5.........28 C2
Jenkins Rd *RUGBYN/HIL* CV21...63 F5
Jenner St *COV* CV1.........31 E2
Jesmond Rd *COV* CV1.........3 H1
Jim Forrest Cl *COVS* CV3.........41 G1
Joanna Dr *COVS* CV3.........39 F5
Joan Ward St *COVS* CV3.........39 G1
Job's La *TLHL/CAN* CV4.........28 D4
Joe Obrien Cl *COVS* CV3.........40 D3
Joe Williams Cl *COVS* CV3.......41 G2
John Grace St *COVS* CV3.........39 G1
John McGuire Crs *COVS* CV3....41 F2
John Nash Sq *KNWTH* CV8.......65 E4
John O'Gaunt Rd *KNWTH* CV8...64 D4
John Rous Av *TLHL/CAN* CV4....37 G2
John Shelton Dr *COVN* CV6......12 D4
John Simpson Cl *KNWTH* CV8...57 F1
Johnson Av *RUGBYS/DCH* CV22.61 G2
Johnson Rd *BDWTH* CV12.........5 H2
  COVN CV6.........23 H3
John St *BDWTH* CV12.........5 H2
John Thwaites Cl
  RUGBYS/DCH CV22.........61 H2
Jonathan Rd *COVE* CV2.........25 E3
Jones Rd *RCOVN/BALC/EX* CV7...5 F4
Jordan Cl *KNWTH* CV8.........65 G5
The Jordans *COVW* CV5.........29 F2
Jordan Well *COV* CV1.........2 E4
Joseph Creighton Cl *COVS* CV3..41 F2
Joseph Luckman Rd
  BDWTH CV12.........5 F1
Joshua Cl *TLHL/CAN* CV4.........28 D4
Joyce Wy *RUGBYS/DCH* CV22....60 B4
Jubilee Crs *COVN* CV6.........22 C4
Jubilee St *RUGBYN/HIL* CV21....61 F1
Jubilee Ter *BDWTH* CV12 *.......5 G1
Judd Cl *BDWTH* CV12.........5 E2
Judds La *COVN* CV6.........13 F4
Judge Cl *RRUGBY* CV23.........46 B4
Judith Wy *RUGBYS/DCH* CV22...60 B4
Julian Cl *COVE* CV2.........25 E3
Juliet Dr *RUGBYS/DCH* CV22.....69 H1
Junction One
  RUGBYN/HIL CV21 *.........47 H3
Junction St *COV* CV1.........2 B5
Junewood Cl *RUGBYN/HIL* CV21.48 C2
Juniper Cl *BDWTH* CV12.........4 C3
Juniper Dr *COVW* CV5.........28 C1

K

Kalfs Dr *RUGBYS/DCH* CV22.....60 C4
Kanzan Rd *COVE* CV2.........14 B4
Kareen Gv *COVS* CV3.........42 B2
Karlingford Cl *COVW* CV5.........38 A1
Kathleen Av *BDWTH* CV12.......4 D4
Kay Cl *RUGBYN/HIL* CV21.......48 B2
Keats Cl *COVE* CV2.........32 C4
Kebull Gn *TLHL/CAN* CV4.........36 D1
Keeling Rd *KNWTH* CV8.........65 G2
Keenan Dr *BDWTH* CV12.........4 C4
Keepers Wk *BDWTH* CV12 *......4 C4
Kegworth Cl *COVN* CV6.........13 H4
Kele Rd *TLHL/CAN* CV4.........37 G2

Kelmscote Rd *COVN* CV6 ....22 A3
Kelsey La *RCOVN/BALC/EX* CV7 ....34 D4
Kelsey's Cl *KNWTH* CV8 ....57 E1
Kelvin Av *COVE* CV2 ....32 C1
Kelway *COVS* CV3 ....33 F5
Kempley Av *COVE* CV2 ....32 B4
Kemps Green Rd
　RCOVN/BALC/EX CV7 ....34 C3
Kendal Ri *COVW* CV5 ....29 F2
Kendon Av *COVN* CV6 ....21 H5
Kendrick Cl *COVN* CV6 ....13 H4
Kenilworth Cl
　RCOVN/BALC/EX CV7 ....34 B3
Kenilworth Rd *COVW* CV5 ....38 D2
　RCOVN/BALC/EX CV7 ....16 D1
　TLHL/CAN CV4 ....51 H3
Kennedy Dr *RUGBYS/DCH* CV22 ..60 D2
Kennet Cl *COVE* CV2 ....24 B3
Kenpas Hwy *COVS* CV3 ....38 D4
Kensington Rd *COVW* CV5 ....30 A5
Kent Cl *COVS* CV3 ....39 H3
Kenthurst Cl *COVW* CV5 ....27 H2
Kentmere Cl *COVN* CV6 ....24 D1
The Kent *RRUGBY* CV23 ....49 F5
　RUGBYN/HIL CV21 ....63 F3
Keppel Cl *RUGBYS/DCH* CV22 .....60 D3
Keppel St *COV* CV1 ....31 F1
Keresley Brook Rd *COVN* CV6 ....22 A1
Keresley Cl *COVN* CV6 ....22 A1
Keresley Green Rd *COVN* CV6 ....22 A2
Keresley Rd *COVN* CV6 ....22 A3
Kerris Wy *COVS* CV3 ....33 F5
Kestrel Cft *COVS* CV3 ....41 G5
Keswick Dr *RUGBYN/HIL* CV21 ....48 B1
Keswick Wk *COVE* CV2 ....33 G2
Keviliok St *COVS* CV3 ....39 G3
Kew Cl *KNWTH* CV8 ....65 H2
Kew Rd *RUGBYN/HIL* CV21 ....47 H5
Keyes Dr *RUGBYS/DCH* CV22 ......60 D3
Kilburn Dr *COVW* CV5 ....30 A3
Kildale Cl *COV* CV1 ....3 G2
Kilderkin Ct *COV* CV1 ....3 F7
Kilsby La *RUGBYN/HIL* CV21 ....63 H5
Kilworth Rd *RUGBYN/HIL* CV21 ....63 G5
Kimberley Cl *COVW* CV5 * 28 C2
Kimberley Rd *BDWTH* CV12 ....5 G1
　KNWTH CV8 ....53 H2
　RUGBYN/HIL CV21 ....48 A5
Kimble Cl *COVW* CV5 ....30 A4
Kineton Rd *COVE* CV2 ....24 B5
　KNWTH CV8 ....65 G3
King Edward Rd *COV* CV1 ....3 H1
　RUGBYN/HIL CV21 ....48 A5
Kingfield Rd *COV* CV1 ....23 E5
King George's Av *COVN* CV6 ....23 G1
King Richard St *COVE* CV2 ....3 J2
Kingsbury Rd *COVN* CV6 ....21 G5
Kingscote Gv *COVS* CV3 ....38 D5
Kingsford Rd *COVN* CV6 ....22 D5
Kings Gdns *BDWTH* CV12 ....5 H3
Kings Gv *COVE* CV2 ....32 A3
King's Hill La *COVS* CV3 ....52 C5
Kingsholm Cl *COVS* CV3 ....33 G5
Kingsland Av *COVW* CV5 ....30 A4
Kingsley Av *RUGBYN/HIL* CV21 ....62 D3
Kingsley Crs *BDWTH* CV12 ....7 E2
Kingsley Ter *COVE* CV2 ....24 C5
Kingsley Wk *COVE* CV2 ....25 E3
Kingsmead Ms *COVS* CV3 ....40 D3
Kings Newnham La
　RRUGBY CV23 ....44 D2
Kings Newnham Rd
　RRUGBY CV23 ....45 E3
Kings Park Dr *COVS* CV3 ....33 G5
Kingston Rd *COVW* CV5 ....30 A4
King St *BDWTH* CV12 ....5 H3
　RUGBYN/HIL CV21 ....47 H5
Kingsway *COVE* CV2 ....31 G3
　RUGBYS/DCH CV22 ....61 H3
Kingswood Cl *COVN* CV6 ....23 E2
King William St *COV* CV1 ....3 H1
Kinlet Cl *COVN* CV6 ....22 D4
Kinman Wy *RUGBYN/HIL* CV21 ....48 B3
The Kintyre *COVE* CV2 ....25 G4
Kinver Cl *COVE* CV2 ....24 D2
Kipling Rd *COVN* CV6 ....22 A3
Kirby Cl *COV* CV1 ....23 E5
　KNWTH CV8 ....43 E4
Kirby Corner Rd *TLHL/CAN* CV4 ...37 G4
Kirby Rd *COVW* CV5 ....30 A4
Kirkby Cl *RUGBYN/HIL* CV21 ....63 G5
Kirkby Rd *RUGBYN/HIL* CV21 ....63 G5
Kirkdale Av *COVN* CV6 ....13 E5
Kirkstone *RUGBYN/HIL* CV21 ....48 C2
Kirkstone Rd *BDWTH* CV12 ....5 F3
Kirton Cl *COVN* CV6 ....22 A2
Kitchener Rd *COVN* CV6 ....23 F2
Kittermaster Rd
　RCOVN/BALC/EX CV7 ....18 A1

Knight Av *COV* CV1 ....3 H6
Knightlow Av *COVS* CV3 ....40 D4
Knightlow Cl *KNWTH* CV8 ....65 H4
Knights Templar Wy
　TLHL/CAN CV4 ....28 D5
Knoll Cft *COVS* CV3 ....39 F3
Knoll Dr *COVS* CV3 ....39 F3
Knotting Wy *COVS* CV3 ....32 B5
Knowle Hl *KNWTH* CV8 ....65 H1
Kynner Wy *COVS* CV3 ....42 A1

L

Laburnum Av *COVN* CV6 ....30 A1
　KNWTH CV8 ....65 F3
Laburnum Cl *BDWTH* CV12 ....4 D3
Laburnum Gv
　RUGBYS/DCH CV22 ....61 F4
Ladbroke Rd *COVW* CV5 ....28 D2
Ladyfields Wy *COVN* CV6 ....12 C4
Lady La *COVN* CV6 ....13 G4
Ladymead Dr *COVN* CV6 ....22 C1
Ladysmock *RRUGBY* CV23 ....48 C1
Lady Warwick Av *BDWTH* CV12 .....5 H3
Lakeside *BDWTH* CV12 ....5 F3
Lake View Rd *COVW* CV5 ....30 A2
Lambeth Cl *COVE* CV2 ....24 D4
Lambourne Cl *COVW* CV5 ....28 D2
Lamb St *COV* CV1 ....2 C2
Lamerton Cl *COVE* CV2 ....24 B5
Lammas Ct *KNWTH* CV8 ....57 F1
Lammas House *COVN* CV6 * 30 B2
Lammas Rd *COVN* CV6 ....30 B2
Lancaster Pl *KNWTH* CV8 ....64 D5
Lancaster Rd
　RUGBYN/HIL CV21 ....47 H5
Lanchester Rd *COVN* CV6 ....22 C5
Lancia Cl *COVN* CV6 ....14 A4
Lancing Rd *BDWTH* CV12 ....7 F2
Landseer Cl *RUGBYN/HIL* CV21 ...63 G4
Laneside *COVS* CV3 ....41 F3
Langbank Av *COVS* CV3 ....40 D1
Langdale Av *COVN* CV6 ....13 E5
Langdale Rd *RUGBYN/HIL* CV21 ...48 B2
Langley Cft *TLHL/CAN* CV4 ....28 D3
Langlodge Rd *COVN* CV6 ....22 C1
Langnor Rd *COVE* CV2 ....24 B4
Langton Cl *COVS* CV3 ....41 F1
Langton Rd *RUGBYN/HIL* CV21 ....62 D3
Langwood *TLHL/CAN* CV4 ....37 G2
Lansdowne Cl *BDWTH* CV12 ....5 F2
Lansdowne Pl
　RUGBYN/HIL CV21 ....62 C2
Lansdowne St *COVE* CV2 ....3 J5
Lant Cl *TLHL/CAN* CV4 ....36 A2
Lapwing Dr *HIA/OLT* B92 ....16 C4
Lapworth Rd *COVE* CV2 ....24 B2
Larch Cl *RUGBYS/DCH* CV22 ....60 C2
The Larches
　RCOVN/BALC/EX CV7 ....5 F5
Larchfields *KNWTH* CV8 ....43 F5
Larch Tree Av *TLHL/CAN* CV4 ......28 D3
Larchwood Rd
　RCOVN/BALC/EX CV7 ....5 G5
Larkfield Wy *COVW* CV5 ....20 D5
Larkin Cl *BDWTH* CV12 ....7 E2
Larkin Gv *COVE* CV2 ....25 E5
Larkspur *RRUGBY* CV23 ....48 C1
Larkspur Gv *BDWTH* CV12 ....4 C3
Latham Rd *COVW* CV5 ....30 B4
Latimer Cl *KNWTH* CV8 ....65 E5
Lauderdale Av *COVN* CV6 ....13 E5
Lauderdale Cl *RRUGBY* CV23 ....46 C5
Laurel Cl *COVE* CV2 ....24 D1
Laurel Dr *RUGBYS/DCH* CV22 ......60 C3
Laurel Gdns *RUGBYS/DCH* CV22 ..61 G4
Laurels Crs *RCOVN/BALC/EX* CV7 ..34 D3
The Laurels *BDWTH* CV12 ....4 C3
　TLHL/CAN CV4 ....38 C3
Lavender Av *COVN* CV6 ....29 H1
Lavender Cl *BDWTH* CV12 ....4 D4
　RRUGBY CV23 ....48 D1
Lavender Hall La
　RCOVN/BALC/EX CV7 ....26 A5
Lawford Cl *COVS* CV3 ....32 D5
Lawford Heath La
　RRUGBY CV23 ....68 A2
Lawford La *RUGBYS/DCH* CV22 ...60 C3
Lawford Rd *RUGBYN/HIL* CV21 ....61 F1
Lawley Cl *TLHL/CAN* CV4 ....28 D4
The Lawns *BDWTH* CV12 ....4 C3
Lawrence Gdns *KNWTH* CV8 ....65 E1
Lawrence Rd
　RCOVN/BALC/EX CV7 ....5 F5
　RUGBYN/HIL CV21 ....62 C1
Lawrence Saunders Rd
　COVN CV6 ....30 C1

Lawrence Sheriff St
　RUGBYN/HIL CV21 ....61 H2
Lea Crs *RUGBYN/HIL* CV21 ....47 E3
Leacrest Rd *COVN* CV6 ....22 B1
Leafield Cl *COVE* CV2 ....25 E3
Leaf La *COVS* CV3 ....39 H4
Leagh Cl *KNWTH* CV8 ....51 G5
Leam Gn *TLHL/CAN* CV4 ....38 A4
Leamington Rd *COVS* CV3 ....39 F4
　KNWTH CV8 ....65 G5
Leas Cl *BDWTH* CV12 ....5 F2
Leasowe's Av *COVS* CV3 ....38 C5
Lea Wk *KNWTH* CV8 ....56 A3
Leeder Cl *COVN* CV6 ....22 D1
Leeming Cl *TLHL/CAN* CV4 ....37 H3
The Lee *COVW* CV5 ....29 F2
Le Hanche Cl
　RCOVN/BALC/EX CV7 ....12 B1
Leicester Cswy *COV* CV1 ....31 E2
Leicester Ct *BDWTH* CV12 ....7 F3
Leicester Rd *BDWTH* CV12 ....5 G1
　RUGBYN/HIL CV21 ....47 H3
Leicester Rw *COV* CV1 ....2 D1
Leicester St *BDWTH* CV12 ....5 G2
　COVS CV3 ....53 F1
Leigh Rd *RUGBYN/HIL* CV21 ....47 G1
Leigh St *COV* CV1 ....3 H1
Leighton Cl *TLHL/CAN* CV4 ....52 A2
Lennon Cl *RUGBYN/HIL* CV21 ......63 H5
Lennox Cl *COVS* CV3 ....41 E3
Lenton's La *COVE* CV2 ....14 C4
Leofric St *COVN* CV6 ....30 B1
Leopold Rd *COV* CV1 ....31 G2
Lesingham Dr *TLHL/CAN* CV4 ....28 B5
Lestock Cl *RUGBYS/DCH* CV22 ....60 D3
Letchlade Cl *COVE* CV2 ....24 B3
Leven Wy *COVE* CV2 ....25 F3
Lever Rd *RUGBYN/HIL* CV21 ....63 F3
Leveson Crs
　RCOVN/BALC/EX CV7 ....34 C3
Levy Cl *RUGBYN/HIL* CV21 ....61 G1
Lewis Rd *COV* CV1 ....31 E1
Leyburn Cl *COVN* CV6 ....23 F1
Leycester Rd *KNWTH* CV8 ....65 E5
Leyes La *KNWTH* CV8 ....65 H2
Leyland Rd *BDWTH* CV12 ....7 E3
　COVW CV5 ....29 G2
Leymere Cl
　RCOVN/BALC/EX CV7 ....18 B2
Leyside *COVS* CV3 ....41 F4
Leys La *RCOVN/BALC/EX* CV7 ......18 B2
Leys Rd *RUGBYN/HIL* CV21 ....63 H5
Library Rd *TLHL/CAN* CV4 ....37 G4
Lichen Gn *TLHL/CAN* CV4 ....38 A4
Lichfield Rd *COVS* CV3 ....39 G1
Lifford Wy *COVS* CV3 ....41 H2
Light La *COV* CV1 ....30 C1
Lilac Av *COVN* CV6 ....30 A1
Lilac Dr *RUGBYS/DCH* CV22 ....60 C2
Lilbourne Rd *RRUGBY* CV23 ....49 F4
Lilley Cl *COVN* CV6 ....22 D1
Lillington Rd *COVE* CV2 ....24 C2
Limbrick Av *TLHL/CAN* CV4 ....28 D5
Lime Gv *KNWTH* CV8 ....65 F3
　TLHL/CAN CV4 ....29 E4
The Limes *BDWTH* CV12 ....4 D3
　RCOVN/BALC/EX CV7 * 12 A3
Limestone Hall La
　RRUGBY CV23 ....44 D5
Lime Tree Av
　RUGBYS/DCH CV22 ....60 C5
　TLHL/CAN CV4 ....28 D4
Linaker Rd *COVS* CV3 ....40 D4
Lincoln St *COV* CV1 ....31 E2
Lincroft Crs *COVW* CV5 ....29 G2
Lindale *RUGBYN/HIL* CV21 ....48 B1
Linden Lea *BDWTH* CV12 ....5 G2
Lindisfarne Dr *KNWTH* CV8 ....65 H3
Lindley Rd *BDWTH* CV12 ....4 C3
　COVS CV3 ....32 A4
Linford Wk *COVE* CV2 ....25 E2
Ling La *RRUGBY* CV23 ....58 C3
Links Rd *COVN* CV6 ....22 C3
Linnell Rd *RUGBYN/HIL* CV21 ......62 D2
Linnet Cl *COVS* CV3 ....41 E4
Linstock Wy *COVN* CV6 ....14 A4
Linwood Dr *COVE* CV2 ....25 E2
Lion Fields Av *COVW* CV5 ....21 E5
Little Church St *COV* CV1 ....31 E2
　RUGBYN/HIL CV21 ....61 H2
Little Cryfield *TLHL/CAN* CV4 ....51 H2
Little Elborow St
　RUGBYN/HIL CV21 ....61 H1
Little Fld *COVE* CV2 ....31 H1
Little Gv *RUGBYS/DCH* CV22 ....62 B3
Little Lawford La
　RRUGBY CV23 ....45 H2
　RUGBYN/HIL CV21 ....46 C2

Little Park St *COV* CV1 2
Little Pennington St
　RUGBYN/HIL CV21 61
Little South St *COV* CV1 * 2
Littlethorpe *COVS* CV3 41
Littleton Cl *KNWTH* CV8 51
Livingstone Av *RRUGBY* CV23 46
Livingstone Rd *COVN* CV6 23
Liza Ct *RUGBYN/HIL* CV21 48
Lloyd Crs *COVE* CV2 32
Lloyd Rd *RUGBYN/HIL* CV21 48
Loach Dr *COVE* CV2 14
Loch St *COVS* CV3 32
Locke Cl *COVN* CV6 22
Lockhart Cl *KNWTH* CV8 65
Lockhurst La *COVN* CV6 23
The Locks *RUGBYN/HIL* CV21 63
Loder Cl *TLHL/CAN* CV4 28
Lodge Rd *COVS* CV3 32
　RUGBYN/HIL CV21 48
Logan Rd *COVE* CV2 24
Lole Cl *COVN* CV6 13
Lollard Cft *COVS* CV3 39
Lomsey Cl *TLHL/CAN* CV4 28
London Rd *COV* CV1 3
　COVS CV3 40
　KNWTH CV8 55
　RRUGBY CV23 57
Long Close Av *COVW* CV5 21
Longfellow Ct *COVE* CV2 32
Longfellow Rd *COVE* CV2 32
Longford Rd *COVN* CV6 13
Longford Sq *COVN* CV6 13
Long Furlong
　RUGBYS/DCH CV22 61
Long La *COVW* CV5 21
Longmoor Dr *COVS* CV3 32
Longrood Rd
　RUGBYS/DCH CV22 69
Long St *BDWTH* CV12 7
Longwood Cl *TLHL/CAN* CV4 37
Lonscale Dr *COVS* CV3 39
Lord Lytton Av *COVE* CV2 32
Lord St *COVW* CV5 30
Lorenzo Cl *COVS* CV3 41
Loudon Av *COVN* CV6 30
Lovell Cl *RCOVN/BALC/EX* CV7 5
Lovell Rd *BDWTH* CV12 5
Loverock Crs
　RUGBYN/HIL CV21 62
Lower Eastern Green La
　COVW CV5 28
Lower Ford St *COV* CV1 3
Lower Hillmorton Rd
　RUGBYN/HIL CV21 62
Lower Holyhead Rd *COV* CV1 2
Lower Ladyes Hills *KNWTH* CV8 ...65
Lower Lea Pl *RUGBYN/HIL* CV21 ..63
Lowe Rd *COVN* CV6 2
Lower Prec *COV* CV1 2
Lower Rd *RCOVN/BALC/EX* CV7 ..15
Lower St *RUGBYN/HIL* CV21 63
Loweswater Rd *COVS* CV3 32
Lowfield Rd *COVS* CV3 32
Lowry Cl *BDWTH* CV12 5
Lowther St *COVE* CV2 24
Loxley Cl *COVE* CV2 24
Lucas Ct *RUGBYN/HIL* CV21 48
Lucerne Cl *COVE* CV2 14
Lucian Cl *COVE* CV2 25
Ludham Pl *RUGBYS/DCH* CV22 60
Ludlow Rd *COVW* CV5 30
Luff Cl *COVS* CV3 40
Lulworth Pk *KNWTH* CV8 65
Lumsden Cl *COVE* CV2 25
Lunar Cl *TLHL/CAN* CV4 38
Lunn Av *KNWTH* CV8 64
Lupton Av *COVS* CV3 32
Luscombe Rd *COVE* CV2 24
Luther Wy *COVW* CV5 32
Lutterworth Rd *COVE* CV2 32
Luxor La *COVW* CV5 20
Lydford Cl *COVE* CV2 24
Lydgate Rd *COVN* CV6 24
Lymesy St *COVS* CV3 39
Lymington Dr *COVN* CV6 14
Lymington Dr *COVN* CV6 14
Lymore Cft *COVE* CV2 25
Lynbrook Rd *COVW* CV5 38
Lynchgate Ct *TLHL/CAN* CV4 * 37
Lynchgate Rd *TLHL/CAN* CV4 37
Lyndale Cl *COVW* CV5 29
Lyndale Rd *COVW* CV5 29
Lyndhurst Cl *COVN* CV6 14
Lyndhurst Cft *COVW* CV5 27
Lyndhurst Rd *RUGBYN/HIL* CV21 ..63
Lyng Cl *COVW* CV5 29
Lynmouth Rd *COVE* CV2 24
Lynton Rd *COVN* CV6 23

ander St *COVS* CV3....................41 E3
halls La *COVN* CV6......................23 F1
ham Rd *RUGBYS/DCH* CV22 ....61 E2
tleton Cl *COVS* CV3....................33 F5

M

caulay Rd *COVE* CV2..................32 C2
RUGBYS/DCH CV2......................61 F5
cbeth Cl *RUGBYS/DCH* CV2........32 C3
cdonald Rd *COVE* CV2.................24 C1
cefield Cl *COVE* CV2...................24 C1
ckenzie Cl *COVW* CV5.................20 D4
dden Pl *RUGBYS/DCH* CV2 ....60 D2
deira Cft *COVW* CV5...................29 H4
gnet La *RUGBYS/DCH* CV2.........60 D4
gnolia Cl *COVS* CV3...................39 E4
idavale Crs *COVS* CV3................39 F4
idenhair Dr *RRUGBY* CV23.........48 C1
in Rd *RCOVN/BALC/EX* CV7 ....18 A2
in St *KNWTH* CV8.......................43 F5
RRUGBY CV23...........................46 B5
RRUGBY CV23...........................49 E4
RRUGBY CV23...........................68 D5
RUGBYN/HIL CV21......................47 E2
RUGBYS/DCH CV2......................60 D4
lam Cl *TLHL/CAN* CV4................28 D5
liory Wy *COVN* CV6....................13 F3
llow Cft *BDWTH* CV12.................4 D3
llow Wy *RRUGBY* CV23...............48 B1
lmesbury Rd *COVN* CV6..............22 B1
lthouse La *KNWTH* CV8...............64 D1
lvern Av *RUGBYS/DCH* CV2........62 C3
lvern Rd *COVW* CV5...................29 H2
RCOVN/BALC/EX CV7.................34 D3
nderley Cl *COVW* CV5.................27 H1
nfield Av *COVE* CV2....................25 F4
nhattan Wy *TLHL/CAN* CV4.........27 H3
nning Wk
RUGBYN/HIL CV21 *...................61 H1
nn's Cl *KNWTH* CV8....................56 A4
nor Ct *KNWTH* CV8 *..................65 F1
nor Est *KNWTH* CV8...................57 E1
nor Hall Ms *COVS* CV3................40 F3
nor House Cl
RUGBYN/HIL CV21......................47 E2
nor House Dr *COV* CV1...............2 C5
nor Rd *COV* CV1.........................2 D6
KNWTH CV8................................65 E1
RUGBYN/HIL CV21......................48 A5
nor Terrace Flats
KNWTH CV8 *.............................65 F1
nor Vw *KNWTH* CV8 *.................57 E1
nse Cl *RCOVN/BALC/EX* CV7 ......5 F4
nsel St *COVS* CV3......................23 F3
ntilla Dr *COVS* CV3....................39 E4
ple Av *RCOVN/BALC/EX* CV7........5 G4
plebeck Cl *COVW* CV5................30 B3
ple Gv *RUGBYN/HIL* CV21...........47 H5
e Maples *BDWTH* CV12...............4 F2
pleton Rd *COVN* CV6..................22 A3
ple Wk *COVN* CV6......................13 C3
pperley Cl *COVE* CV2.................25 F3
rch Wy *COVS* CV3.......................41 E2
rdol Cl *COVE* CV2.......................24 C4
rflow Cl *COVN* CV5.....................29 E2
rlston Wk *COVW* CV5.................29 E2
rlwood Cl *COVN* CV6...................13 G4
rner Crs *COVN* CV6....................22 C5
rner Rd *BDWTH* CV12...................5 F2
rnhull Cl *COV* CV2......................33 E2
rriners La *COVW* CV5.................29 E2
rriott Rd *BDWTH* CV12.................4 C3
COVN CV6.................................30 B2
rshbrook Cl *COVE* CV2...............24 D1
rshdale Av *COVN* CV6.................13 F5
rshfield Dr *TLHL/CAN* CV4.........52 A4
rston La *BDWTH* CV12..................5 F1
rtin Cl *COVW* CV5.......................28 B2
rtindale Rd
RCOVN/BALC/EX CV7...................5 H5
rtin La *RUGBYS/DCH* CV22.........61 E5

Martins Rd *BDWTH* CV12..............4 D4
Marton Ct *RUGBYS/DCH* CV22.....60 C5
The Martyrs' Cl *COVS* CV3...........39 G1
Mary Herbert St *COVS* CV3.........39 G2
Mary Slessor St *COVS* CV3..........41 E2
Marystow Cl *COVW* CV5..............21 E3
Mason Rd *COVN* CV6....................23 G2
Masser Rd *COVN* CV6..................12 D4
Matlock Cl *RUGBYN/HIL* CV21......48 B2
Matlock Rd *COV* CV1..................23 E5
Matterson Rd *COVN* CV6.............30 B3
Maudslay Rd *COVW* CV5..............29 H4
Maureen Cl *TLHL/CAN* CV4.........27 H5
Mavor Dr *BDWTH* CV12.................4 C4
Mawnan Cl *RCOVN/BALC/EX* CV7 ..5 G5
Max Rd *COVN* CV6......................30 A1
Maxstoke Cl
RCOVN/BALC/EX CV7.................18 A2
Maxstoke La
RCOVN/BALC/EX CV7.................18 A1
Maycock Rd *COVN* CV6...............23 E4
Mayfield Cl *BDWTH* CV12..............5 F2
Mayfield Dr *KNWTH* CV8.............65 H3
Mayfield Rd *COVW* CV5...............38 D1
Mayflower Dr *COVE* CV2.............32 C4
May La *RUGBYS/DCH* CV22..........61 E3
Maynard Av *BDWTH* CV12..............4 C5
Mayo Dr *KNWTH* CV8...................65 H3
Mayor's Cft *TLHL/CAN* CV4.........37 G2
May St *COVN* CV6.......................23 F3
McDonnell Dr
RCOVN/BALC/EX CV7.................13 G2
McKinnell Crs *RUGBYN/HIL* CV21..62 D2
McMahon Rd *BDWTH* CV12...........4 D5
Meadfoot Rd *COVS* CV3..............33 G5
Meadowcroft Cl *TLHL/CAN* CV4...37 E1
Meadow Dr *HIA/OLT* B92.............16 B5
Meadow Ri
RCOVN/BALC/EX CV7.................34 D2
Meadow Rd *COVN* CV6................12 C4
KNWTH CV8................................43 F5
RUGBYN/HIL CV21......................47 E3
Meadow St *COV* CV1....................2 C4
Meadowsweet *RRUGBY* CV23.......48 B1
Meadway *COVE* CV2....................24 A5
Medhurst Cl *RUGBYS/DCH* CV22..69 G4
Medina Rd *COVN* CV6..................23 F2
Medland Av *COVS* CV3.................38 C4
Meeting House La
RCOVN/BALC/EX CV7.................34 D3
Melbourne Rd *COVW* CV5............30 B4
Melfort Cl *COVS* CV3..................33 E4
Mellish Ct *RUGBYS/DCH* CV22.....61 F3
Mellish Rd *RUGBYS/DCH* CV22....61 F3
Mellor Rd *RUGBYN/HIL* CV21.......63 G4
Mellowdew Rd *COVE* CV2............24 A5
Mellowship Rd *COVW* CV5...........27 H1
Melrose Av *BDWTH* CV12..............4 C5
Melville Cl *RCOVN/BALC/EX* CV7 ..5 F5
RUGBYS/DCH CV22....................61 F2
Melville Rd *COV* CV1..................30 B3
Mercer Av *COVE* CV2..................31 H1
Mercer Ct *RUGBYS/DCH* CV22.....63 E4
Mercers Meadow
RCOVN/BALC/EX CV7.................12 B2
Mercia Av *KNWTH* CV8................64 D3
Meredith Rd *COVE* CV2...............32 C4
Meriden Cl *HIA/OLT* B92.............16 B4
RCOVN/BALC/EX CV7.................26 D1
Meriden St *COV* CV1....................2 A2
Merlin Cl *RRUGBY* CV23.............48 B4
Merrivale Rd *COVW* CV5.............29 H3
Merryfields Wy *COVE* CV2...........25 F2
Mersey Rd *BDWTH* CV12...............6 D3
Merttens Dr
RUGBYS/DCH CV22....................61 G2
Merynton Av *TLHL/CAN* CV4.......38 B3
Meschines St *COVS* CV3.............39 G3
The Mews *BDWTH* CV12................5 H3
KNWTH CV8................................64 D4
Michael Blanning Pl
RCOVN/BALC/EX CV7 *...............34 C2
Michaelmas Rd *COVS* CV3............2 C7
Michell Cl *COVS* CV3..................40 C1
Mickleton Rd *COVW* CV5.............38 D1
Middle Bickenhill La
HIA/OLT B92................................9 E4
Middleborough Rd *COV* CV1..........2 B1
Middlecotes *TLHL/CAN* CV4.........29 E5
Middlefield Dr *COVS* CV3............33 F5
Middlemarch Rd *COVN* CV6.........22 D4
Middle Ride *COVS* CV3................39 G3
Midland Rd *COVN* CV6................31 F1
Milburn Hill Rd *TLHL/CAN* CV4.....37 G4
Miles Meadow *COVN* CV6............24 A2
Milestone Dr
RUGBYS/DCH CV22....................61 G4
Mile Tree La *COVE* CV2...............15 E1
Milford Cl *COVW* CV5.................21 E5

Millais Cl *BDWTH* CV12................5 F1
Mill Bank Ms *KNWTH* CV8............65 G4
Millbeck *RUGBYN/HIL* CV21.........48 C2
Mill Cl *COVE* CV2.......................14 A5
KNWTH CV8................................57 E1
Mill End *KNWTH* CV8..................65 F1
Millennium Wy *KNWTH* CV8........57 E1
Miller's Cl *RUGBYS/DCH* CV22.....69 E3
Millers Dale Cl
RUGBYN/HIL CV21......................48 B2
Mill Farm Cl *RUGBYS/DCH* CV22..69 G4
Millfields Av *RUGBYN/HIL* CV21...63 E4
Mill Hl *COVS* CV3.......................53 G1
Millhouse Ct *COVN* CV6..............23 G4
Mill La *BDWTH* CV12...................6 D2
COVS CV3.................................33 E4
RRUGBY CV23............................48 D4
Mill Race La *COVN* CV6...............13 H5
Mill Rd *RUGBYN/HIL* CV21...........48 B5
Mill St *BDWTH* CV12...................7 G3
COV CV1...................................2 B1
Milner Cl *BDWTH* CV12................7 G3
Milner Crs *COVE* CV2.................24 D2
Milrose Wy *TLHL/CAN* CV4.........37 E1
Milton Cl *BDWTH* CV12.................6 A4
Milton St *COVE* CV2...................31 H2
Milverton Rd *COVE* CV2..............24 B1
Minster Rd *COV* CV1...................2 A3
Minton Rd *COVE* CV2..................24 D2
Miranda Cl *COVS* CV3.................41 E2
Mitchell Av *TLHL/CAN* CV4.........37 F3
Mitchell Rd *BDWTH* CV12.............5 H3
Moat Av *COVS* CV3....................38 C5
Moat Cl *RRUGBY* CV23................68 D5
Moat Farm Dr *BDWTH* CV12..........6 A3
RUGBYN/HIL CV21......................63 F5
Moat House La *TLHL/CAN* CV4.....37 H2
Modbury Cl *COVS* CV3................39 G4
Molands Br
RCOVN/BALC/EX CV7.................17 E2
Molesworth Av *COVS* CV3...........31 H5
Momus Bvd *COVE* CV2................32 B4
Monarch Cl *RUGBYN/HIL* CV21....48 A2
Monks Cl *RUGBYS/DCH* CV22......60 B4
The Monk's Cft *COVS* CV3...........39 F2
Monksfield Cl *TLHL/CAN* CV4......28 D5
Monks Rd *COV* CV1.....................3 J4
COVS CV3.................................42 B2
Monkswood Crs *COVE* CV2..........24 C3
Monmouth Cl *COVW* CV5.............29 E3
KNWTH CV8................................65 E1
Montague Rd
RUGBYS/DCH CV22....................69 H2
Montalt Rd *COVS* CV3.................39 H2
Montgomery Cl *COVS* CV3...........40 D5
Montgomery Dr
RUGBYS/DCH CV22....................60 D3
Montjoy Cl *COVS* CV3................41 E2
Montpellier Cl *COVS* CV3............39 F3
Montrose Rd
RUGBYS/DCH CV22....................61 H3
Moore Cl *COVN* CV6...................13 H4
The Moorfield *COVS* CV3.............40 B1
Moorlands Av *KNWTH* CV8..........65 E4
Moor St *COVW* CV5....................30 B5
Moreall Mdw *TLHL/CAN* CV4.......52 A1
Morey St *COVN* CV6...................23 F4
Morgans Rd *COVW* CV5..............27 H2
Morland Cl *BDWTH* CV12.............7 G3
Morland Rd *COVN* CV6................12 D5
Morningside *COVW* CV5..............39 E1
Morris Av *COVN* CV6..................32 C2
Morris Cl *RUGBYN/HIL* CV21.......47 G3
Morson Crs *RUGBYN/HIL* CV21....62 D2
Mortimer Rd *KNWTH* CV8...........65 E5
Morton Cl *COVN* CV6..................22 B2
Morton Gdns *RUGBYN/HIL* CV21..62 A2
Mosedale *RUGBYN/HIL* CV21......48 C2
Moseley Av *COVN* CV6................30 B2
Moseley Rd *KNWTH* CV8.............65 G4
Moss Cl *RUGBYS/DCH* CV22.......61 F3
Mossdale Cl *COVN* CV6...............22 B5
Moss Gv *KNWTH* CV8..................51 G5
Mottistone Cl *COVS* CV3............39 G3
Moultrie Rd *RUGBYN/HIL* CV21....62 A2
Mountbatten Av *KNWTH* CV8......65 H4
Mount Dr *BDWTH* CV12................5 F2
Mount Nod Wy *COVW* CV5..........38 A1
Mount Pleasant Rd *BDWTH* CV12..5 F2
Mount St *COVW* CV5..................30 A4
The Mount *COVS* CV3.................39 G1
Mowbray St *COVE* CV2...............3 K2
Moyeady Av *RUGBYS/DCH* CV22..62 D4
Moyle Crs *COVW* CV5.................28 A2
Much Park St *COV* CV1.................2 F5
Mulberry Rd *COVE* CV2...............23 H5
RUGBYS/DCH CV22....................60 C2
Mulliner St *COVN* CV6................31 G1
Murrayfield Wy *COVS* CV3..........33 G5

Murrayian Cl *RUGBYN/HIL* CV21..62 A1
Murray Rd *COVN* CV6..................22 B4
RUGBYN/HIL CV21......................48 B5
Myers Rd *RUGBYN/HIL* CV21.......63 H4
Mylgrove *COVS* CV3...................39 G5
Myrtle Gv *COVW* CV5..................30 A5

N

Nailcote Av *TLHL/CAN* CV4..........27 H5
Nailcote La
RCOVN/BALC/EX CV7.................35 H2
Napier St *COV* CV1......................3 H3
Napton Cl *RUGBYS/DCH* CV22.....69 F1
Napton Gn *COVW* CV5................28 D3
Narberth Wy *COVE* CV2..............25 E4
Nares Cl *RUGBYS/DCH* CV22.......61 F3
Narrowboat Cl *COVN* CV6............14 A2
Naseby Cl *COVS* CV3..................41 G1
Naseby Rd *RUGBYS/DCH* CV22....62 B8
Nason Gv *KNWTH* CV8................65 G2
Navigation Wy *COVN* CV6...........23 H3
Nayler Cl *RUGBYN/HIL* CV21.......48 B3
Neal Ct *COVE* CV2 *...................25 F3
Neale Av *COVW* CV5...................20 D5
Neale Cl *BDWTH* CV12..................7 F4
Needlers End La
RCOVN/BALC/EX CV7.................34 A3
Nelson St *COV* CV1......................3 H1
Nelson Wy *RUGBYS/DCH* CV22....60 D3
Nene Cl *COVS* CV3.....................41 E2
Nesfield Gv *HIA/OLT* B92............16 C4
Nethermill Rd *COVN* CV6............30 B1
Newall Cl *RRUGBY* CV23.............48 D4
New Ash Dr *COVW* CV5...............28 C1
Newbold Cl *COVS* CV3................33 E5
Newbold Rd *RUGBYN/HIL* CV21...47 F3
New Buildings *COV* CV1................2 D3
Newby Cl *COVS* CV3...................39 H3
New Combe Cl
RUGBYS/DCH CV22....................69 G4
Newcombe Rd *COVW* CV5...........30 B5
Newcomen Cl *BDWTH* CV12..........4 C5
Newcomen Rd *BDWTH* CV12.........4 C4
Newdegate Rd *BDWTH* CV12........5 F1
Newdigate Rd *COVN* CV6.............31 G1
Newey Av *BDWTH* CV12...............4 C5
Newey Dr *KNWTH* CV8................65 F5
Newey Rd *COVE* CV2..................32 C2
Newfield Av *KNWTH* CV8.............65 G4
Newfield Rd *COV* CV1.................30 D1
New Green Pk *COVE* CV2 *..........24 C4
Newhall Rd *COVE* CV2................24 C4
Newhaven Cl *COVN* CV6.............21 H5
Newhouse Cft
RCOVN/BALC/EX CV7.................34 C3
Newington Cl *COVN* CV6.............21 G5
Newland La
RCOVN/BALC/EX CV7.................12 C1
Newland Rd *COV* CV1.................31 E1
Newland St *RUGBYS/DCH* CV22...61 F1
Newman Cl *BDWTH* CV12.............5 G1
Newmarket Cl *COVN* CV6............14 A4
Newnham Rd *COV* CV1................31 G1
Newport Rd *COVN* CV6...............23 E2
New Rd *COVN* CV6.....................22 A2
RCOVN/BALC/EX CV7.................12 D2
Newstead Wy *COVS* CV3............33 G5
New St *BDWTH* CV12...................5 H3
BDWTH CV12..............................7 F3
KNWTH CV8................................65 E1
RUGBYS/DCH CV22....................61 F1
Newton Cl *COVE* CV2.................25 E4
Newton Manor La
RRUGBY CV23............................48 B1
Newton Rd *RRUGBY* CV23...........49 E3
Newtown Rd *BDWTH* CV12...........5 F3
New Union St *COV* CV1................2 D5
Nicholas Everton Cl
KNWTH CV8................................43 F4
Nicholls St *COVE* CV2..................3 J1
Nickson Rd *TLHL/CAN* CV4.........36 D1
Nightingale La *COVW* CV5...........38 A1
Niven Cl *COVW* CV5...................20 D5
Noble Dr *RUGBYS/DCH* CV22......60 B4
Nod Ri *COVW* CV5......................29 E3
Nolan Cl *COVN* CV6....................13 E3
Nordic Drift *COVE* CV2................25 F5
Norfolk St *COV* CV1.....................2 A3
Norfolk Ter *TLHL/CAN* CV4..........37 H2
Norman Ashman Coppice
COVS CV3.................................42 B2
Norman Av *COVE* CV2................25 E4
Norman Place Rd *COVN* CV6........21 H4
Norman Rd *RUGBYN/HIL* CV21....47 G3
Northampton La
RUGBYS/DCH CV22....................69 G3

North Av *BDWTH* CV12......6 A3
  BHAMNEC B40......8 D3
  COVE CV2......31 H3
North Brook Rd *COVN* CV6......21 G3
Northcote Rd
  RUGBYS/DCH CV22......61 G2
Northey Rd *COVS* CV3......23 E3
Northfield Rd *COV* CV1......3 H5
North Rd *RRUGBY* CV23......49 E4
North St *COVE* CV2......31 H1
  RUGBYN/HIL CV21......61 H1
Northumberland Rd *COV* CV1......30 B3
Northvale Cl *KNWTH* CV8......65 G1
North Vw *COVE* CV2......25 F2
Northway *BHAMNEC* B40......8 D3
  RUGBYN/HIL CV21 *......61 H1
Norton Gra *COVE* CV2......21 F5
Norton Hill Dr *COVE* CV2......24 D5
Norton Leys *RUGBYS/DCH* CV22...70 B1
Norwich Dr *COVS* CV3......39 E4
Norwood Gv *COVE* CV2......24 D1
Nova Cft *COVS* CV5......27 H2
Nuffield Rd *COVN* CV6......23 H4
Nuneaton Rd *BDWTH* CV12......5 G1
Nunts La *COVN* CV6......12 C5
Nunts Park Av *COVN* CV6......12 C4
Nutbrook Av *TLHL/CAN* CV4......28 B4

O

Oak Cl *BDWTH* CV12......5 H1
  KNWTH CV8......54 A2
Oakdale Rd *COVS* CV3......42 B2
Oakey Cl *COVN* CV6......13 G4
Oakfield Rd *COVN* CV6......30 A1
  RUGBYS/DCH CV22......61 G1
Oakford Dr *COVN* CV6......20 C5
Oakham Crs *BDWTH* CV12......7 G3
The Oaklands *TLHL/CAN* CV4......28 D4
Oak La *COVN* CV6......19 H2
Oakmoor Rd *COVN* CV6......13 H5
Oaks Pl *COVN* CV6......13 H5
Oaks Rd *KNWTH* CV8......64 D5
The Oaks *BDWTH* CV12......5 E4
Oak St *RUGBYS/DCH* CV22......61 G2
Oak Tree Av *COVS* CV3......38 D4
Oak Tree Rd *COVS* CV3......41 H2
Oak Wy *TLHL/CAN* CV4......28 A4
Oakworth Cl *COVE* CV2......25 E3
Oatlands Cl *COVN* CV6......12 C4
Oban Rd *COVN* CV6......13 G3
Oberon Cl *RUGBYS/DCH* CV22...69 H1
Occupation Rd *COVE* CV2......32 B3
Oddicombe Cft *COVS* CV3......39 G4
Offa Dr *KNWTH* CV8......65 F2
Okehampton Rd *COVS* CV3......39 H4
Okement Gv *RRUGBY* CV23......46 C4
Olaf Pl *COVE* CV2......25 F4
Old Church Rd *COVN* CV6......23 G2
Old Crown Ms *COVE* CV2......14 C3
Oldfield Rd *COVW* CV5......29 G3
Oldham Av *COVE* CV2......32 C2
Old House La
  RCOVN/BALC/EX CV7......10 D1
Old Leicester Rd
  RUGBYN/HIL CV21......47 H2
Old Meeting Yd *BDWTH* CV12......5 G2
Old Mill Av *TLHL/CAN* CV4......38 A4
Old Rd *RCOVN/BALC/EX* CV7......18 D2
Old Station Rd *HIA/OLT* B92......16 A1
Old Waste La
  RCOVN/BALC/EX CV7......35 F3
Old Winnings Rd
  RCOVN/BALC/EX CV7......12 A2
The Old Yd *COVE* CV2......25 E4
Olive Av *COVE* CV2......32 C1
Oliver St *COVN* CV6......23 G5
  RUGBYN/HIL CV21......61 G1
Olivier Wy *COVE* CV2......25 G3
Olton Av *COVW* CV5......28 B2
Olympus Cl *COVW* CV5......19 G3
Omar Rd *COVE* CV2......32 C4
Omega Pl *RUGBYN/HIL* CV21......48 A5
Onley La *RUGBYS/DCH* CV22......71 H2
Onley Ter *TLHL/CAN* CV4......37 H2
Oratory Dr *COVS* CV3......40 D3
Orchard Cl *COVS* CV3......33 E5
Orchard Crs *COVS* CV3......39 F1
Orchard Dr *COVN* CV6......27 H2
Orchard La *KNWTH* CV8......65 G2
Orchard Wy *RUGBYS/DCH* CV22...61 E4
Orchid Cl *BDWTH* CV12......4 C3
Orchid Wy *RRUGBY* CV23......48 C1
Ordnance Rd *COVN* CV6......31 F1
Orion Crs *COVE* CV2......24 D1
Orlando Cl *RUGBYS/DCH* CV22...69 H1
Orlescote Rd *TLHL/CAN* CV4......38 A3

Orpington Dr *COVN* CV6......13 E4
Orson Leys *RUGBYS/DCH* CV22...61 G5
Orton Rd *COVN* CV6......12 D5
Orwell Cl *RRUGBY* CV23......49 F4
Orwell Rd *COV* CV1......3 J6
Osbaston Cl *COVW* CV5......28 B2
Osborne Rd *COVW* CV5......38 D1
Oslo Gdns *COVE* CV2......25 F4
Osprey Cl *COVE* CV2......25 F4
Oswald Wy *RUGBYS/DCH* CV22...61 E1
Oswin Gv *COVE* CV2......32 B2
Othello Cl *RUGBYS/DCH* CV22...69 H2
Outermarch Rd *COVN* CV6......22 D4
Oval Rd *RUGBYS/DCH* CV22......62 C4
Overberry Cl *COVE* CV2......24 C1
Overdale Rd *COVW* CV5......29 F3
Overslade Crs *COVN* CV6......21 H4
Overslade La *RUGBYS/DCH* CV22..61 F4
Overslade Manor Dr
  RUGBYS/DCH CV22......61 G4
Over St *COVN* CV6......23 H3
Owenford Rd *COVN* CV6......22 D4
Ox Cl *COVE* CV2......23 H5
Oxendon Wy *COVS* CV3......41 F1
Oxford Canal Pth
  RUGBYN/HIL CV21......63 H4
Oxford Canal Wk *RRUGBY* CV23..46 D1
Oxford Rd *KNWTH* CV8......55 G3
Oxford St *COV* CV1......3 H3
  RUGBYN/HIL CV21......62 B1
Oxhayes Cl *RCOVN/BALC/EX* CV7..34 D3
Oxley Dr *COVS* CV3......53 F1

P

Packington Av *COVW* CV5......21 E5
Packington La
  RCOVN/BALC/EX CV7......9 F3
Packwood Av
  RUGBYN/HIL CV21......63 G4
Packwood Gn *COVW* CV5......28 D3
Paddocks Cl *KNWTH* CV8......57 F1
The Paddocks *BDWTH* CV12......7 E2
Paddox Cl *RUGBYS/DCH* CV22...63 E4
Padstow Rd *TLHL/CAN* CV4......36 D1
Page Rd *TLHL/CAN* CV4......36 D2
Paget Ct *COVE* CV2......14 A5
Pailton Cl *COVE* CV2......24 C1
Pake's Cft *COVN* CV6......30 B1
Palermo Av *COVS* CV3......39 H3
Palmer La *COV* CV1......2 D3
Palmer's Cl *RUGBYN/HIL* CV21...63 G4
Palmerston Rd *COVW* CV5......38 C1
Palm Tree Av *COVE* CV2......24 B1
Pancras Cl *COVE* CV2......24 D2
Pandora Rd *COVE* CV2......24 D4
Pangbourne Rd *COVE* CV2......24 B3
Pangfield Pk *COVW* CV5......29 F2
Pantolf Pl *RUGBYN/HIL* CV21...47 F2
Papenham Gn *TLHL/CAN* CV4...37 F1
Paradise St *COV* CV1......3 F6
  RUGBYN/HIL CV21......62 B1
Paradise Wy *COVE* CV2......25 F2
Paragon Wy
  RCOVN/BALC/EX CV7......5 G5
Parbrook Cl *TLHL/CAN* CV4......36 D1
Park Av *COVN* CV6......12 D5
Park Cl *KNWTH* CV8......65 G2
Park Ct *RUGBYN/HIL* CV21 *......47 H5
Parkend *RUGBYN/HIL* CV21......48 A2
Park Farm Cl
  RUGBYS/DCH CV22......61 E2
Parkfield Dr *KNWTH* CV8......65 G2
Parkfield Rd
  RCOVN/BALC/EX CV7......12 B2
  RUGBYN/HIL CV21......47 E5
Parkgate Rd *COVN* CV6......12 C5
Park Hl *KNWTH* CV8......65 G2
Parkhill Dr *COVW* CV5......28 C2
Park Hill La *COVW* CV5......28 D1
Parkland Cl *COVN* CV6......12 D5
Park La *RCOVN/BALC/EX* CV7......26 A4
The Park Paling *COVS* CV3......39 H3
Park Rd *BDWTH* CV12......5 G3
  COV CV1......2 D6
  KNWTH CV8......65 F1
  RUGBYN/HIL CV21......47 H5
Parkside *COVN* CV6......3 F5
Parkstone Rd *COVN* CV6......23 G1
Park St *COVN* CV6......23 F4
Park View Cl
  RCOVN/BALC/EX CV7......13 H1
Parkville Cl *COVN* CV6......12 D5
Parkville Hwy *COVN* CV6......12 C5
Park Wk *RUGBYN/HIL* CV21......47 H5
Parkway *COVE* CV2......25 G3
Park Wood La *TLHL/CAN* CV4......36 C2

Parnell Cl *RUGBYN/HIL* CV21......61 G1
Parrotts Gv *COVE* CV2......14 C3
Parry Rd *COVE* CV2......24 A4
Parson's Nook *COVE* CV2......31 H1
Partridge Cft *COVN* CV6......23 H2
Patricia Cl *TLHL/CAN* CV4......27 H5
Patrick Br *HIA/OLT* B92......17 E4
Patterdale *RUGBYN/HIL* CV21...48 C3
Pauline Av *COVN* CV6......24 A1
Pavilion Wy *COVW* CV5......30 A3
Paxmead Cl *COVN* CV6......22 B1
Paxton Rd *COVN* CV6......30 B2
Paynell Cl *COVN* CV6......22 C1
Payne's La *COV* CV1......3 J3
  RUGBYN/HIL CV21......61 E1
Peacock Av *COVE* CV2......25 E2
Pears Cl *KNWTH* CV8......65 E2
Pearson Av *COVN* CV6......24 A2
Pear Tree Wy
  RUGBYS/DCH CV22......60 C3
Peat Cl *RUGBYS/DCH* CV22......61 F3
Pebblebrook Wy *BDWTH* CV12...5 H3
Pebworth Cl *COVW* CV5......29 E3
Peckstone Cl *COV* CV1......3 F7
Peel Cl *COVN* CV6......23 F5
Peel La *COVN* CV6......31 G1
Peel St *COVN* CV6......23 G5
Pegmill Cl *COVS* CV3......40 A1
Peliam Bend *TLHL/CAN* CV4......27 H3
Pembroke Cl *BDWTH* CV12......4 B4
Pembrook Rd *COVN* CV6......22 D1
Pembury Av *COVN* CV6......13 H5
Penarth Gv *COVS* CV3......41 G2
Pencraig Cl *KNWTH* CV8......65 E2
Pendenis Cl *COVN* CV6......23 H3
Pendigo Wy *BHAMNEC* B40......8 C4
Pendred Rd *RUGBYS/DCH* CV22..61 F2
Pennington Ms
  RUGBYN/HIL CV21......61 G1
Pennington St
  RUGBYN/HIL CV21......61 H1
Pennington Wy *COVN* CV6......23 F3
Penny Park La *COVN* CV6......12 A5
Penrose Cl *TLHL/CAN* CV4......37 F2
Penryhn Cl *KNWTH* CV8......65 H2
Pensilva Wy *COV* CV1......3 H1
Pepper La *COV* CV1......2 D4
Pepys Cnr *TLHL/CAN* CV4......28 B3
Perchfoot Cl *COV* CV1......3 F7
Percival Rd *RUGBYS/DCH* CV22..62 C4
Percy Crs *KNWTH* CV8......64 D5
Percy Rd *KNWTH* CV8......64 D5
Percy St *COV* CV1......2 A3
Peregrine Dr *COVW* CV5......28 D1
Perimeter Rd *BHAMNEC* B40......8 A4
Perkins Gv *RUGBYN/HIL* CV21...63 E3
Permian Cl *RUGBYN/HIL* CV21...48 B3
Pershore Pl *TLHL/CAN* CV4......38 B3
Perth Ri *COVW* CV5......28 B2
Peters Wk *COVN* CV6......13 H4
Petitor Crs *COVE* CV2......24 B2
Pettiver Crs *RUGBYS/DCH* CV21..63 E3
Peverill Dr *COVS* CV3......39 E4
Peyto Cl *COVN* CV6......22 D1
Pheasant Cl *BDWTH* CV12......4 C4
Pheasant Oak *TLHL/CAN* CV4......27 H4
Phipps Av *RUGBYN/HIL* CV21...63 E3
Phoenix Wy *COVN* CV6......23 F1
Pickard Cl *RUGBYN/HIL* CV21...48 D2
Pickford Grange La *COVW* CV5...19 H4
Pickford Green La *COVW* CV5...19 H5
Pickford Wy *COVW* CV5......29 E1
Pikers La *RCOVN/BALC/EX* CV7...10 D5
Pilgrims Wk
  RCOVN/BALC/EX CV7......12 B3
Pilkington Rd *COVW* CV5......38 A1
Pilling Cl *COVE* CV2......25 E3
Pinders La *RUGBYN/HIL* CV21 *...48 A5
Pine Gv *RUGBYN/HIL* CV21......63 F3
The Pines *BDWTH* CV12......4 D5
  TLHL/CAN CV4 *......36 C2
Pine Tree Av *TLHL/CAN* CV4......28 D4
Pine Tree Rd *BDWTH* CV12......5 H1
Pinewood Dr *COVS* CV3......42 B2
Pinewood Gv *COVW* CV5......39 E1
Pinfold St *RUGBYN/HIL* CV21......61 H1
Pinley Flds *COVS* CV3......40 C1
Pinner's Cft *COVE* CV2......31 H1
Pinnock Pl *TLHL/CAN* CV4......28 C5
Piper's La *KNWTH* CV8......65 F5
Pipewell Cl *RUGBYS/DCH* CV22..60 D3
Pipkin Ct *COV* CV1......3 G7
Placid Cl *TLHL/CAN* CV4......27 H3
Plantagenet Dr
  RUGBYS/DCH CV22......70 A1
Planter Cl *RUGBYS/DCH* CV22...60 D3
Plants Hill Crs *TLHL/CAN* CV4...28 B5
Plexfield Rd *RUGBYS/DCH* CV22..60 D3

Pleydell Cl *COVS* CV3......40
Plomer Cl *RUGBYS/DCH* CV22...60
Plowman St *RUGBYN/HIL* CV21...61
Plymouth Cl *COVE* CV2......24
Poitiers Rd *COVS* CV3......39
Polperro Dr *COVW* CV5......28
Pomeroy Cl *TLHL/CAN* CV4......36
Pondthorpe *COVS* CV3......41
Pontypool Av *COVS* CV3......41
Pool Cl *RUGBYS/DCH* CV22......61
Pool Cottages *KNWTH* CV8 *......53
Poole Rd *COVN* CV6......22
Poolside Gdns *COVS* CV3......38
Pope St *RUGBYS/DCH* CV22......61
Poplar Av *BDWTH* CV12......6
Poplar Gv *KNWTH* CV8......56
  RUGBYN/HIL CV21......47
Poplar Rd *COVW* CV5......30
Poppy Ct *COVS* CV3 *......41
Poppy Dr *RRUGBY* CV23......48
Poppyfield Ct *TLHL/CAN* CV4......52
Porchester Cl *COVS* CV3......33
Porlock Cl *COVS* CV3......39
Porter Cl *TLHL/CAN* CV4......36
Portland Pl *RUGBYN/HIL* CV21...62
Portland Rd *RUGBYN/HIL* CV21..62
Portree Av *COVS* CV3......33
Portsea Cl *COVS* CV3......39
Portway Cl *TLHL/CAN* CV4......36
Portwrinkle Av *COVN* CV6......24
Postbridge Rd *COVS* CV3......39
Potters Green Rd *COVE* CV2......24
Potters Rd *BDWTH* CV12......4
Potton Cl *COVS* CV3......41
Potts Cl *KNWTH* CV8......65
Poultney Rd *COVN* CV6......22
Pound Cl *RCOVN/BALC/EX* CV7...26
Powell Rd *COVE* CV2......31
Powis Gv *KNWTH* CV8......65
The Precinct *COV* CV1......2
Prentice Cl *RRUGBY* CV23......46
Preston Cl *TLHL/CAN* CV4......37
Pretorian Wy *RUGBYN/HIL* CV21..47
Pridmore Rd *COVN* CV6......23
Primrose Cl *RRUGBY* CV23......48
Primrose Dr *BDWTH* CV12......4
Primrose Hill St *COV* CV1......3
Prince of Wales Rd *COVW* CV5...29
Princes Cl *COVS* CV3......40
Princes Dr *KNWTH* CV8......51
Princess Dr *COVN* CV6......23
Princess St *COVN* CV6......23
Princes St *RUGBYN/HIL* CV21......61
Princethorpe Wy *COVS* CV3......41
Prince William Cl *COVN* CV6......21
Prior Deram Wk *TLHL/CAN* CV4...37
Priors Cl *RCOVN/BALC/EX* CV7...34
Priorsfield Rd *COVN* CV6......30
  KNWTH CV8......50
Priors Harnall *COV* CV1......31
The Priors *BDWTH* CV12......5
Priory Ct *COVW* CV5 *......30
Priory Cft *KNWTH* CV8......65
Priory Pl *COV* CV1 *......2
Priory Rd *KNWTH* CV8......43
  KNWTH CV8......65
Priory Rw *COV* CV1......2
Priory St *COV* CV1......2
Privet Rd *COVE* CV2 *......24
Progress Cl *COVS* CV3......41
Progress Wy *COVS* CV3......41
Projects Dr *RUGBYN/HIL* CV21...48
Prospect Wy *RUGBYN/HIL* CV21..48
Providence St *COVW* CV5......38
Pudding Bag La *RRUGBY* CV23...68
Puma Wy *COV* CV1......3
Pumphouse Cl *COVN* CV6......14
Purcell Rd *COVN* CV6......23
Purefoy Rd *COVS* CV3......39
Purlieu La *KNWTH* CV8......65
Pytchley Rd *RUGBYS/DCH* CV22..62
Pyt Pk *COVW* CV5......29

Q

The Quadrant *COV* CV1 *......2
Quarry Cl *RUGBYN/HIL* CV21......47
Quarryfield La *COV* CV1......3
Quarry Rd *KNWTH* CV8......64
Quarrywood Gv *COVE* CV2......39
Queen Isabel's Av *COVS* CV3......39
Queen Margaret's Rd
  TLHL/CAN CV4......37
Queen Mary's Rd *COVN* CV6......23
Queen Philippa St *COVS* CV3......39
Queen's Cl *KNWTH* CV8......65

ensferry Cl
   UGBYS/DCH CV22......**60** D4
ensland Av COVW CV5......**30** A4
ensland Gdns BDWTH CV12...**5** E3
en's Rd COV CV1......**2** A5
   NWTH CV8......**65** E4
   RUGBY CV23......**44** B2
en St BDWTH CV12......**5** H3
   OV CV1......**3** F1
   UGBYN/HIL CV21......**61** H1
en Victoria Rd COV CV1...**2** B3
en Victoria St
   ......**62** B1
m Cl COVN CV6......**23** H1 ... n Cl COVS CV3......**40** C2
lletts Cl COVN CV6......**23** H1
nton Pk COVS CV3......**39** G2
nton Rd COV CV1......**2** E7
rn Wy COVS CV3......**41** F2

R

cliffe Rd COVW CV5......**38** C1
ford Rd COV CV1......**2** C1
   OV CV6......**22** B5
nor Wk COVE CV2......**25** E3
lan Cl KNWTH CV8......**65** G2
lan St COV CV1......**3** G3
way St RRUGBY CV23......**46** B5
way Ter BDWTH CV12 *......**5** H3
   UGBYN/HIL CV21......**48** A5
nsbrook Av
   UGBYS/DCH CV22......**62** D4
eigh Rd COV CV2......**32** A3
ph Rd COVN CV6......**30** A1
aby Rd CHWD/FDBR/MGN B37...**8** A3
nsay Crs COVS CV3......**21** E4
dy Rd COV CV2......**3** J1
dall Rd KNWTH CV8......**65** E4
adle St COVN CV6......**30** C1
akine Cl RUGBYN/HIL CV21...**47** E2
som Rd COVN CV6......**23** F3
ulf Cft COVS CV3......**39** F2
hael Cl COVW CV5......**29** F3
hbone Cl
   COVN/BALC/EX CV7......**12** B2
   UGBYN/HIL CV21......**63** F4
iffe Rd RUGBYS/DCH CV22...**61** G5
en Cragg Rd COVW CV5......**38** B1
nglass RUGBYN/HIL CV21...**48** C2
nsdale Rd COVE CV2......**32** B3
nsholst TLHL/CAN CV4 *...**38** A4
nsthorpe Cl COVS CV3......**41** F1
grave Cl COVE CV2......**25** G3
hill Rd RRUGBY CV23......**46** B5
dland Cl COVE CV2......**24** C1
dland La KNWTH CV8......**55** H1
d La COVN CV6......**31** F1
   NWTH CV8......**50** C4
d Lodge Dr
   UGBYS/DCH CV22......**61** F4
druth Cl COVN CV6......**23** H3
thorne Gv KNWTH CV8......**51** G4
es Dr COVS CV3......**39** F5
ve Dr KNWTH CV8......**65** F3
ency Ct COVW CV5......**38** C1
ency Dr COVS CV3......**38** C4
   NWTH CV8......**65** E4
gent Pl RUGBYN/HIL CV21...**47** H5
gent St BDWTH CV12......**5** H1
   OV CV1......**2** A6
   UGBYN/HIL CV21......**61** H1
gent Ct COVN CV6......**22** B2
gina Crs COVE CV2......**25** F4
gis Wk COVE CV2......**25** E4
mbrandt Cl COVW CV5......**29** F3
membrance Rd COVS CV3...**41** E3
naissance Ct COVS CV3......**38** C4
nison Rd BDWTH CV12......**4** D4
nolds Cl COVW CV5......**29** F4
nown Av COVW CV5......**29** F5
ston Dr COVN CV6......**24** A1
servoir Rd RUGBYN/HIL CV21...**48** B3
x Cl TLHL/CAN CV4......**36** C1

Reynolds Cl RUGBYN/HIL CV21......**63** G4
Reynolds Rd BDWTH CV12......**5** F1
Ribble Cl BDWTH CV12......**6** D3
Ribble Rd COVS CV3......**3** K5
Richard Joy Cl COVN CV6......**22** D1
Richards Cl KNWTH CV8......**65** E2
Richardson Wy COVE CV2......**25** G3
Richmond Rd RUGBYN/HIL CV21...**62** B2
Richmond St COVE CV2......**31** H3
Riddings Hl
   RCOVN/BALC/EX CV7......**34** D2
The Riddings COVW CV5......**38** A2
Ridge Cl COVE CV2......**20** D5
Ridge Dr RUGBYN/HIL CV21...**48** C5
Ridgethorpe COVS CV3......**41** F4
Ridgeway Av COVS CV3......**39** F3
Ridgley Rd TLHL/CAN CV4...**36** C1
Rigdale Cl COVE CV2......**32** D4
Riley Cl KNWTH CV8......**65** H3
Ringway Hill Cross COV CV1...**2** B2
Ringway Queens COV CV1...**2** B5
Ringway Rudge COV CV1...**2** B4
Ringway St Johns COV CV1...**2** B5
Ringway St Nicholas COV CV1...**2** D2
Ringway St Patricks COV CV1...**2** D6
Ringway Swanswell COV CV1...**2** E1
Ringway Whitefriars COV CV1...**3** F3
Ringwood Hwy COVE CV2...**2** D1
Ripon Cl COVW CV5......**20** D3
Risborough Cl COVW CV5...**29** F3
River Cl BDWTH CV12......**3** E5
River Ct COV CV1 *......**1** F5
Riverford Cft TLHL/CAN CV4...**52** A1
Riverside Cl COVS CV3......**40** A3
Riverslea Rd COVS CV3......**32** B5
Robbins Ct RUGBYS/DCH CV22...**63** E4
Robert Cl COVS CV3......**40** D5
Robert Cramb Av TLHL/CAN CV4...**37** E1
Robert Hill Cl RUGBYN/HIL CV21...**63** F3
Robert Rd RCOVN/BALC/EX CV7...**5** E5
Robertson Cl RRUGBY CV23...**49** F4
Robin Hood Rd COVS CV3...**40** D3
Robinson Rd BDWTH CV12...**5** A1
Robotham Cl RUGBYN/HIL CV21...**47** G3
Rocheberie Wy
   RUGBYS/DCH CV22......**61** G4
Rochester Rd COVW CV5...**38** B1
Rock Cl COV CV6......**24** A2
Rocken End COVN CV6......**23** E3
Rock La RCOVN/BALC/EX CV7...**11** F1
Rocky La KNWTH CV8......**66** A4
Rodhouse Cl TLHL/CAN CV4...**28** A5
Rodney Cl RUGBYS/DCH CV22...**60** D3
Rodway Dr COVW CV5......**28** A2
Rodyard Wy COV CV1......**3** F7
Rokeby St RUGBYN/HIL CV21...**62** B1
Roland Av COVN CV6......**12** C5
Roland Mt COVN CV6......**12** C5
Rollason Cl COVN CV6......**22** D3
Rollason Rd COVN CV6......**22** D3
Rollasons Yd COVN CV6 *...**13** H5
Roman Rd COVE CV2......**32** A3
Roman Wy COVS CV3......**53** G1
   RUGBYN/HIL CV21......**47** H2
Romford Rd COVN CV6......**22** C1
Romney Pl RUGBYS/DCH CV22...**61** G5
Romsley Rd COVN CV6......**22** D5
Ro-oak Rd COVN CV6......**30** A1
Rookery La COVN CV6......**12** C5
Roosevelt Dr TLHL/CAN CV4...**28** B4
Roper Cl RUGBYN/HIL CV21...**63** F4
Rosaville Crs COVW CV5......**20** D5
Rose Av COVN CV6......**30** A1
Roseberry Av COVE CV2......**24** A2
Rose Cottages
   RUGBYN/HIL CV21 *......**61** F1
Rose Cft KNWTH CV8......**64** D1
Rosegreen Cl COVS CV3......**39** H3
Rosehip Dr COVE CV2......**24** A5
Roseland Rd KNWTH CV8......**65** E5
Roselands Av COVE CV2......**24** B3
Rosemary Cl TLHL/CAN CV4...**28** B3
Rosemount Cl COVE CV2......**24** D4
Rosemullion Cl
   RCOVN/BALC/EX CV7......**5** G5
Rosewood Av
   RUGBYS/DCH CV22......**61** G4
Ross Cl COVW CV5......**28** D1
Rosslyn Av COVN CV6......**21** H5
Rotherham Rd COVN CV6......**22** C1
Rothesay Av TLHL/CAN CV4...**29** E4
Rothley Dr RUGBYN/HIL CV21...**48** D2
Roughknowles Rd
   TLHL/CAN CV4......**36** C3
Rouncil La KNWTH CV8......**65** E5
Round Av RRUGBY CV23......**46** B4
Round House Rd COVS CV3...**40** B1
Rounds Gdns RUGBYN/HIL CV21...**61** G1
Rounds Hl KNWTH CV8......**64** D5

Round St RUGBYN/HIL CV21...**61** G1
Rover Rd COV CV1 *......**2** C4
Rowan Cl COVS CV3......**42** C2
Rowan Dr RUGBYS/DCH CV22...**60** C2
Rowan Gv COVE CV2......**24** D1
The Rowans BDWTH CV12......**4** D3
Rowcroft Rd COVE CV2......**25** F5
Rowe Cl RUGBYN/HIL CV21...**63** G4
Rowington Cl COVN CV6......**21** G5
Rowland St RUGBYN/HIL CV21...**61** G1
Rowley Dr COVS CV3......**40** C5
Rowley La COVS CV3......**41** E5
Rowley Rd COVS CV3......**40** D5
   KNWTH CV8......**54** A1
Rowley's Green La COVN CV6...**13** F4
Rowse Cl RUGBYN/HIL CV21...**48** B2
The Row KNWTH CV8 *......**54** A2
Royal Cl RUGBYN/HIL CV21 *...**61** G1
Royal Crs COVS CV3......**40** D4
Royal Oak La BDWTH CV12...**12** D1
Royal Oak Yd BDWTH CV12 *...**5** G1
Royston Cl COVS CV3......**33** F3
Rubens Cl COVW CV5......**29** F3
Rudgard Rd COVN CV6......**13** H4
Rugby Rd BDWTH CV12......**7** F3
   COVS CV3......**42** B1
   KNWTH CV8......**43** F4
   RRUGBY CV23......**45** E4
   RUGBYS/DCH CV22......**69** F1
Runnymede Dr
   RCOVN/BALC/EX CV7......**34** D4
Rupert Brooke Rd
   RUGBYS/DCH CV22......**61** F5
Rupert Rd COVN CV6......**22** C3
Rushmoor Dr COVW CV5......**30** A3
Rushton Cl RUGBYN/HIL CV21...**63** G3
Ruskin Cl RUGBYS/DCH CV22...**70** B1
Russell Av RUGBYS/DCH CV22...**69** H3
Russell St COV CV1......**2** E1
Russell St North COV CV1 *...**31** E2
Russelsheim Wy
   RUGBYS/DCH CV22......**61** H2
Russet Gv TLHL/CAN CV4 *...**52** A1
Rutherglen Av COVS CV3......**40** B3
Rutland Cl RUGBYN/HIL CV21...**62** D2
Rutland Cft COVS CV3......**41** G1
Rydal Cl COVW CV5......**21** E3
   RUGBYN/HIL CV21......**48** C3
Rye Hl COVW CV5......**20** D5
Rye Meadow KNWTH CV8......**50** D2
Rye Piece Ringway BDWTH CV12...**5** G2
Ryhope Cl BDWTH CV12......**4** B4
Rylston Av COVN CV6......**22** B2
Ryton Br KNWTH CV8......**55** E1
Ryton Cl TLHL/CAN CV4......**37** G1

S

Saddington Rd COVS CV3......**41** F1
Sadler Gdns BDWTH CV12......**5** H3
Sadler Rd COVN CV6......**22** B4
Saffron Cl RRUGBY CV23......**48** C1
St Agatha's Rd COVE CV2......**31** H3
St Agnes La COV CV1 *......**2** D2
St Andrews Crs
   RUGBYS/DCH CV22......**61** H4
St Andrew's Rd COVW CV5...**38** C1
St Ann's Rd RUGBYS/DCH CV22...**61** F3
St Ann's Rd COVE CV2......**31** H3
St Augustine's Wk COVN CV6...**22** B4
St Austell Rd COVE CV2......**32** D3
St Bartholemews Cl COVS CV3...**33** F4
St Catherine's Cl COVS CV3...**40** C1
St Christian's Cft COVS CV3...**39** G1
St Christian's Rd COVS CV3...**39** H1
St Columba's Cl COV CV1......**2** C1
St Davids Orch COVS CV3......**41** G2
St Elizabeth's Rd COVN CV6...**23** F4
St Georges Av
   RUGBYS/DCH CV22......**61** G4
St George's Rd COV CV1......**3** J4
St Giles Rd RCOVN/BALC/EX CV7...**13** E2
St Helen's Wy COVW CV5......**21** E3
St Ives Rd COVE CV2......**32** C3
St James' La COVS CV3......**40** D4
St John's Av KNWTH CV8......**65** F4
   RUGBYS/DCH CV22......**62** D4
St John's La RRUGBY CV23...**46** B4
St Johns St COV CV1......**3** F5
   KNWTH CV8......**65** E4
St John St RUGBYN/HIL CV21...**47** H5
St Jude's Crs COVS CV3......**41** G2
St Lawrence's Rd COVN CV6...**23** G2
St Leonard's Wk KNWTH CV8...**55** H1
St Luke's Rd COVN CV6......**23** E1
St Margaret Rd COV CV1......**3** J5

St Margarets Av KNWTH CV8...**43** F5
St Mark's Av RUGBYS/DCH CV22...**60** D5
St Martin's Rd COVS CV3......**53** F5
St Mary's Ct KNWTH CV8......**65** E4
St Mary St COV CV1......**2** D4
St Michael's Rd COVE CV2...**31** H3
St Nicholas Av KNWTH CV8...**65** E4
St Nicholas St COV CV1......**30** D2
St Osburg's Rd COVE CV2...**31** H3
St Paul's Rd COVN CV6......**23** F5
St Peter's Ct COV CV1 *......**3** G1
St Peters Rd RUGBYN/HIL CV21...**62** B2
St Thomas Ct COV CV1 *......**2** A5
St Thomas' Rd COVN CV6...**13** G5
St Thomas's Ct COV CV1......**2** A5
Salcombe Cl COVS CV3......**41** E3
Salemorton Ct
   RUGBYS/DCH CV22......**69** F1
Salford Cl COVE CV2......**31** H1
Salisbury Av COVS CV3......**39** F3
Salisbury Cl KNWTH CV8......**57** E1
Salt La COV CV1......**2** D4
Sam Gault Cl COVS CV3......**41** F2
Sammons Wy TLHL/CAN CV4...**28** A5
Sampson Cl COVE CV2......**24** B2
Sanby Cl BDWTH CV12......**5** F1
Sanders Rd COVN CV6......**14** A2
Sandford Cl COVE CV2......**14** C5
Sandford Wy
   RUGBYS/DCH CV22......**69** G4
Sandgate Crs COVE CV2......**32** C4
Sandhurst Gv COVN CV6......**30** C1
Sandilands Cl COVE CV2......**32** D2
Sandown Av COVN CV6......**23** F1
Sandown Rd RUGBYN/HIL CV21...**48** B5
Sandpiper Rd COVE CV2......**14** A5
Sandpits La
   RCOVN/BALC/EX CV7......**21** H1
Sandringham Cl TLHL/CAN CV4...**37** E2
Sandwick Cl COVS CV3......**41** G1
Sandy La COVN CV6......**30** D1
   RUGBYN/HIL CV21......**61** F1
Santos Cl COVS CV3......**41** G1
Sapcote Gv COVN CV6......**14** A4
Sapphire Ct COVE CV2 *......**25** G2
Sapphire Ga COVE CV2......**32** B4
Sarawak Pl RUGBYS/DCH CV22...**60** C4
Saunders Av BDWTH CV12...**5** G3
Saunton Cl COVW CV5......**21** E2
Saunton Rd RUGBYS/DCH CV22...**61** G3
Savannah Cl TLHL/CAN CV4...**27** H3
Saville Gv KNWTH CV8......**65** H1
Saxon Cl COVS CV3......**42** C2
   RUGBYS/DCH CV22......**60** B4
Saxon Rd COVE CV2......**32** A2
Scafell RUGBYN/HIL CV21......**48** C2
Scafell Cl COVW CV5......**28** D2
Scarborough Wy TLHL/CAN CV4...**37** E2
Scarman Rd TLHL/CAN CV4...**37** C4
Scholars Dr RUGBYS/DCH CV22...**60** C4
Scholfield Rd
   RCOVN/BALC/EX CV7......**12** B2
School Bell Ms KNWTH CV8 *...**67** E4
School Cl COVS CV3......**3** K5
Schoolfield Gv
   RUGBYN/HIL CV21......**61** G1
School Gdns RUGBYN/HIL CV21...**63** E4
School House La COVE CV2...**25** F5
School La KNWTH CV8......**65** E2
   RCOVN/BALC/EX CV7......**9** H1
   RCOVN/BALC/EX CV7......**13** F1
School Rd BDWTH CV12......**7** F3
School St KNWTH CV8......**43** F5
   RRUGBY CV23......**45** E4
   RUGBYN/HIL CV21......**61** G1
   RUGBYS/DCH CV22......**69** G4
The Scothill COVN CV6......**22** A2
Scots Cl RUGBYS/DCH CV22...**60** D5
Scots La COVN CV6......**22** A5
Scott Rd KNWTH CV8......**64** D5
Seabroke Av RUGBYS/DCH CV22...**61** G1
Seaford Cl COVN CV6......**14** A4
Seagrave Rd COV CV1......**3** G5
Sealand Dr BDWTH CV12......**5** E2
Sear Hills Cl
   RCOVN/BALC/EX CV7......**34** C3
Seathwaite RUGBYN/HIL CV21...**48** B2
Sebastian Cl COVS CV3......**40** C4
Second Av COVS CV3......**32** B5
Second Exhibition Av
   BHAMNEC B40......**8** B4
Sedgemere Gv
   RCOVN/BALC/EX CV7......**34** D4
Sedgemoor Rd COVS CV3......**40** C4
Sedlescombe Pk
   RUGBYN/HIL CV21......**48** B2
Seed Field Cft COVS CV3......**39** H2
Seekings Dr KNWTH CV8......**65** G3
Sefton Rd TLHL/CAN CV4......**38** B3

Selborne Rd *RUGBYS/DCH* CV22....61 E4
Selsey Cl *COVS* CV3....................40 D5
Selside *RUGBYN/HIL* CV21.........48 C2
Selworthy Rd *COVN* CV6..............13 E5
Seneschal Rd *COVS* CV3...............39 H2
Sephton Dr *COVN* CV6.................14 B2
Severn Rd *BDWTH* CV12.................6 D2
  COV CV1.................................3 J6
Sevilla Cl *COVS* CV3....................33 F4
Sewall Hwy *COVE* CV2.................32 C1
  COVN CV6..............................23 H3
Seymour Cl *COVS* CV3.................40 D4
Seymour Rd *RUGBYN/HIL* CV21....48 B3
Shadowbrook Rd *COVN* CV6........30 B1
Shaftesbury Av
  RCOVN/BALC/EX CV7................12 B1
Shaftesbury Rd *COVW* CV5..........38 C1
Shakespeare Av *BDWTH* CV12........6 A3
Shakespeare Gdns
  RUGBYS/DCH CV22...................61 F5
Shakespeare St *COVE* CV2...........32 A3
Shakleton Rd *COVW* CV5.............30 B4
Shanklin Rd *COVS* CV3................40 C5
Shapfell *RUGBYN/HIL* CV21.........48 C2
Sharp Cl *COVN* CV6.....................22 D1
Sharpley Ct *COVE* CV2 *..............25 F3
Sharratt Rd *BDWTH* CV12..............5 E3
Sheldrake Cl *COVS* CV3...............33 F5
Shelfield Cl *COVW* CV5................29 C5
Shelley Cl *BDWTH* CV12.................6 A4
Shelley Ct *COVE* CV2...................32 B3
Shelley Rd *COVE* CV2..................32 B3
Shellon Cl *COVS* CV3...................41 G1
Shelton Sq *COV* CV1.....................2 C4
Shenstone Av
  RUGBYN/HIL CV21...................62 D3
Shenstone Dr
  RCOVN/BALC/EX CV7................34 B3
Shepherd Cl *TLHL/CAN* CV4........28 C3
Sherbourne Ar *COV* CV1 *..............2 D3
Sherbourne Crs *COVW* CV5..........29 H2
Sherbourne St *COVW* CV1............30 B4
Sheridan Cl *RUGBYS/DCH* CV22...61 G5
Sheriff Av *TLHL/CAN* CV4............37 G2
Sheriff Rd *RUGBYN/HIL* CV21.......62 C2
Sheriffs Orch *COV* CV1...................2 C5
Sherington Av *COVW* CV5............29 F3
Sherlock Rd *COVW* CV5...............29 G3
Sherwood Jones Cl *COVN* CV6......22 C5
Shetland Cl *COVW* CV5................28 D2
Shevlock Wy *COVN* CV6...............23 H5
Shillingstone Cl *COVE* CV2...........33 F2
Shilton La *BDWTH* CV12.................7 G4
  COVE CV2...............................24 D1
Shipston Rd *COVE* CV2................24 B5
Shirebrook Cl *COVE* CV2..............24 C2
Shire Cl *COVN* CV6......................24 A1
The Shires *RUGBY* CV23..............45 F3
Shirlett Cl *COVE* CV2...................14 A4
Shirley La *RCOVN/BALC/EX* CV7....27 F1
Shirley Rd *COVE* CV2...................25 E4
Shorncliffe Rd *COVN* CV6.............21 H5
Shortfield Cl
  RCOVN/BALC/EX CV7................34 C2
Shortlands *RCOVN/BALC/EX* CV7..13 C4
Shortley Rd *COVS* CV3.................39 H1
Short St *COV* CV1..........................3 F5
Shortwheat Hl *RUGBY* CV23.........48 C1
Shottery Cl *COVW* CV5................29 E3
Showell La
  RCOVN/BALC/EX CV7................19 E2
The Shrubberies *TLHL/CAN* CV4...38 B5
Shuckburgh Crs
  RUGBYS/DCH CV22...................62 C4
Shulman's Wk *COVE* CV2.............24 C4
Shultern La *TLHL/CAN* CV4..........38 A3
Shuna Cft *COVE* CV2....................25 F4
Shuttle St *COVN* CV6...................24 A3
Shuttleworth Rd *RRUGBY* CV23....49 E4
Sibree Rd *COVS* CV3...................40 C5
Sibton Cl *COVE* CV2....................24 B2
Sidbury Rd *COVN* CV6..................22 D5
Siddeley Av *COVS* CV3.................31 H5
  KNWTH CV8............................64 D4
The Sidings *RUGBYN/HIL* CV21....48 A5
Sidmouth Cl *COVE* CV2................24 B4
Sidney Rd *RUGBYS/DCH* CV22.....62 C4
Silksby St *COVS* CV3...................39 G1
Silver Birch Av *BDWTH* CV12.........4 D3
Silver Birch Cl *COVS* CV3.............42 C2
Silverdale Cl *COVE* CV2...............14 A4
Silverstone Dr *COVN* CV6.............13 F3
Silver St *COV* CV1.........................2 D2
Silverton Rd *COVE* CV2...............23 G4
Silver Trees Dr *BDWTH* CV12........7 E1
Simon Stone St *COVN* CV6...........23 F3
Simpson Gv *COVS* CV3................40 D3
Sinclair Dr *COVN* CV6..................14 B2
Singer Cl *COVN* CV6....................23 H3

Sir Henry Parkes Rd
  TLHL/CAN CV4........................37 H2
Sir Thomas White's Rd
  COVW CV5..............................30 A4
Sir William Lyons Rd
  TLHL/CAN CV4........................37 H3
Sir Winston Churchill Pl
  COVS CV3...............................42 B2
Siskin Cl *RRUGBY* CV23..............48 B1
Siskin Dr *COVS* CV3....................54 D2
Siskin Pkwy East *COVS* CV3.........54 D3
Siskin Pkwy West *COVS* CV3........54 C3
Skipton Gdns *COVE* CV2..............24 A5
Skipworth Rd *COVS* CV3..............41 H1
Sky Blue Wy *COV* CV1...................3 J3
Slade Rd *RUGBYN/HIL* CV21........62 B2
Sleath's Yd *BDWTH* CV12.............5 G2
Sledmere Cl *COVE* CV2................14 A5
Sleets Yd *BDWTH* CV12.................5 F3
Smarts Rd *BDWTH* CV12...............5 E4
Smercote Cl *BDWTH* CV12.............4 C1
Smithford Wy *COV* CV1.................2 D3
Smiths Orch *RUGBYN/HIL* CV21...62 B1
Smith St *BDWTH* CV12.................4 D4
  COVN CV6...............................31 G1
Smiths Wd *BDWTH* CV12 *............5 G1
Smithy La *RRUGBY* CV23.............45 E4
Smorrall La *BDWTH* CV12..............4 A3
Snape Rd *COVE* CV2....................32 D1
Soden Cl *COVS* CV3.....................41 E3
Soden's Av *KNWTH* CV8...............55 H3
Solent Dr *COVE* CV2....................25 F2
Solihull Pkwy
  CHWD/FDBR/MGN B37.............8 C1
Somerly Cl *COVS* CV3..................41 C1
Somerset Rd *COV* CV1.................30 D1
Somers Rd *RCOVN/BALC/EX* CV7..72 A5
  RCOVN/BALC/EX CV7................17 C2
  RUGBYS/DCH CV22...................61 E2
Sommerville Rd *COVE* CV2...........32 B2
Soredale Cft *COVS* CV3................33 F5
Sorrel Cl *TLHL/CAN* CV4...............28 B5
Sorrel Dr *RRUGBY* CV23..............48 C1
Southam Cl *TLHL/CAN* CV4..........36 D2
Southam Rd *RUGBYS/DCH* CV22...69 C4
South Av *COVE* CV2.....................31 H4
Southbank Rd *COVN* CV6.............29 H1
  KNWTH CV8............................65 E2
Southbrook Rd
  RUGBYS/DCH CV22...................61 H3
South Car Park Rd
  BHAMNEC B40.........................8 D5
Southcott Wy *COVE* CV2..............25 E2
Southey Rd *RUGBYS/DCH* CV22...61 F5
Southfield Dr *KNWTH* CV8...........65 F1
Southfield Rd
  RUGBYS/DCH CV22...................62 B3
Southleigh Av *COVW* CV5............38 C3
Southport Cl *COVS* CV3...............40 C4
South Rdg *COVW* CV5..................29 E2
South Rd *RRUGBY* CV23..............49 E4
South St *COV* CV1..........................3 H4
  RUGBYN/HIL CV21...................48 C3
South View Rd *RRUGBY* CV23......46 A5
South Wy *BHAMNEC* B40...............8 B5
Sovereign Rd *COVW* CV5..............30 A4
Sovereign Rw *COVW* CV5.............30 B4
Sparkbrook St *COV* CV1.................3 H2
Sparta Cl *RUGBYN/HIL* CV21........47 H3
Speedway La *KNWTH* CV8............43 E2
Speedwell Cl *BDWTH* CV12............4 C3
  RRUGBY CV23.........................48 D2
Speedwell Dr
  RCOVN/BALC/EX CV7................34 B3
Spencer Av *COVW* CV5................30 B5
Spencer Rd *COVW* CV5..................2 B7
Spencer's La
  RCOVN/BALC/EX CV7................35 G1
Sphinx Dr *COVS* CV3...................32 A5
Spicer Pl *RUGBYS/DCH* CV22.......61 E3
Spindle St *COV* CV1....................23 E5
Spinney Cl *COVS* CV3..................42 D2
The Spinney *RRUGBY* CV23..........46 B4
  TLHL/CAN CV4........................52 B1
Spitfire Cl *COVW* CV5..................29 F5
Spon End *COV* CV1.......................30 B3
Spon St *COV* CV1..........................2 B3
Spottiswood Cl
  RUGBYS/DCH CV22...................60 B4
Spring Cl *COV* CV1........................3 H2
Springfield Crs *BDWTH* CV12.........5 C3
Springfield Pl *COV* CV1................31 E2
Springfield Rd *COV* CV1...............31 E2
Spring La *KNWTH* CV8..................65 F2
Spring Rd *COVN* CV6...................23 G3
  RCOVN/BALC/EX CV7................15 F2
Spring St *RUGBYN/HIL* CV21........62 B1
The Square *COVE* CV2 *...............25 F2
  RUGBYS/DCH CV22...................69 H4

Squires Cft *COVE* CV2..................25 E2
Squires Wy *TLHL/CAN* CV4...........38 A4
Stable Yd *KNWTH* CV8 *...............53 H2
Stadium Cl *COVN* CV6..................23 E1
Stafford Cl *BDWTH* CV12...............7 F3
Staircase La *COVW* CV5...............21 G3
Stamford Av *COVS* CV3................39 F3
Standard Av *TLHL/CAN* CV4.........28 D5
Standish Cl *COVE* CV2.................32 D4
Stanier Av *COV* CV1.....................30 B3
Stanley Rd *COVW* CV5.................38 C1
  RUGBYS/DCH CV22...................62 D3
Stansfield Gv *KNWTH* CV8...........66 A3
Stanway Rd *COVW* CV5...............38 D1
Staples Cl *BDWTH* CV12................7 F3
Starcross Cl *COVE* CV2................24 B4
Stare Gn *TLHL/CAN* CV4..............38 A4
Stareton Cl *TLHL/CAN* CV4..........38 B3
Starley Rd *COV* CV1......................2 B4
Starley Wy
  CHWD/FDBR/MGN B37.............8 A2
Startin Rd *RCOVN/BALC/EX* CV7...13 G1
Station Av *TLHL/CAN* CV4............36 C1
Station Link Rd
  CHWD/FDBR/MGN B37.............8 B4
Station Rd *HIA/OLT* B92...............16 B4
  KNWTH CV8............................65 E3
  RCOVN/BALC/EX CV7................34 D2
  RUGBY CV23..........................49 E3
Station Sq *COV* CV1......................2 C6
Station St East *COVN* CV6............23 C4
Station St West *COVN* CV6...........23 E3
Station Tower *COV* CV1 *...............2 C6
Staveley Wy *RUGBYN/HIL* CV21...48 C3
Staverton Cl *COVW* CV5...............28 D2
Staverton Leys
  RUGBYS/DCH CV22...................61 H5
Steele St *RUGBYS/DCH* CV22.......61 E1
Steeping Rd *RRUGBY* CV23..........46 C4
Steeplefield Rd *COVN* CV6 *.........30 A4
Stennels Cl *COVN* CV6.................22 A3
Stephenson Rd
  RCOVN/BALC/EX CV7................14 A1
Stephen St *RUGBYN/HIL* CV21.....61 G1
Stepney Rd *COVE* CV2.................31 H2
Stepping Stones Rd *COVW* CV5....30 A2
Stevenson Rd *COVN* CV6..............22 B3
Stewart Cl *TLHL/CAN* CV4............29 C4
Stirling Cl *COVS* CV3...................41 G1
Stivichall Cft *COVS* CV3...............39 E3
Stockley Rd *COVN* CV6.................14 A2
Stocks Ct *RUGBYS/DCH* CV22......61 G4
Stocks La *RRUGBY* CV23..............68 D4
The Stocks *RUGBYS/DCH* CV22 *..69 G4
Stockton Rd *COV* CV1..................31 F2
Stoke Gn *COVS* CV3....................31 H3
Stoke Park Ms *COVE* CV2 *...........31 H3
Stoke Rw *COVE* CV2....................31 H2
Stonebridge Hwy *COVS* CV3........39 F5
Stonebrook Wy *COVN* CV6...........13 C5
Stonebury Av *COVW* CV5.............28 B2
Stonefield Cl *COVE* CV2...............25 F3
Stonehall Rd *RUGBYS/DCH* CV22..60 B4
Stonehaven Dr *COVS* CV3............53 F1
Stonehills *RUGBYN/HIL* CV21.......48 B2
Stonehouse La *COVS* CV3............40 D5
Stone House La
  RCOVN/BALC/EX CV7................10 C2
Stoneleigh Av *COVW* CV5............38 C2
  KNWTH CV8............................65 F1
Stoneleigh Cl *KNWTH* CV8...........65 F1
Stoneleigh Rd *KNWTH* CV8..........65 F1
  TLHL/CAN CV4........................52 A2
Stone Meadow
  RCOVN/BALC/EX CV7................12 B2
Stoneton Crs
  RCOVN/BALC/EX CV7................34 B3
Stoney Ct *COVS* CV3...................41 H2
Stoney Rd *COV* CV1......................2 D7
Stoney Stanton Rd *COV* CV1..........2 E1
Stoneywood Rd *COVE* CV2...........25 F2
The Stoop *COVS* CV3...................33 G5
Stowe Pl *TLHL/CAN* CV4..............27 H5
Stradey Cl *COVS* CV3...................33 G5
Stratford St *COVE* CV2.................31 H2
Strath Cl *RUGBYN/HIL* CV21.........63 F5
Strathmore Av *COV* CV1.................3 C5
Strawberry Flds
  RCOVN/BALC/EX CV7................18 A2
Strawberry Wk *COVE* CV2............24 C1
Streamside Cl *COVW* CV5............20 D3
Stretton Av *COVS* CV3.................40 D4
Stretton Rd *RRUGBY* CV23...........57 F4
Stuart Ct *COVN* CV6....................23 H3
Stubbs Cl *BDWTH* CV12.................5 F1
Stubbs Gv *COVE* CV2...................32 A1
Studland Av *RUGBYN/HIL* CV21....63 E3
Studland Gn *COVE* CV2................33 F2
Sturley Cl *KNWTH* CV8.................65 G1

Sturminster Cl *COVE* CV2.............33
Styvechale Av *COVW* CV5............38
Suffolk Cl *BDWTH* CV12.................5
  COVW CV5..............................29
Sullivan Rd *COVN* CV6.................24
Sunbury Rd *COVS* CV3.................40
Suncliffe Dr *KNWTH* CV8..............65
Sundew St *COVE* CV2...................24
Sundorne Cl *COVS* CV3................28
Sunningdale Av *COVN* CV6...........23
  KNWTH CV8............................65
Sunnybank Av *COVS* CV3.............40
Sunnyside Cl *COVW* CV5..............30
  RCOVN/BALC/EX CV7................34
Sunnyside La
  RCOVN/BALC/EX CV7................34
Sunshine Cl *KNWTH* CV8..............65
Sun St *RUGBYN/HIL* CV21............62
Sunway Gv *COVS* CV3..................39
Sussex Rd *COVW* CV5..................30
Sutherland Av *COVW* CV5.............30
Sutherland Dr *BDWTH* CV12...........5
Sutton Av *COVW* CV5...................28
Sutton Stop *COVN* CV6.................14
Swallowdean Rd *COVN* CV6..........21
Swallow Rd *COVN* CV6..................22
Swanage Gn *COVE* CV2................33
Swancroft Rd *COVE* CV2..............31
Swan La *COVE* CV2........................3
Swanswell St *COV* CV1...................3
Swift Cl *KNWTH* CV8....................65
Swift Pk *RUGBYN/HIL* CV21.........47
Swift Rd *COV* CV1..........................2
Swift's Cnr *COVS* CV3..................39
Swillington Rd *COVN* CV6.............30
Swinburne Av *COVE* CV2...............32
Swindale Cft *COVS* CV3................33
Sycamore Gv *RUGBYN/HIL* CV21..47
Sycamore Rd *COVE* CV2...............24
The Sycamores *BDWTH* CV12.........4
Sydnall Flds *COVN* CV6................13
Sydnall Rd *COVN* CV6...................13
Sylvan Dr *COVS* CV3....................38
Synkere Cl *RCOVN/BALC/EX* CV7..12
Sywell Leys *RUGBYS/DCH* CV22...70

T

Tachbrook Cl *COVE* CV2................24
Tackford Rd *COVN* CV6.................23
Tainters Hl *KNWTH* CV8................65
Talisman Cl *KNWTH* CV8...............65
Talland Av *COVN* CV6...................23
Tallants Cl *COVN* CV6...................23
Tallants Rd *COVN* CV6..................23
Tamar Cl *RRUGBY* CV23...............46
Tamar Rd *BDWTH* CV12..................6
Tamworth Rd
  RCOVN/BALC/EX CV7................11
Tanners Gv *COVN* CV6..................13
Tanners' La
  RCOVN/BALC/EX CV7................27
Tanyard Cl *TLHL/CAN* CV4............27
Tapcon Wy *COVE* CV2...................33
Tappinger Gv *KNWTH* CV8............65
Tarlington Rd *COVN* CV6...............21
Tarn Cl *BDWTH* CV12......................5
Tarquin Cl *COVS* CV3....................41
Tarragon Cl *COVE* CV2.................24
Tarrant Wk *COVE* CV2..................33
Taunton Wy *COVN* CV6.................22
Tavistock Wk *COVE* CV2...............24
Taylor Cl *KNWTH* CV8...................65
Tay Rd *COVN* CV6........................22
Teachers Cl *COVN* CV6.................30
The Tea Gdn *BDWTH* CV12.............4
Teasel Cl *RRUGBY* CV23...............48
Ted Pitts La *COVW* CV5................21
Tee Tong Rd *RUGBY* CV23............46
Telephone Rd *COVS* CV3...............32
Telfer Rd *COVN* CV6......................22
Telford Rd *RCOVN/BALC/EX* CV7....5
Templar Av *TLHL/CAN* CV4...........37
Templars' Flds *TLHL/CAN* CV4.......37
Temple Av *RCOVN/BALC/EX* CV7...27
Temple St *RUGBYS/DCH* CV22......62
Tenby Cl *BDWTH* CV12...................5
Teneriffe Rd *COVN* CV6................23
Tennant Cl *RUGBYS/DCH* CV22.....62
Tennyson Av *RUGBYS/DCH* CV22..61
Tennyson Cl *KNWTH* CV8..............65
Tennyson Rd *COVE* CV2...............32
Ten Shilling Dr *TLHL/CAN* CV4......36
Terracotta Dr *COVE* CV2 *............31
Terry Rd *COV* CV1..........................3
Tewkesbury Dr *BDWTH* CV12.........5
Thackeray Cl *RUGBYS/DCH* CV22..61

ckhall St *COVE* CV2 3 J1
mes Cl *BDWTH* CV12 6 D2
mley Rd *COVN* CV6 30 B2
Thatchings
UGBYS/DCH CV22 * 69 H4
bes Cl *COVW* CV5 19 G3
ddingworth Cl *COVS* CV3 41 F1
na Gdns *COVN* CV6 23 H2
:kthorn Cl *KNWTH* CV8 65 G4
nbler Rd *TLHL/CAN* CV4 37 H2
'd Exhibition Av
HAMNEC B40 8 B3
'lestane Cl *KNWTH* CV8 65 H1
'lmere *RUGBYN/HIL* CV21 48 B2
'lmere Cl *TLHL/CAN* CV4 28 B3
'lmere Rd *BDWTH* CV12 5 F3
'sk Rd *COVS* CV3 39 F4
stle Wy *RRUGBY* CV23 48 C1
stley Fld East *COVN* CV6 22 A5
stley Fld North *COVN* CV6 22 B4
stley Fld South *COVN* CV6 22 A5
stley Fld West *COVN* CV6 22 A5
mas Landsdail St *COVS* CV3 2 E7
mas Lane St *COVN* CV6 23 H2
mas Naul Cft *TLHL/CAN* CV4 28 C3
mas Sharp St *TLHL/CAN* CV4 37 F2
mas St *BDWTH* CV12 5 F3
OV CV1 * 2 A4
mas Wy *RRUGBY* CV23 46 B4
mpsons La
COVN/BALC/EX CV7 11 H2
mpsons Rd
COVN/BALC/EX CV7 11 H2
mson Cl *RUGBYN/HIL* CV21 48 A3
rnby Av *KNWTH* CV8 65 F4
rn Cl *RUGBYN/HIL* CV21 48 B3
rney Rd *COVE* CV2 24 A5
rnhill Ct *COV* CV1 * 31 E1
rnhill Rd *COV* CV1 31 E1
rnton Cl *COVW* CV5 27 H2
rnton Ct *TLHL/CAN* CV4 29 E4
eadneedle St *COV* CV1 22 D5
ee Spires Av *COVN* CV6 30 B1
uppence Cl *TLHL/CAN* CV4 36 D3
rlaston Dr *RUGBYS/DCH* CV22 69 E1
rlestone Rd *COVN* CV6 22 A3
rnmill Rd *RRUGBY* CV23 46 D4
er Cl *COVW* CV5 28 C2
er Wy *RUGBYN/HIL* CV21 47 G2
eswell Cl *COVS* CV3 33 F5
marsh Cl *RCOVN/BALC/EX* CV7 34 B3
Hill La *TLHL/CAN* CV4 28 B5
Hurst Dr *TLHL/CAN* CV4 28 A4
hurst Dr *TLHL/CAN* CV4 28 A4
wood Av *COVW* CV5 28 B2
ber Ct *RUGBYS/DCH* CV22 62 B3
othy Gv *TLHL/CAN* CV4 29 E5
cagel Gv *KNWTH* CV8 65 G3
tern Wy *BDWTH* CV12 5 H3
'ale Ri *KNWTH* CV8 65 G1
rton Gv *COVE* CV2 32 C1
rton Rd *COVE* CV2 32 C1
eycourt Rd *COVN* CV6 13 H5
il Cft *TLHL/CAN* CV4 38 A5
do Cl *COVW* CV5 29 F5
ard Cl *COVE* CV2 33 E1
Brown St
UGBYN/HIL CV21 62 B1
Henderson Cl *COVS* CV3 41 G2
son Av *COVN* CV6 30 B2
Ward Cl *COVS* CV3 41 E2
bridge Rd *COVS* CV3 40 B3
o's Dr *BDWTH* CV12 4 D4
o's Heath *BDWTH* CV12 4 D4
Rd *RCOVN/BALC/EX* CV7 15 G2
bay Rd *COVW* CV5 29 F2
castle Cl *COVN* CV6 23 G4
cross Av *COVE* CV2 32 B1
point Cl *COVE* CV2 24 B4
rance Rd *RUGBYN/HIL* CV21 61 G1
rington Av *TLHL/CAN* CV4 37 E1
wood Cl *TLHL/CAN* CV4 37 E3
nes Cl *COVE* CV2 24 B4
e Ct *RRUGBY* CV23 46 C4
er Rd *BDWTH* CV12 5 F3
UGBYS/DCH CV22 62 B3
ver St *COV* CV1 2 D2
n Feilds Cl *COVW* CV5 21 E4
nsend Cft *COVS* CV3 39 F2
nsend La *RRUGBY* CV23 46 C5
nsend Rd
UGBYN/HIL CV21 62 C1
path Cl *COVN* CV6 14 A2
mor Cl *COVN* CV6 23 G2
lington Rd *COVW* CV5 28 C2
dale Cl *TLHL/CAN* CV4 36 C1
orest Rd *COVS* CV3 40 D1
orrick Rd
COVN/BALC/EX CV7 13 H1

Tregullan Rd
RCOVN/BALC/EX CV7 5 G5
Treherne Rd *COVN* CV6 22 C3
Trelawney Rd
RCOVN/BALC/EX CV7 13 H1
Trenance Rd
RCOVN/BALC/EX CV7 13 H1
Treneere Rd
RCOVN/BALC/EX CV7 5 F5
Trensale Av *COVN* CV6 30 A2
Trentham Gdns *KNWTH* CV8 65 H2
Trentham Rd *COV* CV1 31 G2
Trent Rd *BDWTH* CV12 6 D3
Tresillian Rd *RCOVN/BALC/EX* CV7 5 G5
Treviscoe Cl
RCOVN/BALC/EX CV7 13 H1
Trevor Cl *TLHL/CAN* CV4 36 C1
Trevor White Dr
RUGBYS/DCH CV22 62 A3
Trevose Av *RCOVN/BALC/EX* CV7 14 A1
The Triangle *COVW* CV5 29 E2
Trident Rd
LGN/SDN/BHAMAIR B26 8 A4
Trimpley Dr *COVN* CV6 22 D5
Trinity La *COV* CV1 2 D3
Trinity Pk *HIA/OLT* B92 * 8 B5
Trinity St *COV* CV1 2 E3
Triumph Cl *COVE* CV2 32 D3
Trossachs Rd *COVW* CV5 28 C3
Troughton Crs *COVN* CV6 30 B1
Troutbeck Rd *COVW* CV5 28 C2
Troyes Cl *COVS* CV3 39 G2
Truggist La
RCOVN/BALC/EX CV7 35 E1
Trussell Wy *RUGBYS/DCH* CV22 60 A4
Tudor Av *COVW* CV5 28 C3
Tulip Tree Av *KNWTH* CV8 65 G2
Tulliver Cl *BDWTH* CV12 5 G1
Tulliver St *COVN* CV6 30 C1
Turchil Rd *RUGBYS/DCH* CV22 60 B4
Turlands Cl *COVE* CV2 25 F4
Turner Cl *BDWTH* CV12 5 F1
RUGBYN/HIL CV21 63 G4
Turner Rd *COVW* CV5 29 G3
Turnpike Cl
RCOVN/BALC/EX CV7 34 C2
Turton Wy *KNWTH* CV8 65 H3
Tutbury Av *TLHL/CAN* CV4 38 B4
Twickenham Wy *COVS* CV3 33 G5
Tybalt Cl *COVS* CV3 40 D4
Tylney Cl *COVS* CV3 33 G4
Tynemouth Cl *COVE* CV2 14 C3
Tynward Cl *COVS* CV3 39 E4
Tysoe Cft *COVS* CV3 41 G1

U

Ufton Cft *COVW* CV5 28 D3
Ullswater Rd *BDWTH* CV12 5 F3
COVS CV3 32 D5
Ulverscroft Rd *COVS* CV3 39 F2
Ulverston *RUGBYN/HIL* CV21 48 C2
The Underpass *BHAMNEC* B40 8 C4
Unicorn Av *COVW* CV5 28 B2
Unicorn La *COVW* CV5 28 D2
Union Pl *COVN* CV6 13 G4
Union St *RUGBYS/DCH* CV22 61 H2
University Rd *TLHL/CAN* CV4 37 G5
Uplands *COVE* CV2 31 H1
Upper Eastern Green La
COVW CV5 27 H1
Upperfield Wy *COVS* CV3 33 F5
Upper Hill St *COV* CV1 2 B2
Upper Ladyes Hills *KNWTH* CV8 65 F1
Upper Pk *COVS* CV3 41 E4
Upper Prec *COV* CV1 2 D3
Upper Ride *COVS* CV3 41 E4
Upper Rosemary Hl
KNWTH CV8 65 E2
Upper Spon St *COV* CV1 30 B4
Upper Spring La *KNWTH* CV8 51 E5
Upper Well St *COV* CV1 2 C2
Upper York St *COV* CV1 2 A5
Upton Rd *RUGBYS/DCH* CV22 61 E1
Utrillo Cl *COVW* CV5 29 F3
Uxbridge Av *COVS* CV3 32 B4

V

Vale Cl *RUGBYN/HIL* CV21 63 F4
Valencia Rd *COVS* CV3 33 F4
The Vale *COVS* CV3 40 C1
Valley Rd *COVE* CV2 23 H5
Van Dyke Cl *COVW* CV5 29 F3
Vanguard Av *COVW* CV5 29 F5
Vanguard Rd
LGN/SDN/BHAMAIR B26 8 A4
Vardon Dr *COVS* CV3 39 G5
Vauxhall Av *TLHL/CAN* CV4 29 F5
Vauxhall Cl *COV* CV1 3 H2
Vauxhall St *COV* CV1 3 H2
Vecqueray St *COV* CV1 3 H4
Ventnor Cl *COVE* CV2 32 D3
Vere Rd *RUGBYN/HIL* CV21 63 E3
Vernon Av *RUGBYS/DCH* CV22 62 D4
Vernon Cl *COV* CV1 3 H2
Viaduct Cl *RUGBYN/HIL* CV21 48 C5
Vicarage Gdns *KNWTH* CV8 * 65 F5
Vicarage Hl *RUGBYN/HIL* CV21 48 D5
Vicarage La
RCOVN/BALC/EX CV7 13 E1
RUGBYS/DCH CV22 69 H4
Vicarage Rd *KNWTH* CV8 67 E1
RUGBYS/DCH CV22 61 G2
Victoria Av *RUGBYN/HIL* CV21 61 G1
Victoria Ct *COVW* CV5 * 29 G2
Victoria St *COV* CV1 3 F1
RUGBYN/HIL CV21 61 F1
Victory Rd *COVN* CV6 23 F3
Villa Cl *BDWTH* CV12 7 E4
Villa Crs *BDWTH* CV12 7 E4
Villa Rd *COVN* CV6 22 C5
Villiers Rd *KNWTH* CV8 65 G2
Villiers St *COVE* CV2 3 K2
Vincent St *COV* CV1 2 A4
Vinecote Rd *COVN* CV6 13 G4
Vine St *COV* CV1 3 F2
Violet Cl *BDWTH* CV12 4 D3
COVE CV2 24 B1
RRUGBY CV23 48 D1
Virginia Rd *COV* CV1 3 G2
Vogue Cl *COV* CV1 3 G2

W

Wade Av *COVS* CV3 39 E4
Wainbody Av North *COVS* CV3 38 D4
Wainbody Av South *COVS* CV3 38 C5
Wakefield Cl *COVS* CV3 41 G2
Walford Pl *RUGBYS/DCH* CV22 63 E4
Walkers Orch *KNWTH* CV8 67 E1
Walkers Wy *BDWTH* CV12 5 E4
KNWTH CV8 65 E5
Wallace Rd *COVN* CV6 22 B3
Wall Hill Rd
RCOVN/BALC/EX CV7 10 D4
Walnut St *COVE* CV2 24 A1
Walnut Tree Cl *KNWTH* CV8 65 F4
Walnut Wy *RUGBYS/DCH* CV22 60 C3
Walsall St *TLHL/CAN* CV4 37 F2
Walsgrave Gdns *COVE* CV2 25 F4
Walsgrave Rd *COVE* CV2 31 H3
Walsh La *RCOVN/BALC/EX* CV7 18 D1
Walter Scott Rd *BDWTH* CV12 5 H4
Walton Cl *COVS* CV3 41 F2
Wanley Rd *COVS* CV3 39 G3
Wansfell Cl *TLHL/CAN* CV4 37 F2
Wappenbury Cl *COVE* CV2 24 B1
Wappenbury Rd *COVE* CV2 24 C2
Warden Rd *COVN* CV6 22 C5
The Wardens Av *COVW* CV5 21 E5
The Wardens *KNWTH* CV8 65 H2
Wareham Gn *COVE* CV2 33 F1
Waring Wy *RUGBYS/DCH* CV22 69 H3
Warmington Cl *COVS* CV3 41 F1
Warmwell Cl *COVE* CV2 33 E2
Warner Rw *COVN* CV6 23 G4
Warren Cl *KNWTH* CV8 55 H3
Warren Fld *KNWTH* CV8 55 H3
Warren Gn *TLHL/CAN* CV4 37 E1
Warren Rd *RUGBYS/DCH* CV22 62 C3
Warton Cl *KNWTH* CV8 65 H3
Warwick Av *COVW* CV5 38 D2
Warwick La *COV* CV1 2 D4
Warwick Rd *COVS* CV3 2 C6
KNWTH CV8 57 F1
KNWTH CV8 65 E4
Warwick Rw *COV* CV1 2 C5
Warwick St *COVW* CV5 38 C1
RUGBYS/DCH CV22 61 H2
Washbrook La *COVW* CV5 20 D2
Wasperton Cl *COVS* CV3 41 G1
Waste La *COVN* CV6 21 H2
RCOVN/BALC/EX CV7 35 F4
Watch Cl *COV* CV1 2 B3
Watcombe Rd *COVE* CV2 24 D3
Watercall Av *COVS* CV3 39 F4
Waterfall Cl
RCOVN/BALC/EX CV7 18 B2
Waterford Wy *COVS* CV3 32 B5
Waterloo St *COV* CV1 3 H1
Waterman Rd *COVN* CV6 31 G1
Waterside *COV* CV1 2 D1
COVN CV6 14 B2
Waterside Dr *RUGBYN/HIL* CV21 48 B3
Watersmeet Gv *COVE* CV2 24 A5
Watersmeet Rd *COVE* CV2 24 A5
Water Tower La *KNWTH* CV8 65 E1
Watery La *RCOVN/BALC/EX* CV7 10 A3
RCOVN/BALC/EX CV7 12 B4
Watling Rd *KNWTH* CV8 65 G1
Watson Rd *COVW* CV5 29 G4
Watson Wy
RCOVN/BALC/EX CV7 * 34 D2
Watts La *RUGBYN/HIL* CV21 63 G4
Wavebeck Ct *RRUGBY* CV23 46 C4
Waveley Rd *COV* CV1 30 B3
Wavendon Cl *COVE* CV2 25 E2
Waverley Rd *KNWTH* CV8 65 F4
RUGBYN/HIL CV21 63 F3
Weaver Dr *RRUGBY* CV23 46 D5
Weavers Wk *COVN* CV6 24 A3
Webb Dr *RRUGBY* CV23 48 C1
Webb Ellis Rd
RUGBYS/DCH CV22 61 F2
Webster Av *KNWTH* CV8 65 G1
Webster Steet *COVN* CV6 23 F4
Wedgewood Cl *COVE* CV2 24 D3
Wedon Cl *TLHL/CAN* CV4 36 D2
Welby Ga *RCOVN/BALC/EX* CV7 34 B3
Welford Pl *COVN* CV6 23 E4
Welford Rd *RUGBYN/HIL* CV21 48 B5
Welgarth Av *COVN* CV6 21 H5
Welland Cl *RRUGBY* CV23 46 C4
Welland Rd *COV* CV1 3 J6
Wellesbourne Rd *COVW* CV5 28 D3
Wellfield Cl
RCOVN/BALC/EX CV7 35 E4
Wellington Gdns *COV* CV1 * 30 B4
Wellington St *COV* CV1 3 G1
Wells St *RUGBYN/HIL* CV21 62 A1
Well St *COV* CV1 2 D2
Welsh Rd *COVE* CV2 32 A2
Welton Pl *RUGBYS/DCH* CV22 62 C4
Wendiburgh St *TLHL/CAN* CV4 37 F2
Wendover Ri *COVW* CV5 29 F2
Wentworth Dr *COVN* CV6 12 C4
Wentworth Rd
RUGBYS/DCH CV22 61 G3
Wesley Rd *RUGBYN/HIL* CV21 63 F4
Wessex Cl *BDWTH* CV12 5 F1
West Av *BDWTH* CV12 6 A3
COVE CV2 31 H4
COVN CV6 12 B3
Westbourne Gv
RUGBYS/DCH CV22 61 G3
Westbury Ms *COVE* CV2 * 31 H3
Westbury Rd *COVW* CV5 29 G1
Westcliffe Dr *COVS* CV3 39 E4
Westcotes *TLHL/CAN* CV4 29 E5
Westfield Rd *RUGBYS/DCH* CV22 61 G2
Westgate Rd *RUGBYN/HIL* CV21 62 D3
Westhill Rd *COVN* CV6 22 A5
Westleigh Av *COVW* CV5 38 C2
West Leyes *RUGBYN/HIL* CV21 61 G1
Westminster Rd *COV* CV1 2 B6
Westmorland Rd *COVE* CV2 33 E2
Westonbirt Cl *KNWTH* CV8 65 H1
Weston Cl *RUGBYS/DCH* CV22 69 G3
Weston La *BDWTH* CV12 7 E2
Weston St *COV* CV1 3 F1
West Rdg *COVW* CV5 28 D1
West St *COV* CV1 3 H3
RRUGBY CV23 46 B5
West View Rd
RUGBYS/DCH CV22 61 E2
Westwood Heath Rd
TLHL/CAN CV4 36 B3
Westwood Rd *COVW* CV5 30 B5
RUGBYS/DCH CV22 63 E5
Westwood Wy *TLHL/CAN* CV4 36 D3
Wetherell Wy *RUGBYN/HIL* CV21 48 B2
Wexford Rd *COVE* CV2 24 C2
Whaley's Cft *COVN* CV6 22 B3
Wharf Rd *COVN* CV6 31 G1
Whateley's Dr *KNWTH* CV8 65 F3
Wheate Cft *TLHL/CAN* CV4 28 C4
Wheatfield Rd
RUGBYS/DCH CV22 60 D3
Wheelwright La *COVN* CV6 12 D4
Wheler Rd *COVS* CV3 40 B1
Whernside *RUGBYN/HIL* CV21 48 B2
Whetstone Dr
RUGBYN/HIL CV21 48 D2
Whichcote Av
RCOVN/BALC/EX CV7 18 B2
Whiley Cl *RRUGBY* CV23 49 E4
Whimbrel Cl *RRUGBY* CV23 48 B1
Whitaker Rd *COVW* CV5 29 F2
Whitburn Rd *BDWTH* CV12 4 B4
Whitchurch Wy *TLHL/CAN* CV4 37 E2

Whitebeam Cl *TLHL/CAN* CV4......28 A5
Whitefield Cl *TLHL/CAN* CV4......36 C3
Whitefriars Dr
  RUGBYS/DCH CV22..................60 B3
White Friars La *COV* CV1.................3 F5
White Friars St *COV* CV1.................3 F4
Whitehall Rd *RUGBYN/HIL* CV21...62 A2
Whitehead Dr *KNWTH* CV8.......65 H1
Whitehead Gv
  RCOVN/BALC/EX CV7............34 C2
Whitehorse Cl *COVN* CV6...........14 A2
Whitelaw Crs *COVW* CV5.............21 E5
Whitemoor Rd *KNWTH* CV8........65 F3
Whiteside Cl *COVS* CV3..............41 G1
Whites Rw *KNWTH* CV8..............65 F5
Whitestitch La
  RCOVN/BALC/EX CV7............18 A1
White St *COV* CV1..........................3 F2
Whitley Village *COVS* CV3...........40 A2
Whitmore Park Rd *COVN* CV6....12 D5
Whitnash Cl
  RCOVN/BALC/EX CV7............34 B3
Whitnash Gv *COVE* CV2...............32 C1
Whittle Cl *COVS* CV3...................41 G1
  RUGBYS/DCH CV22...................61 E5
Whitworth Av *COVS* CV3..............32 A5
Whoberley Av *COVW* CV5.............29 G3
Whoberley Ct *COVW* CV5 *.........29 F3
Wickham Cl *COVN* CV6................22 A1
Wickmans Dr *TLHL/CAN* CV4......27 H4
Widdecombe Cl *COVE* CV2..........24 C3
Widdrington Rd *COV* CV1............30 D1
Wiggins Cl *RUGBYN/HIL* CV21...63 G5
Wigston Rd *COV* CV2...................25 F3
  RUGBYN/HIL CV21...................63 F3
Wildcroft Rd *COVW* CV5..............29 F4
Wildey Rd *BDWTH* CV12................4 C3
Wildmoor Cl *COVE* CV2...............14 A4
Willenhall La *COVS* CV3...............41 G2
William Arnold Cl *COVE* CV2......31 H2
William Bree Rd *COVW* CV5.........27 H1
William Bristow Rd *COVS* CV3....39 H2
William Cree Cl *KNWTH* CV8......57 E1
William Groubb Cl *COVS* CV3......41 F2
William Kirby Cl *TLHL/CAN* CV4...28 D5
William McCool Cl *COVS* CV3......41 G2
William McKee Cl *COVS* CV3.......41 F2
William St *BDWTH* CV12................6 A2
  RUGBYN/HIL CV21...................62 A1
Willis Gv *BDWTH* CV12..................5 H2
Willoughby Av *KNWTH* CV8.......64 D4
Willoughby Cl *COVS* CV3.............41 F1
Willoughby Pl
  RUGBYS/DCH CV22..................62 C4

Willow Brook Rd *KNWTH* CV8......43 F5
Willow Ctyd *COVE* CV2.................24 C4
Willow Gv *TLHL/CAN* CV4.............29 F4
Willowherb Cl *COVS* CV3.............41 G1
Willow La *RUGBYS/DCH* CV22....62 B2
Willow Meer *KNWTH* CV8.............65 G2
The Willows *BDWTH* CV12..............4 D3
Wilmcote Gn *COVW* CV5..............28 D3
Wilmot Cl *RCOVN/BALC/EX* CV7...34 C1
Wilson Cl *RUGBYS/DCH* CV22.....60 D2
Wilson Gn *COVS* CV3...................33 E5
Wilson Gv *KNWTH* CV8...............65 H3
Wilson's La *COVN* CV6.................13 G3
Wilton Rd *RCOVN/BALC/EX* CV7...34 C3
Wiltshire Cl *BDWTH* CV12..............5 F2
  COVW CV5............................29 E3
Wimborne Dr *COVE* CV2..............33 E2
Winceby Pl *TLHL/CAN* CV4...........28 A5
Winchat Cl *COVS* CV3..................33 E5
Winchester St *COV* CV1.................3 G2
Windermere Av *COVS* CV3............32 D5
  COVW CV5............................28 B2
Windermere Cl
  RUGBYN/HIL CV21...................48 B2
Winding House La *COVN* CV6......12 D3
Windmill Cl *KNWTH* CV8..............65 F1
The Windmill Hl *COVW* CV5.........20 D4
Windmill La
  RCOVN/BALC/EX CV7............10 A2
  RCOVN/BALC/EX CV7............35 E5
  RUGBYS/DCH CV22..................69 E3
Windmill Pk
  RCOVN/BALC/EX CV7 *.........35 E5
Windmill Rd *COVN* CV6...............13 H5
Windridge Cl *COVS* CV3..............40 D3
Windrush Wy *RRUGBY* CV23......46 C4
Windsor Ct *TLHL/CAN* CV4...........29 E4
Windsor St *COV* CV1.......................2 A4
  RUGBYN/HIL CV21...................62 B1
Windy Arbour *KNWTH* CV8..........65 G4
Winfield St *RUGBYN/HIL* CV21....62 C1
Wingfield Wy *COVN* CV6..............22 B1
Wingrave Cl *COVW* CV5...............20 D5
Winifred Av *COVW* CV5................30 B5
Winnallthorpe *COVS* CV3............41 F3
Winsford Av *COVW* CV5...............29 F2
Winsford Cl
  RCOVN/BALC/EX CV7............34 B3
Winsham Wk *COVS* CV3...............53 F1
Winspear Cl
  RCOVN/BALC/EX CV7............18 A2
Winster Cl *RCOVN/BALC/EX* CV7...12 B1
Winston Av *COVE* CV2.................24 C2
Winston Cl *COVE* CV2 *...............24 C3

Winterton Rd *BDWTH* CV12...........7 F4
Winwick Pl *RUGBYS/DCH* CV22...60 D2
Wise Gv *RUGBYN/HIL* CV21.........63 E2
Wisley Gv *KNWTH* CV8................65 H2
Withybrook Cl *COVE* CV2.............24 C1
Withybrook Rd *BDWTH* CV12........7 H3
Witnell Rd *COVN* CV6..................22 D5
Wolfe Rd *TLHL/CAN* CV4.............37 E2
Wolsey Rd *RUGBYS/DCH* CV22...69 H2
Wolston Ct *RUGBYS/DCH* CV22...60 C5
Wolston La *KNWTH* CV8..............56 B3
Wolston Wy *COVS* CV3................40 D3
Wolverton Rd *COVW* CV5............28 D3
Wolvey Rd *BDWTH* CV12................7 H3
Woodburn Cl *COVW* CV5.............29 E2
Woodclose Av *COVN* CV6.............22 A5
Woodcote Av *KNWTH* CV8...........64 C1
Woodcraft Cl *TLHL/CAN* CV4......28 C4
Woodend Cft *TLHL/CAN* CV4......28 B5
Woodfield Rd *COVW* CV5.............38 B1
Woodford Cl
  RCOVN/BALC/EX CV7............13 E3
Woodhams Rd *COVS* CV3.............54 D1
Wood Hill Ri *COVN* CV6...............22 C2
Woodhouse Cl *COVS* CV3............41 F1
Woodland Av *COVW* CV5..............38 C2
Woodland Rd *KNWTH* CV8...........51 G5
Woodlands Ct *COVW* CV5 *.........38 D1
Woodlands La *BDWTH* CV12...........4 D1
Woodlands Rd *BDWTH* CV12..........4 D2
  COVS CV3..............................42 C2
Woodleigh Rd *TLHL/CAN* CV4......37 E4
Woodmill Meadow *KNWTH* CV8...65 F1
Woodridge Av *COVW* CV5............20 C5
Woodroffe Wk *COVN* CV6............13 H4
Woodshires Rd *COVN* CV6...........13 G3
Woodsia Cl *RRUGBY* CV23...........48 C1
Woodside Av North *COVS* CV3....38 D3
Woodside Av South *COVS* CV3....38 C4
Woodside Pk
  RUGBYN/HIL CV21...................47 H4
Woods Piece
  RCOVN/BALC/EX CV7............12 A2
Woodstock Rd *COVS* CV3.............39 G2
Wood St *BDWTH* CV12....................5 F1
  RUGBYN/HIL CV21...................47 H4
Woodway Cl *COVE* CV2...............24 D3
Woodway La *COVE* CV2...............25 E4
Woodway Wk *COVE* CV2..............24 D5
Woolgrove St *COVN* CV6.............13 H5
Wootton St *BDWTH* CV12..............5 H2
Worcester Cl *COVW* CV5..............21 E4
Worcester Rd *KNWTH* CV8.........65 G4
Worcester St *RUGBYN/HIL* CV21...47 H5

Wordsworth Dr *KNWTH* CV8........65
Wordsworth Rd *BDWTH* CV12........6
  COVE CV2.............................32
  RUGBYS/DCH CV22..................70
Worsdell Cl *COV* CV1......................2
Worsfold Cl *COVW* CV5................20
Wortley Cl *RUGBYS/DCH* CV22...60
Wrenbury Dr *COVN* CV6...............13
Wren St *COVE* CV2...........................3
Wright St *COV* CV1........................31
Wrigsham St *COVS* CV3...................2
Wroxall Dr *COVS* CV3....................40
Wyatt Ct *BDWTH* CV12 *................5
Wych-Elm Cl *RUGBYS/DCH* CV22...60
Wychwood Av *COVS* CV3..............39
Wycliffe Gv *COVE* CV2..................32
Wycliffe Rd West *COVE* CV2.........32
Wye Cl *BDWTH* CV12.......................7
Wykeley Rd *COVE* CV2..................32
Wyken Av *COVE* CV2.....................32
Wyken Cft *COVE* CV2....................32
Wyken Grange Rd *COVE* CV2.......32
Wyken Wy *COVE* CV2....................31
Wyke Rd *COVE* CV2.......................32
Wyld Ct *COVW* CV5.......................29
Wyley Rd *COVN* CV6......................30
Wyncote Cl *KNWTH* CV8...............65
Wynter Rd *RUGBYS/DCH* CV22....61
Wythburn Wy
  RUGBYN/HIL CV21...................48
Wyver Crs *COVE* CV2....................32

Y

Yardley St *COV* CV1..........................3
Yarmouth Gn *TLHL/CAN* CV4........36
Yarningale Rd *COVS* CV3..............40
Yarrow Cl *RRUGBY* CV23 *...........48
Yates Av *RUGBYN/HIL* CV21.........47
Yelverton Rd *COVN* CV6................22
Yew Cl *COVS* CV3...........................40
Yewdale Crs *COVE* CV2.................24
The Yews *BDWTH* CV12...................4
York Av *BDWTH* CV12......................6
York Cl *COVS* CV3.........................40
York St *COV* CV1..............................2
  RUGBYN/HIL CV21...................61
Yule Rd *COVE* CV2........................32

Index - featured places

Abbey Clinic
  COVW CV5............................30 B5
Abbey Fields Swimming Pool
  KNWTH CV8.............................64 D2
Abbey Industrial Estate
  COVE CV2.............................25 E5
  COVE CV2.............................32 D1
Abbots Farm Infant School
  RUGBYN/HIL CV21...................62 D2
Abbots Farm Junior School
  RUGBYN/HIL CV21...................63 E2
Abbotsford School
  KNWTH CV8.............................65 E1
Albion Industrial Estate
  COVN CV6.............................23 E4
Alderman Callow School
  TLHL/CAN CV4.......................37 F3
Alderman Green
  Primary School *COVE* CV2...14 B5
Aldermans Green
  Industrial Estate
  COVE CV2.............................24 D1
Aldermoor Farm
  Primary School
  COVS CV3.............................40 C1
Aldermoor Lane
  Welfare Clinic
  COVS CV3.............................31 H5
Alice Stevens Special School
  COVS CV3.............................40 B4
Allesley Hall Primary School
  COVW CV5............................29 E2
Allesley Hotel
  COVW CV5............................21 E5
Allesley Park Medical Centre
  COVW CV5............................29 F2
Allesley Primary School
  COVW CV5............................20 D4

All Saints CE Infant School
  BDWTH CV12............................5 H3
All Saints Cemetery
  COVW CV5............................21 F5
All Saints CE Primary School
  COV CV1.................................3 H6
All Souls RC Primary School
  COVW CV5............................29 H4
Alpha Business Park
  COVE CV2.............................24 C2
Alvis Retail Park
  COVW CV5............................30 B2
Annie Osborn
  Primary School
  COVE CV2.............................24 C4
Arches Business Centre
  RUGBYN/HIL CV21...................48 B4
Arches Industrial Estate
  COVW CV5............................30 B3
  RUGBYN/HIL CV21...................48 B4
Arden Forest Infant School
  BDWTH CV12............................6 D2
The Arena
  COV CV1.................................2 B4
Arts Centre Cinema
  TLHL/CAN CV4.......................37 G5
Ash Green School
  RCOVN/BALC/EX CV7............13 E2
Ashlawn School
  RUGBYS/DCH CV22..................62 D5
Aston Industrial Estate
  BDWTH CV12............................6 A3
AT7 Sports Centre
  COVN CV6.............................23 H4
Avon Industrial Estate
  RUGBYN/HIL CV21...................48 B4
Avon Valley School
  RUGBYN/HIL CV21...................47 F3

Bablake Junior School
  COV CV1.................................2 B1
Bablake School
  COVN CV6.............................2 A1
Baginton Fields Special School
  COVS CV3.............................40 C5
Balsall Common Health Clinic
  RCOVN/BALC/EX CV7............34 C2
Balsall Common Primary School
  RCOVN/BALC/EX CV7............34 C4
Barkers Butts RFC
  COVW CV5............................19 H3
Barrs Hill School &
  Community College
  COVN CV6.............................30 C2
Bawnmore County
  Infant School
  RUGBYS/DCH CV22..................61 F5
Bayton Road Industrial Estate
  RCOVN/BALC/EX CV7............14 A1
Bede Shopping Arcade
  BDWTH CV12............................5 G2
Bedworth Cemetery
  BDWTH CV12............................5 H1
Bedworth Health Centre
  BDWTH CV12............................5 G3
Bedworth Leisure Centre
  BDWTH CV12............................5 G3
Bedworth RFC
  BDWTH CV12............................5 E4
Belgrade Theatre
  COV CV1.................................2 C3
Bell Green Health Centre
  COVE CV2.............................24 B2
Berkswell CE Primary School
  RCOVN/BALC/EX CV7............26 B3
Berkswell Windmill
  RCOVN/BALC/EX CV7............35 E5

Best Western
  Weston Hall Hotel
  BDWTH CV12............................7
Bickenhill Trading Estate
  CHWD/FDBR/MGN B37.........
Big Apple Bowling
  RUGBYN/HIL CV21...................48
Bilton CE Junior School
  RUGBYS/DCH CV22..................69
Bilton Grange School
  RUGBYS/DCH CV22..................70
Bilton High School
  RUGBYS/DCH CV22..................60
Bilton Industrial Estate
  COV CV1.................................3
Bilton Infant School
  RUGBYS/DCH CV22..................60
Binley Business Park
  COVS CV3.............................33
Binley Industrial Estate
  COVS CV3.............................41
Binley Woods Primary School
  COVS CV3.............................42
Birmingham International
  Airport
  LGN/SDN/BHAMAIR B26.......
Bishopgate Business Park
  COV CV1.................................3
Bishop Ullathorne RC
  Comprehensive School
  TLHL/CAN CV4.......................38
Bishop Wulstan RC High
  School
  RUGBYS/DCH CV22..................6
Blue Coat CE School
  COV CV1................................
BMI Meriden Hospital
  COVE CV2.............................21

...min Road Industrial Estate
  ...VE CV2 ....32 D1
...'s Hospital & Bablake
  ...d School COV CV1 ....2 B3
...ghton Leigh County Junior
  ...hool
  ...GBYN/HIL CV21 ....48 B2
...ghton Leigh Infant School
  ...GBYN/HIL CV21 ....48 C2
...ghton Road Industrial
  ...tate
  ...GBYN/HIL CV21 ....48 A3
...don Court Leofric
  ...siness Park
  ...VS CV3 ....41 H2
...don Wood Golf Club
  ...WTH CV8 ....42 B4
...ge Works Industrial Estate
  ...WTH CV8 ....65 F3
...d Heath Community
  ...imary School
  ...VN CV6 ....23 F5
...d Heath School
  ...VN CV6 ....23 F4
...d Lane Trading Estate
  ...HL/CAN CV4 ....27 H2
...d Street Health Centre
  ...VN CV6 ....23 G4
...d Street Old Boys RFC
  ...VS CV3 ....42 A1
...d Street RFC
  ...VE CV2 ....24 B3
...ke Special School
  ...GBYS/DCH CV22 ....61 G3
...klands Grange Hotel
  ...VW CV5 ....29 G1
...nsover Community
  ...hool
  ...UGBY CV23 ....48 C1
...nsover Hall Hotel
  ...GBYN/HIL CV21 ....48 A1
...sall Road Industrial Estate
  ...VW CV5 ....37 H1
...on Green CE Primary
  ...hool 50 A1
...rs Leap Industrial Estate
  ...GBYN/HIL CV21 ....48 C5
...s Park Arena
  ...V CV2 ....30 B4
...ton Castle School
  ...VE CV2 ....32 D2
...ton Centre
  ...VE CV2 ....25 E5
...banile Hotel
  ...VE CV2 ....25 F3
...ey Garden Cemetery
  ...HL/CAN CV4 ....38 A3
...ey Gardens Crematorium
  ...HL/CAN CV4 ....38 A3
...on Park Primary School
  ...HL/CAN CV4 ....38 A4
...n Evans CE Infant School
  ...WTH CV12 ....5 F3
...n Maggs CE Junior School
  ...WTH CV12 ....5 G3
...nal Newman RC School &
  ...mmunity College
  ...VN CV6 ....22 A1
...nal Wiseman RC School
  ...VE CV2 ....24 D2
...s Business Centre
  ...V CV1 ....31 E1
...e Place Industrial Estate
  ...V CV1 ....3 G1
...e Sixth Form Centre
  ...WTH CV8 ....65 E5
...edral Lanes Shopping
  ...ntre
  ...V CV1 ....2 D3
...ton Grange Primary
  ...hool
  ...GBYS/DCH CV22 ....60 B3
...al City Industrial Estate
  ...VN CV6 ....31 G1
...al Six Retail Park
  ...VS CV3 ....2 B6
...hace Hotel
  ...VS CV3 ....40 C4
...e Primary School
  ...VS CV3 ....40 D3
...nge Business Park
  ...V CV1 ....31 E1
...y Tree Sports Club
  ...VN CV6 ....23 F1
...unt Pre Preparatory
  ...hool
  ...V CV1 ....2 D6
...lesmore Welfare Clinic
  ...VS CV3 ....39 H3

Christ the King Catholic Infant School
  COVN CV6 ....22 A5
Christ the King RC Junior School
  COVN CV6 ....22 A4
Church Lawford Business Centre
  RRUGBY CV23 ....44 D4
Cineworld
  RUGBYN/HIL CV21 ....48 A3
City Arcade
  COV CV1 ....2 C4
City College Coventry
  COVW CV5 ....30 B4
  KNWTH CV8 ....65 E3
  TLHL/CAN CV4 ....28 C5
City Farm
  COV CV1 ....3 G1
City Walls & Gate
  COV CV1 ....2 E2
Clarendon House Hotel
  KNWTH CV8 ....65 E4
Clifford Bridge Primary School
  COVS CV3 ....33 F3
Clifton Road Cemetery
  RUGBYN/HIL CV21 ....62 B1
Clifton upon Dunsmore CE Primary School
  RRUGBY CV23 ....49 E4
Clifton upon Dunsmore Churchyard
  RRUGBY CV23 ....49 F3
Clinton Combined School
  KNWTH CV8 ....64 D4
The Clock Towers Shopping Centre
  RUGBYN/HIL CV21 ....61 H1
Combe Abbey Country Park
  COVS CV3 ....33 F3
Common Lane Industrial Estate
  KNWTH CV8 ....51 H5
Copsewood School
  COVN CV6 ....12 C5
Corley CC
  RCOVN/BALC/EX CV7 ....11 F2
Corley School
  RCOVN/BALC/EX CV7 ....11 E2
Corpus Christi RC Primary School
  COVS CV3 ....41 E2
Coundon Court School & Community College
  COVN CV6 ....21 H4
  COVN CV6 ....23 F4
Coundon Primary School
  COVN CV6 ....29 H1
Courthouse Green Primary School
  COVN CV6 ....23 H3
Courtyard by Marriott
  KNWTH CV8 ....55 E1
Coventry Airport
  COVS CV3 ....54 B3
Coventry Athletics Track
  TLHL/CAN CV4 ....37 G3
Coventry Business Park
  COVW CV5 ....29 G5
  TLHL/CAN CV4 ....29 F4
Coventry Cathedral & Visitor Centre
  COV CV1 ....2 E3
Coventry City FC (Jaguar Arena)
  COVN CV6 ....13 F5
Coventry Golf Club
  COVS CV3 ....53 G2
Coventry Grammar School
  COVW CV5 ....30 A5
Coventry Hearsall Golf Club
  COVW CV5 ....38 C1
Coventry Muslim School
  COVN CV6 ....23 F3
Coventry Preparatory School
  COVW CV5 ....39 E1
Coventry RFC
  COVN CV6 ....30 B2
Coventry Road Cemetery
  BDWTH CV12 ....5 G3
Coventry Sports Centre
  COV CV1 ....3 F3
The Coventry Toy Museum
  COV CV1 ....3 F4
Coventry Trading Estate
  COVS CV3 ....54 D3
Coventry Transport Museum
  COV CV1 ....2 D2

Coventry University
  COV CV1 ....2 E3
Coventry University Technocentre
  COV CV1 ....3 F6
Coventry Welsh RFC
  COVN CV6 ....13 G2
The Crescent School
  RUGBYS/DCH CV22 ....61 E4
Criterion Theatre
  COVW CV5 ....38 D1
Croop Hill Cemetery
  RUGBYS/DCH CV22 ....61 E2
Cross Point Business Park
  COVE CV2 ....25 H3
Cross Road Industrial Estate
  COVE CV2 ....23 G4
Dalehouse Lane Industrial Estate
  KNWTH CV8 ....51 H5
Dartmouth Special School
  COVE CV2 ....24 C5
Davenport Lodge School
  COVW CV5 ....39 E1
Deedmore Special School
  COVE CV2 ....24 B3
The Dr Phillips Shopping Centre
  COVE CV2 ....24 C2
Dunchurch Boughton CE Junior School
  RUGBYS/DCH CV22 ....69 F4
Dunchurch Infant School
  RUGBYS/DCH CV22 ....69 G4
Dunchurch Trading Estate
  RRUGBY CV23 ....68 B3
Durbar Avenue Industrial Estate
  COVN CV6 ....23 E3
Earl Place Business Park
  TLHL/CAN CV4 ....29 E5
Earlsdon Business Centre
  COVW CV5 ....38 C1
Earlsdon Primary School
  COVW CV5 ....30 B5
Eastern Green Junior School
  COVW CV5 ....28 A1
Eastlands CP School
  RUGBYN/HIL CV21 ....62 C2
Eastlands Court Business Centre
  RUGBYN/HIL CV21 ....62 B1
Eastwood Business Village
  COVS CV3 ....33 E5
Edgewick Community Primary School
  COVN CV6 ....23 F3
Edgwick Park Industrial Estate
  COVN CV6 ....23 G3
Electric Wharf
  COVN CV6 ....30 D1
Elliott's Field Retail Park
  RUGBYN/HIL CV21 ....48 A2
Elmdon Trading Estate
  CHWD/FDBR/MGN B37 ....8 A2
English Martyrs RC Primary School
  RUGBYS/DCH CV22 ....63 E5
Ensign Business Centre
  TLHL/CAN CV4 ....37 E3
Ernesford Grange Primary School
  COVS CV3 ....32 D5
Ernesford Grange School & Community School
  COVS CV3 ....41 E1
Exhall Business Park
  RCOVN/BALC/EX CV7 ....5 G5
Exhall Cedars Infant School
  RCOVN/BALC/EX CV7 ....5 G5
Exhall Grange Special School
  RCOVN/BALC/EX CV7 ....13 E3
Finham Park School
  COVS CV3 ....38 D5
Finham Primary School
  COVS CV3 ....53 E1
Fletchamstead Highway Industrial Estate
  COVW CV5 ....38 A2
Fletchworth Gate Industrial Estate
  COVW CV5 ....37 H1
Foleshill Cemetery
  COVN CV6 ....23 H1
Foleshill CE Primary School
  COVN CV6 ....23 H1
Foleshill Leisure Centre
  COVN CV6 ....23 E4
Fords Hospital
  COV CV1 ....2 C4

Forum Health Centre
  COVE CV2 ....32 C2
Fosse Wayside Industrial Estate
  RUGBYN/HIL CV21 ....48 C5
Foxford School & Community Arts College
  COVN CV6 ....13 H3
Frank Whittle Primary School
  COVE CV2 ....25 E3
Frederick Bird Primary School
  COVE CV2 ....31 G1
Gallagher Business Park
  COVN CV6 ....13 F4
Gallagher Retail Park
  COVE CV2 ....23 G3
GEC Management College
  RUGBYS/DCH CV22 ....69 H4
George Fentham Endowed Primary School
  HIA/OLT B92 ....16 B5
Glebe Farm Industrial Estate
  RUGBYN/HIL CV21 ....47 G2
Godiva Trading Estate
  COVN CV6 ....23 G3
Good Shepherd RC Primary School
  COVN CV6 ....23 G2
Goodyers End Primary School
  BDWTH CV12 ....4 D5
Gosford Industrial Estate
  COV CV1 ....3 H4
Gosford Park Primary School
  COV CV1 ....3 K5
The GPT Golf Club
  COVS CV3 ....32 C5
Grange Farm Primary School
  COVS CV3 ....39 E4
Grangehurst Primary School
  COVE CV2 ....14 A4
Great Central Way Industrial Estate
  RUGBYN/HIL CV21 ....48 C5
Grosvenor Hotel
  RUGBYN/HIL CV21 ....62 A1
Grovelands Industrial Estate
  RCOVN/BALC/EX CV7 ....13 H2
Gulson Road Clinic
  COV CV1 ....3 G4
Haigs Hotel
  RCOVN/BALC/EX CV7 ....34 C2
Hales Industrial Park
  COVN CV6 ....13 F4
Hanford Close Industrial Estate
  COVN CV6 ....23 F5
Harnall Lane Industrial Estate
  COV CV1 ....31 E2
Harnall Lane Medical Centre
  COV CV1 ....31 E2
Harris CE High School
  RUGBYS/DCH CV22 ....61 G3
Hawkesbury Field School
  COVE CV2 ....14 B5
Hawkesbury Lock Industrial Centre
  COVN CV6 ....14 A2
Hazelhead Industrial Estate
  COV CV1 ....3 J5
Hearsall Primary School
  COVW CV5 ....30 B4
Heart of England School
  RCOVN/BALC/EX CV7 ....34 C3
Heath Business Centre
  KNWTH CV8 ....58 A3
Henley College Coventry
  COVE CV2 ....32 A3
  COVN CV6 ....24 A2
Henley College ECDL Centre
  COVN CV6 ....22 B4
Henley Industrial Park
  COVE CV2 ....24 B4
Henry Bellairs CE Junior School
  BDWTH CV12 ....6 A2
Henry Hinde Infant School
  RUGBYS/DCH CV22 ....60 D3
Henry Hinde Junior School
  RUGBYS/DCH CV22 ....60 C2
Henry Parkes Primary School
  TLHL/CAN CV4 ....37 H1
Herald Business Park
  COVS CV3 ....41 G2
Herbert Art Gallery & Museum
  COV CV1 ....2 E4
Hereward College
  TLHL/CAN CV4 ....28 C5
Hill Farm Primary School
  COVN CV6 ....22 C4
Hillfields Health Centre
  COV CV1 ....3 F1

Hillmorton Primary School
RUGBYN/HIL CV21 ....63 G4
Holbrook Park Industrial Estate
COVN CV6 ....23 E3
Holbrook Primary School
COVN CV6 ....23 F2
Hollyfast Primary School
COVN CV6 ....21 H4
Holy Family RC J & I School
COVN CV6 ....12 C5
Homefield School
RUGBYS/DCH CV22 ....70 A3
Hood Street Industrial Estate
COV CV1 ....3 G3
Hornchurch Close Industrial
Estate *COV* CV1 ....2 D7
Hospital of St Cross
RUGBYS/DCH CV22 ....62 A3
Hotel Ibis
COVS CV3 ....40 A3
COV CV1 ....2 E6
Howes Primary School
COVS CV3 ....39 G4
Hunters Lane Industrial Estate
RUGBYN/HIL CV21 ....47 H4
Hylands Hotel
COVS CV3 ....39 F1
IKEA store Coventry
COV CV1 ....2 B4
Jaguar Daimler Heritage Centre
COVW CV6 ....21 E3
John Gulson Primary School
COV CV1 ....31 E1
John Shelton Primary School
COVN CV6 ....13 E4
Joseph Cash J & I School
COVN CV6 ....22 D4
Junction One Retail Park
RUGBYN/HIL CV21 ....48 A3
Kenilworth Business Centre
KNWTH CV8 ....65 F4
Kenilworth Castle
KNWTH CV8 ....64 C2
Kenilworth Cemetery
KNWTH CV8 ....64 D4
Kenilworth Golf Club
KNWTH CV8 ....66 A1
Kenilworth RFC
KNWTH CV8 ....66 A3
Kenilworth School
KNWTH CV8 ....65 H2
Kenilworth Wardens CC
KNWTH CV8 ....65 H4
Ken Marriott Leisure Centre
RUGBYS/DCH CV22 ....62 A2
Keresley Grange
Primary School
COVN CV6 ....22 A2
Keresley Health Centre
RCOVN/BALC/EX CV7 ....12 A2
Keresley Newland Primary
School
RCOVN/BALC/EX CV7 ....12 A1
Kingfield Industrial Estate
COVN CV6 ....22 D5
King Henry VIII School
COVS CV3 ....2 B7
Knightlow CE (Aided) Primary
School
RRUGBY CV23 ....57 E5
Lawford Heath Industrial
Estate *RRUGBY* CV23 ......59 F5
Lawrence Sheriff School
RUGBYN/HIL CV21 ....62 A1
Leigh CE Primary School
TLHL/CAN CV4 ....28 A5
Leyland School
BDWTH CV12 ....5 G2
Limbrick Wood
Primary School
TLHL/CAN CV4 ....28 C3
Little Heath Industrial Estate
COVN CV6 ....23 H1
Little Heath Primary School
COVN CV6 ....23 G2
Lodge Farm Campsite
RRUGBY CV23 ....60 C2
London Road Cemetery
COVS CV3 ....39 H1
Longford Medical Centre
COVN CV6 ....13 H3
Longford Park Primary School
COVN CV6 ....13 H5
Long Lawford Cemetery
RRUGBY CV23 ....46 B4
Long Lawford Primary School
RRUGBY CV23 ....46 B4
Lunt Roman Fort
KNWTH CV8 ....53 H1

Lyng Hall School
COV CV2 ....24 B5
Lythalls Lane Industrial Estate
COVN CV6 ....23 F2
Macdonald Brandon Hall
Hotel & Spa *KNWTH* CV8 ......42 D4
Macdonald De Montfort Hotel
KNWTH CV8 ....64 D3
Maguire Industrial Estate
TLHL/CAN CV4 ....36 D1
Manor Hotel
RCOVN/BALC/EX CV7 ....18 C2
Manor Park Primary School
COVS CV3 ....39 F2
Mansfield Medical Centre
COVS CV3 ....31 H4
Martyr's Memorial
COV CV1 ....2 E6
The Meadows Special School
TLHL/CAN CV4 ....28 B3
Mega Bowl
COVE CV2 ....25 G3
Meriden CE Primary School
RCOVN/BALC/EX CV7 ....18 B1
Meriden Green Business Park
COVW CV6 ....19 G3
Middlemarch Business Park
COVS CV3 ....54 C3
Midland Air Museum
KNWTH CV8 ....54 C1
Midland Oak Industrial Estate
COVN CV6 ....23 F2
Midland Oak Trading Estate
COVN CV6 ....23 F1
Midlands Sports Centre
for the Disabled
TLHL/CAN CV4 ....36 B2
Midland Trading Estate
RUGBYN/HIL CV21 ....47 H3
Moat House Primary School
COVE CV2 ....24 C2
Moseley Primary School
COVN CV6 ....30 B2
Mount Nod Primary School
COVW CV5 ....28 D3
Nailcote Hall Hotel
RCOVN/BALC/EX CV7 ....35 H2
Nation Agricultural Centre
KNWTH CV8 ....66 D3
National Exhibition Centre
BHAMNEC B40 ....8 C3
National Motorcycle Museum
HIA/OLT B92 ....9 E5
Newbold FC
RUGBYN/HIL CV21 ....47 E3
Newbold Leisure Centre
RUGBYN/HIL CV21 ....47 E2
Newbold Riverside
Primary School
RUGBYN/HIL CV21 ....47 F3
Newdigate Primary School
BDWTH CV12 ....4 B4
New Inn Industrial Estate
COVN CV6 ....23 G1
New Oxford Medical Centre
COV CV1 ....2 C2
Nicholas Chamberlaine School
BDWTH CV12 ....6 A2
Northbrook Sports Club
COVN CV6 ....21 G3
Northlands Primary School
RUGBYN/HIL CV21 ....48 A5
North Warks & Hinckley
College
BDWTH CV12 ....5 G2
North Warwickshire Golf Club
RCOVN/BALC/EX CV7 ....17 G3
Novotel
COVN CV6 ....13 G2
LGN/SDN/BHAMAIR B26 .....8 A4
Oakfield Primary School
RUGBYS/DCH CV22 ....61 G2
Odeon Cinema
COV CV1 ....2 E4
One Stop Medical Centre
COV CV1 ....2 C2
Orchard Retail Park
COVS CV3 ....41 E5
Our Lady of the Assumption
RC Primary School
TLHL/CAN CV4 ....28 B5
Paddox Primary School
RUGBYS/DCH CV22 ....62 C4
Parkgate Primary School
COVN CV6 ....12 C5
Park Hill Junior School
KNWTH CV8 ....65 H1
Park Hill Primary School
COVW CV5 ....28 D2

Parkside Business Park
COV CV1 ....2 E6
Park Street Industrial Estate
COVN CV6 ....23 F4
Pattison College
COVS CV3 ....31 H4
Peacock Hotel
COVE CV2 ....65 E4
Pearl Hyde Primary School
COVE CV2 ....33 F1
Playbox Theatre
KNWTH CV8 ....65 F3
Potters Green Primary School
COVE CV2 ....24 D1
Premier Travel Inn
BHAMNEC B40 ....8 D1
COVS CV3 ....42 A1
RCOVN/BALC/EX CV7 ....34 B1
President Kennedy
Comprehensive School &
Community College
COVN CV6 ....12 B4
Princes Drive Industrial Estate
KNWTH CV8 ....51 F4
Priors Field CP School
KNWTH CV8 ....50 C5
Priory Theatre
KNWTH CV8 ....65 E2
Priory Visitor Centre
COV CV1 ....2 E3
Provost Williams CE
Primary School
KNWTH CV8 ....55 H3
Race Leys Infant School
BDWTH CV12 ....5 G2
Race Leys Junior School
BDWTH CV12 ....5 G1
Radford Primary School
COVN CV6 ....30 C1
Ravensdale Primary School
COVE CV2 ....32 B2
Read Street Industrial Estate
COV CV1 ....3 H3
Regent Health Centre
RUGBYN/HIL CV21 ....47 H5
Richard Lee Primary School
COVE CV2 ....32 C3
Rokeby Infant School
RUGBYS/DCH CV22 ....61 H4
Rokeby Junior School
RUGBYS/DCH CV22 ....61 H4
Rowleys Green Industrial
Estate
COVN CV6 ....13 F4
Rugby Athletics Track
RUGBYS/DCH CV22 ....62 A3
Rugby FC
RUGBYS/DCH CV22 ....61 F2
Rugby Golf Club
RUGBYN/HIL CV21 ....48 D5
Rugby High School for Girls
RUGBYS/DCH CV22 ....69 H1
Rugby School
RUGBYS/DCH CV22 ....61 H2
Rugby School Museum
RUGBYN/HIL CV21 ....61 H1
Rugby School Sports Centre
RUGBYS/DCH CV22 ....62 A2
Rugby Theatre
RUGBYN/HIL CV21 ....61 H1
Rugby Welsh RFC
RUGBYN/HIL CV21 ....61 G1
Ryton Organic Gardens
KNWTH CV8 ....56 D3
Sacred Heart RC
Primary School
COVE CV2 ....31 H3
St Andrews CC Primary &
Middle School
RUGBYN/HIL CV21 ....48 C5
St Andrews CE Infant School
COVW CV5 ....27 H1
St Andrews RUFC
RUGBYS/DCH CV22 ....62 C5
St Annes RC Primary School
COVS CV3 ....40 C3
St Augustines RC
Primary School
KNWTH CV8 ....50 D5
St Bartholomews CE
Primary School
COVS CV3 ....41 F1
St Christopher Primary School
COVS CV3 ....29 G2
St Elizabeths RC
Primary School
COVN CV6 ....23 F1
St Francis RC Combined School
BDWTH CV12 ....5 G2

St Giles Junior School
RCOVN/BALC/EX CV7 ....18 C3
St Gregorys RC Primary School
COVE CV2 32
St James CE Junior School
BDWTH CV12 5
St James Medical Centre
COVS CV3 40
St John Fisher RC
Primary School
COVE CV2 32
St Johns CE Primary School
COVW CV5 28
St John's Hospital
COV CV1 2
St Johns Primary School
KNWTH CV8 64
St John the Divine CE
Primary School
COVS CV3 40
St John Vianney RC
Primary School
COVW CV5 27
St Josephs School
KNWTH CV8 51
St Margarets CE
Primary School
KNWTH CV8 64
St Maries Catholic Infant
School
RUGBYS/DCH CV22 61
St Maries RC Junior School
RUGBYS/DCH CV22 61
St Mary & St Benedict RC
Primary School
COV CV1 2
St Mary's Priory
COV CV1 2
St Matthews Bloxam CE School
RUGBYS/DCH CV22 62
St Nicholas CE Combined
School
KNWTH CV8 64
St Osburgs RC Primary School
COV CV1 2
St Oswalds CE Primary School
RUGBYS/DCH CV22 61
St Patricks RC Primary School
COVE CV2 32
St Pauls Cemetery
COVN CV6 30
St Peter & St Paul RC
Primary School
COVE CV2 32
St Thomas More RC
Primary School
COVS CV3 29
Sandy Lane Business Park
COV CV1 3
Seven Stars Industrial Estate
COVS CV3 40
Sherbourne Fields School
COVW CV6 21
Shilton Lane Industrial Estate
BDWTH CV12 14
Showcase Cinemas
COVE CV2 25
Sidney Stringer Community
Technology College
COV CV1 2
Sir Frank Whittle Business
Centre
RUGBYN/HIL CV21 61
Skydome Leisure Complex
COV CV1 2
Somers Wood Caravan Park
RCOVN/BALC/EX CV7 19
Southfield Primary School
COV CV1 3
Sowe Valley Primary School
COVS CV3 33
Sparkbrook Street
Industrial Estate
COV CV1 3
Spon Gate Primary School
COV CV1 2
Stag Industrial Estate
COVN CV6 23
Stanton Bridge Primary School
COVN CV6 30
Star Industrial Park
COVE CV2 33
Station Street West Business
Park
COVN CV6 23
Status Business Centre
COVW CV5 21
Stivichall Primary School
COVS CV3 39

Acknowledgements

Schools address data provided by Education Direct

Petrol station information supplied by Johnsons

Garden centre information provided by

Garden Centre Association · Britains best garden centres

Wyevale Garden Centres

The statement on the front cover of this atlas is sourced, selected and quoted
from a reader comment and feedback form received in 2004

Notes

AA **Street by Street** QUESTIONNAIRE

Dear Atlas User
Your comments, opinions and recommendations are very important to us.
So please help us to improve our street atlases by taking a few minutes
to complete this simple questionnaire.

You do not need a stamp (unless posted outside the UK). If you do not want to remove this page from your street atlas, then photocopy it or write your answers on a plain sheet of paper.

Send to: Marketing Assistant, AA Publishing, 14th Floor Fanum House,
Freepost SCE 4598, Basingstoke RG21 4GY

ABOUT THE ATLAS...

Please state which city / town / county you bought:

_____

Where did you buy the atlas? (City, Town, County)

_____

For what purpose? (please tick all applicable)

To use in your local area ☐   **To use on business or at work** ☐

Visiting a strange place ☐   **In the car** ☐   **On foot** ☐

Other (please state)

_____

Have you ever used any street atlases other than AA Street by Street?

Yes ☐   **No** ☐

If so, which ones?

_____

Is there any aspect of our street atlases that could be improved?
(Please continue on a separate sheet if necessary)

_____
_____
_____

Please list the features you found most useful:

_____

_____

Please list the features you found least useful:

_____

_____

_____

LOCAL KNOWLEDGE...

Local knowledge is invaluable. Whilst every attempt has been made to make the information contained in this atlas as accurate as possible, should you notice any inaccuracies, please detail them below (if necessary, use a blank piece of paper) or e-mail us at *streetbystreet@theAA.com*

_____

_____

_____

ABOUT YOU...

Name (Mr/Mrs/Ms) _____

Address _____

_____ **Postcode** _____

Daytime tel no _____

E-mail address _____

Which age group are you in?

Under 25 ☐   **25-34** ☐   **35-44** ☐   **45-54** ☐   **55-64** ☐   **65+** ☐

Are you an AA member?   YES ☐   **NO** ☐

Do you have Internet access?   YES ☐   **NO** ☐

_____

Thank you for taking the time to complete this questionnaire. Please send it to us as soon as possible, and remember, you do not need a stamp (unless posted outside the UK).

We may use information we hold about you to, telephone or email you about other products and services offered by the AA, we do NOT disclose this information to third parties.

Please tick here if you do not wish to hear about products and services from the AA. ☐

ML034y